Emotional Sandwiches®

Emotional Sandwiches

Warning!
All Fillings Contain Perspectives

Sarah Ashley Neal

Copyright © 2018 Sarah Ashley Neal

Emotional Sandwiches® is a registered trademark owned by Sanartina Ltd

The moral right of the author has been asserted.

Apart from any fair dealing for the purposes of research or private study, or criticism or review, as permitted under the Copyright, Designs and Patents Act 1988, this publication may only be reproduced, stored or transmitted, in any form or by any means, with the prior permission in writing of the publishers, or in the case of reprographic reproduction in accordance with the terms of licences issued by the Copyright Licensing Agency. Enquiries concerning reproduction outside those terms should be sent to the publishers.

Matador
9 Priory Business Park,
Wistow Road, Kibworth Beauchamp,
Leicestershire. LE8 0RX
Tel: 0116 279 2299
Email: books@troubador.co.uk
Web: www.troubador.co.uk/matador
Twitter: @matadorbooks

ISBN 978 1788038 461
British Library Cataloguing in Publication Data.
A catalogue record for this book is available from the British Library.

Printed and bound by CPI Group (UK) Ltd, Croydon, CR0 4YY
Typeset in 12 pt Minion Pro by Troubador Publishing Ltd, Leicester, UK

Matador is an imprint of Troubador Publishing Ltd

Dedicated to my Mum
for all of the reasons she knows to be true

The Menu

Article 22: The Power of Your Mind	1
How to Approach an Emotional Sandwich	8
The Essential Ingredient	13

Course 1
Fillings Containing Mixed Seeds:

Discovery and Exploration	19
SOMETIMES: Taking Ownership	22
PATH: Appearances Aren't Everything!	27
CHOICE: Join the Brigade and Get in Line!	43
HOPE: Bridging the Gap	55

Course 2
Fillings Experienced in Moderation:

Balance and Management	67
CONFIDENCE: The Waiting Room	70
NORMAL: The Puppeteer	84
CONTROL: The Double Acts	93
DARKNESS: The Rainbow Effect	105

Course 3
Fillings Enriched with Good Nutrition:

Understanding and Respect	113
TIME: Speed Limits Apply	116

PATIENCE: It's Not the Speed That Counts!	126
TRUST: Emotional Contracts	141
JUDGEMENT: Reading Between the Lines	153

Course 4

Fillings Containing Anti-Nutrients:	
Limitations and Acceptance	169
FAILURE: Sugar Isn't Always the Enemy!	172
FEAR: The Holiday Complex	183
GUILT: It's About the Response-ability	193
NEED: Desires and Delusions	205

Course 5

Fillings to Educate the Taste Buds:	
Learning and Development	217
HONEST: Choosing the Right Policy	221
BLAME: Lying Down On the Job	233
FORGIVE: The Multi-Step Equation	245
HUMBLE: Making a Connection	260

The Last Word	274
The Final Interview	280
The Folders of Your Mind	289

Article 22

The Power of Your Mind

"News Flash, News Flash: Sandwiches cause reactions! All fillings contain perspectives."

*

Imagine, for a moment, that you have just read this announcement while sitting in your doctor's waiting room, staring into oblivion. The unusual headline jumped off the page and abruptly entered your field of vision uninvited. Boom! While you appeared to be in a world of your own, the 'empty stare' was but an illusion. You were simply taking precautions and mentally wrapping yourself in Clingfilm to safeguard against those who were trafficking contagious bacterium. And you weren't quite sure who they were. At this point, you didn't actually know what you were playing host to either, or if it was all in your mind.

Out of curiosity you picked up the article which went on to say, "The effects may be more noticeable when perspectives are digested for the first time." Another line read something about 'managing your reactions'. Skipping over that paragraph for fear of being lured into having to 'do something' far too serious, given it was a Monday morning, you settled for the more philosophical bit that followed:

"Although fillings by nature don't tend to fix anything or

anyone (all on their own), it is the fusion of new flavours which filter through that has the potential to make a difference. Where possible, I've resisted using artificial additives, keeping them all home-grown and thoughtfully packaged to subtly entertain."

Beginning to feel as though the author was talking directly to you, and on a personal level, you couldn't help but sense that you were being groomed; being prepared to go on a journey where even your own doctor wasn't equipped to send you. Uncertain at this stage if a recipe was in hiding, you decided to read more before shaking the magazine to find out – a risk not worth taking, judging by the forlorn patients lounging around the room. Any sudden movement was bound to prompt a zombie uprising, disrupting your flow of concentration.

The fanciful language seemed unconventional and appeared to draw you in. Even if there was nothing edible to look forward to, you were still intrigued to find out more about the 'Emotional Sandwiches'. What did you have to lose? After all, what didn't educate was apparently going to entertain. Anyway, some light reading would come in especially useful while allowing your phantom illness to get its act together and make up its mind if it wanted to come or go – ideally, within the next few minutes.

Looking up at the clock, the doctor was running reliably late. Great! This provided the perfect excuse for you to give yourself permission to get sucked further into any abstract ideas that were certain to lie ahead and probably satisfied the writer's inward desire to exaggerate, too. The next chunk of narration only validated your gut feeling, shedding more light on the 'News Flash' that had recently illuminated your imagination.

"Each Emotional Sandwich may provoke an emotional response that impacts positively on how you feel about yourself, relationships, work, family and general life as you know it! Equally they could wind you up leaving you mildly irritated. This is a common side effect associated with not being in the mood really, in which case I suggest you explore them another day. Otherwise, keep going, as one sandwich contains enough filling to contaminate you with an increased sense of self-awareness if you are in the mood for some light reflection.

Just like food in my opinion. Some days, you don't have an appetite for that something you seemingly enjoyed the day before. Yet, on another day, it returns with a vengeance reminding you how sublime it tastes and you can't imagine how on earth you could become bored with it. Putting food aside is something that I find hard to do. The thought of it runs through my veins in the same way that words flow through my mind. Constantly! Food and words bring meaning to my life and they both have the power to make me feel emotional."

Emotional?! All this talk about food was making you hungry. The author had no idea how emotional you were about to get. Not only were you reading about the potential for food to make you feel irritable, you had skipped breakfast, making certain that the lack of it had the potential to do the same. Apparently, it was wise to fast so the results from any impending tests weren't skewed – even if your thoughts were getting twisted, in response to starvation!

"So, what is the book 'Emotional Sandwiches' about, if it isn't about 'real' food? Well, it is most definitely about an exploration of how several words that appear in our vocabulary come to mean so much more to us than just a string of letters that we'd learned to assemble at school. Their arrangement can be questioned later. A word can be placed on trial, at any point in the future, and tried far beyond the dictionary definition it has been assigned. Do you have any vivid memories of standing in a 'spelling test line' at primary school?"...

Unable to stop yourself from blurting the word 'No' – out loud – you turned to the lady beside you and apologised profusely for your vocal outburst, telling her that you had no recollection of being involved in a military operation at such a young age. Aware that this superfluous information only confused her further, judging by her look of angst, you went on to learn more about the author's own experience:

"I remember it all too well. It snaked around the doll-sized desks (seemingly for miles) before reaching the teacher. I recall the pressure expanding in my head as I fought hard to keep the letters in the right order, too afraid to breathe in case they fell apart. Finally they emerged in one piece – so did I! The next step involved placing the final creations into sentences in such a way that their meanings made sense. Little did I know that this would take the next forty years to do! This time I gave myself permission to sit down as I continued my quest to squeeze them into lines that breathed new life into their meaning. Although some of us still refuse to negotiate their meaning, in spite of the context, I think a word can be forgiven more easily for existing in isolation. Do you?

After all, if words could talk, what would they say? A word may tell us something about what they are and their relationships with other words. People they work alongside would get a mention – as would the stories that belong to them. Words would describe the roles they play and their ability to influence in one way or another; how their interviews, to play a part in Emotional Sandwiches, didn't start off as planned, because—"

Rudely interrupted by the sound of an unhealthy tannoy system broadcasting your name, you reluctantly put the article down and made your way to the surgery, wondering why you had gone to the doctor's in the first place. What were you expecting them to do – or say? Offer up a diagnosis, a prognosis or simply make a prediction? Any of these would be acceptable today, based on the fact that all of your aches and pains that you'd experienced last night had appeared to abandon you en route this morning. Concerned, at first, that you'd lost them in transit, you seemed pleased when they did eventually reappear (just as your name was called) if only to confirm that you hadn't gone mad. It was also a reminder that something was still amiss. You just didn't know what!

Were you simply having a reaction to a bad day; a difficult year; or come to think of it, a challenging life…? Then again, maybe life has been kind to you. This doesn't alter the fact that the unwelcome symptoms you were now experiencing, once again (probably about to be rejected by the medics on the grounds that they didn't appear life threatening), still require your attention. Or, maybe your attention simply needed to be directed elsewhere, for a while, to allow them the opportunity to disappear altogether.

Perhaps there isn't a medical quick fix for every time a symptom sneezes. Maybe the white coat army can do little more than palm your symptoms off onto two little words, suggesting that you could be 'run down'. And in your heart, you predicted that would be their conclusion. Run down by what, though, had to be the next step to explore. Ideally, you'd come up with a logical answer before considering the notion that an alien intervention had taken place. Explaining that you'd collided with a UFO at some point during your sleep cycle probably wouldn't go down too well with the white coat army either. Yes, there had to be a logical reason that didn't involve Sci-Fi!

Dismissing such ludicrous thoughts, you wondered if it was possible for your physical body to let you know when it's unhappy with the way you are taking care of yourself. Some of the things we do don't actually serve us well; yet, we keep on doing them anyway!

Our emotions talk to us and our reactions tell us how well we're coping. We may not listen to the entire message, choosing to distance ourselves from lingering too long in our own head space (or heart space) fearful that we might be opening Pandora's Box. A place where we'll find these messages stored, sitting tight, in readiness to increase our self-awareness if we so choose. Then those we ignore, which get left behind, generally find another way of manifesting and can sometimes appear as an ailment which requires medical attention. But often we need to do something differently; think differently; behave differently… and when we don't, we may turn to Blame to come up with a good excuse about why our own wellbeing is not feeling as well as it could be!

In wonderment, you told yourself, "That all seems rather logical", chuffed that, clearly, the Monday blues were lifting as your thoughts were beginning to wake up. You knocked on the doctor's door, wondering if they'd agree too had you had more time to explain your sudden epiphany. Overcome with a sense of déjà vu, while turning the handle, you suddenly recalled that Blame was one of the words in the article to which your eyes had tried remarkably well to avoid paying any attention, unconsciously absorbing it by accident. Now was not the time to engage with Pandora's Box. The blues were lifting – but they hadn't been vanquished!

All of a sudden it registered, while you were hastily thanking the doctor for their time and not their diagnosis! What if you had already dialled into your very own self-awareness contact centre, unknowingly, while scanning the article? What if an emotional shift was suddenly underway, even if you hadn't consciously intended to make one? Wincing with embarrassment, you scanned the room quickly on your way out to ensure that no one had noticed that you were about to undergo a process of transformation. Into what, it was too early to know. A new stream of consciousness was beginning to flow.

On departure, as you pushed the door open with the ball of your foot (to mitigate the risk of catching anything else, other than the blues you'd caught that morning), you realised you had yet to read the last section of the article! Inhaling deeply, you returned to the waiting room, seizing the magazine unsuspectingly. If the article had been fortuitously placed on the table, then the serendipitous moment had to exist as something to be exploited and you could always pop it back through the letterbox tomorrow. Reluctant to run, to avoid tripping over Guilt on the way out, you decided to walk with a purpose in pursuit of finding your own answers within – somehow.

Emotional Sandwiches, here you come…

How to Approach an Emotional Sandwich

The Emotional Sandwiches are not dangerous! Yes, I can tell you now that their fillings carry a warning but this is only because they are influential and challenging little characters, full of charm and wisdom. Who said a reaction is always a bad thing? What did you do when you received your first valentine card? React with suspicion, no doubt, as you eagerly opened it wondering if you'd recognise the handwriting and what it would say – what would it mean? I bet you were more than capable of making it fit your own ideas at the time. The sandwiches are no different. You'll approach one with distrust until you recognise something about it that touches your heart until you work out what valentine message it has for you. You will make the word fit, somehow.

They are going to appear along your path in stages but ultimately the Emotional Sandwiches will end up mingling with each other on and off. Besides, if all these characters started talking at once, right from the beginning, you wouldn't have a clue what each one was trying to say. It would be distracting to listen to their competing voices resulting in a gradual crescendo of white noise. So I have created the ideal opportunity to take this love affair with words and insert them into a menu that promises to deliver each course with pride and respect, allowing each moment to be savoured and discussed with emotion or relished in silent reflection.

There are five courses altogether. Just as you would tuck into a selection of tapas in a Spanish tasca, to enjoy a small bite of something to eat, I'd like you to approach each sandwich with the same amount of interest. Later on, all the fillings can be modified and perspectives can be added or removed to suit your own individual palate. So go ahead: 'Coach the artist within you to create'.

Of course, if you wanted to eat at a carvery, and indulge in a mountain of food in one go, you could have downloaded the contents of a thesaurus, in no particular order, yourself. Yet, this would only represent a bunch of words that continue to sit uncomfortably on each page, awaiting a storyline, as if they have been shuffled from one orphanage to another with no one taking the time to pay each of them a little attention, and giving each a voice that would one day allow them to make a stand and shout out – in upper case – "I HAVE FEELINGS TOO!" This sounds exhausting already!

Every word that crosses your path wants to have a relationship with you at some point in time and be understood. They want to play a part in your life, that's all. It is how we approach them and get to know them better that probably matters the most. Just ignoring them when they are clearly trying to tell us something can be detrimental to our wellbeing.

I reckon that, on occasions, they feel vulnerable as they saunter along your path. At times, you may feel vulnerable when you come across some words that resonate with you more than others as you take an opportunity to explore and decide which ones these are. A friend of mine suggested that they are certainly venerable words, describing them as deserving of respect. I totally agree with him. After sense-checking its definition, elsewhere, others seemed to be of the same opinion. And you may come to the same conclusion.

What else can I tell you about Emotional Sandwiches that won't jeopardise your chances of reacting naturally, over the page? Well, it does have a beginning, middle and end, and I'd like to introduce you to each section in order as you read it for the first time (you're already well past the starting line). This can help you to get the best out of each sandwich and promises to move you along at a comfortable pace. It will inspire you to go to that place where self-awareness inhabits and increases with each stretch of the imagination. You may also find it useful to dip in and out of the book, at a later date, when you feel drawn to one sandwich in particular.

I may throw in a cheeky idea that encapsulates multidimensional concepts and, who knows, they may even be delivered by alien intelligence along the way. A different language can sound nonsense until it is understood; you should have seen the sandwiches before they were decorated with punctuation! The wonderful thing is that Nonsense makes sense to someone. Once you have formed a close relationship with the emotional characters that await you, then Sense may reach out to you in ways you had never considered. Perspectives are personal and we don't all like the same seasonings, for one reason or another.

During this exploration of words, you may notice your own quirky facial expressions taking a hold as they accompany you along the way. So, look out for any rise taking place either side of the mouth, commonly known as a smile or smirk, and a further twisting of the mouth back and forth as the nose follows without complaint. A possible distension of the bottom lip can be indicative of thoughts being processed, yet to be digested along with an eye squint to make it complete. Any nodding up and down is a particularly good sign. A tilt to one side is just a pause for reflection and on occasions a side-to-side movement may suggest a mild intolerance to that particular sandwich; it is unlikely to prevent you from continuing. A little chat to yourself about the fact that these are just ideas will likely do the trick. Go on, give it a go and tell me I'm right…

No, the Emotional Sandwiches didn't start off their adventure as planned. The selection of words had plucked up the courage to attend a one-to-one interview and wanted to prove to me that they were worthy of being assigned a character in a book. By the end of their interview I had to decide which ones were most likely to involve you emotionally or had the potential to evoke an emotional response.

Unbeknown to them, however, on arrival they had all walked into a filming studio by mistake. Somehow, they'd taken a short cut – in the wrong direction (it's amazing what we do when we follow the lead). Anyhow, this blunder had them dangerously close to being screen-tested to play a romantic part alongside a French detective in a TV series, aptly named, I Will Hold You to Each Word, My Darling. That storyline is neither here nor there… Thankfully, they all managed to back out of the group audition with dignity as it looked set to become an orgy of words, as opposed to a solitary affair that I had envisioned for them.

While it would take a passionate wordsmith to arrange for all these words to meet in the same place at exactly the same time, the Emotional Sandwiches also exude a passion of their own, on a par with enthusiasm throughout each course. Who knows, maybe in the future they'll get to go on stage after all, reuniting to discuss their personal shortcomings once they've had an opportunity to go under the spotlight, separately, and be paid attention.

I finally took them under my wing, giving each of them the opportunity to tell me their stories. Any concerns that you may have about focusing on one word (thinking this could lack excitement) can be eliminated as they each prove to be quite capable of listening to their own voice whilst telling you a story – themed or otherwise.

So, moving on from that bit of housekeeping, I would like to invite you to read on and have the opportunity to find out for yourself rather than be unduly influenced, by me. So as my guest, firstly, let me introduce you to the star of the show which appears in every filling, shape shifting to its heart's content while taking on a character of its own. Sandwiched between layers of emotions, it is the very powerful and versatile… W*O*R*D.

Drum roll please!

The Essential Ingredient

How a word is exercised can be exciting and intriguing. It can take you on adventures way past your comfort zone, leading you into unknown territory where challenging debates and areas of conflict can have a habit of momentarily halting you in your tracks. What started out as a mere stroll in the park on a sunny day suddenly became a mountain climb over rocky terrain. The word you're exploring appeared simple and self-explanatory on the surface, but has now taken on a new meaning – to you!

Words you have been using within everyday conversation suddenly seem more meaningful. Read in a new light, their scope for interpretation expands and the exploration begins. The mind's computer switches on. The option now to determine your current position on a word is going to be set in motion as you draw on past experiences and assimilate new concepts. How you connect with a word can change over time. Consider how words can affect you differently and in different ways at different times. Not only are they each awarded a definition to support their own existence which permits us to use them in context, it is the context in which they are used that often needs the permission.

Of course, a word is harmless until it is applied and used in context, whether it is read or spoken. Only then, when subjected to interpretation, can it be accused of causing harm and is often sentenced before being proved innocent! Words that are strung together with conviction and sincerity can soon lose their appeal when they are woven into a new script. Using the same words in a completely different order gives rise to new meanings and new audiences.

A word will have a relationship with you. It can have an attraction and a powerful energy, cropping up frequently in your own vocabulary or in those around you, and up to now the repetition has either gone unnoticed, or has been quietly observed from the sidelines as requiring attention. Yet, what that attention should entail often remains in question. Even when it doesn't seem to pose any threat it can still be deserving of that intellectual contemplation all the same. Taking time out to explore some of these relationships with words can be private and personal yet useful to all of us.

Take a simple example and think about your least favourite food. Imagine you pick up a sandwich on the buffet table at your best friend's wedding, having no idea it contains any unfavourable ingredients. You utter the word 'disgusting', having taken a bite, and suddenly projectile vomit into the nearest napkin. What is the impact of this mortifying moment? In this case, I'd hope that the words 'marriage' and 'disgust' didn't form a lasting relationship for you. Some word associations can play havoc on your own mental wellbeing, reminding you of a situation until the link is broken. But in your own life, you are likely to be familiar with the words that deserve your time and attention, and recognise the impact they have on your behaviours or feelings in any given situation, good or bad.

It isn't easy to be honest about how you feel, about how particular words make you feel. In their presence, you can suddenly become beholden or intimidated but, likewise, liberated when you learn to manage your reactions in their presence and own the space their letters leave behind instead of allowing that vacant space to become an unhealthy shadow.

What about when we use a word loosely to describe that something which seems at the time indescribable? It is often chosen as the 'one-size-fits-all' attempt to explain that something that needs elaboration. Yet, the thought of having to explain further that it wasn't the most ideal of choices just leaves you exhausted. You find yourself ending the sentence with, "Well, that isn't the word I wanted to use but you know what I mean?!" Err, no!

On the other hand, you can sense when a word has been used to avoid that unknown territory situation referred to at the start. Any alternative, whilst being more relevant and quite possibly honest, would just leave you feeling less empowered in its company. This is because it can take you to places you dare not go but sincerely want to explore, if only to understand the viewpoints and opinions held on them. It can lead you into cultural dilemmas, untimely confrontations and unexpected challenges that take you into shades of grey, and ignorance is not always a 'get-out-of-jail-free' card.

At one time or another, you will have learned that some words simply become obsolete and are far too provocative to use anymore. What was once OK is now 'not OK'. And it can take time to get up to speed on why that is and re-educate your brain to think twice before using it. However, some words haven't been officially barred, yet still appear to be worth changing. For example, organisations often redefine everyday words, sanitising our language, pre-empting a word with an intended use instead of allowing its meaning to shine through innocently without an automated caveat of apologetic drivel trailing behind. This happens because we have either lost our ability to distinguish between right and wrong, or mollycoddled to the extent that we are off the hook if we have misunderstood. A concluding sentence, informally apologising, ultimately ensures that anything lost in translation cannot be recovered unlawfully! On occasions, walking into work, for some of us, feels more like crossing over into a parallel universe that offers you corporate immunity, where popularity wins over originality.

I've been wondering, for at least ten minutes, if there is another word I could use to refer to the 'star of the show' and avoid repetition, without renaming 'word' altogether. There isn't. It oozes authority and means what it means; a dictionary will define the noun succinctly and the part it plays in sentence formation. I've no plans to compete, leaving such exquisite compositions to the experts. But having explored 'word' with a little context, using fragments of my imagination to bring it alive, we can go on to call it all the names under the sun – for fun.

So, let me welcome you to a world of perspectives that sits within a fairground of rollercoasters and candyfloss. You will go up and you'll go down as you journey through a labyrinth of ifs and buts, becoming entangled in a sticky cobweb of sugary delight that equally melts away as quickly as that all-important thought passing through your mind, consuming you momentarily yet soon to be forgotten. Only a trail of agitation lingers as a short reminder that you cannot control everything all the time. Even your own memory divorces you on occasions and hides the replay button, keeping the words on the tip of your tongue until you give in and move on!

Emotional Sandwiches is a playground for the devil's advocates and the literary artists who throw you the angles and torment you with alternatives, only to rub them away to create space on their blackboards for more of the same, once the chalk dust settles. As with any artists' impressions starting out their lives as label free, neither right nor wrong, good nor bad, perspectives soon develop as a result of an experience having left its mark or from a creative imagination that doesn't hold any prisoners.

Perspectives can be interesting and funny, dark and mysterious, positive and negative, yet open to suggestion. But when do we notice we have these points of view? It's when we pick up the paint brush and make something out of nothing; when we read between lines and see only the ramblings of madness staring back instead of the sanity that is asking to be understood; when we twist words around and sense their confusion only to leave ourselves utterly confused in the process, about what it is we actually believe (or want to believe)! We greet our perspectives with uncertainty or seek refuge in their certainty and what seems unquestionable at the time. Then another suggestion pops up and we wrestle with them, all over again.

So really, when do we begin a relationship with our own perspectives and with those that belong to other people? Surely, it's as soon as we are born. What do you reckon? Isn't that when we begin the discovery and exploration of ourselves in relation to the world we live in? We search in different ways to find a *balance* and *manage* our expectations, striving to *understand* and *respect* nature's gifts in order to keep us grounded whilst greeting the *limitations* and *acceptance* part of the trip with kindness. No wonder that, at times, *learning* how to cope with our challenges in life and *developing* our coping strategies stirs up a few emotions!

So, there we have it! The five main courses captured in one paragraph, exemplifying a word-search puzzle for beginners that isn't too taxing on the imagination, although the next step asks you to focus a little more. From time to time reflect along the passageways that lay ahead as they lead you around corners, across bridges and down garden paths where only you will know if you've trespassed! They will stretch your imagination as you pass through waterfalls, climb out of avalanches and jump out of aeroplanes, and have you feeling like a superhero in no time – and that's before you go on an adventure! As you brush up against royalty and socialise with science, you'll soon feel rejuvenated as you make new friends along the way.

Play with the words that greet you on your journey and ask yourself, "What is my relationship to them now and during various stages of my life?" Notice how they may have evolved and why. Thank yourself for making the time to still question, challenge and reflect on life, being open to change in an ever-changing world and dare to be you while no one is watching.

Go on then. Get stuck into your first course – you must be hungry.

Course 1

Fillings Containing Mixed Seeds

Discovery and Exploration

'Sometimes we follow a path, make a choice and hope it turns out OK.'

Uncertainty goes hand in hand with discovery and exploration. The more you explore the more certain you can be that your discoveries will be full of surprises. The challenge is to accept them for what they are – good, bad or indifferent – and managing your reactions will be the fun part. No one said that was going to be easy!

Choices await you every step of the way as an army of opportunities marches towards you, each one waving a list of expectations to accompany its mission, brushing up against you, eagerly fighting for attention as though already in battle with no grounds to surrender until you make that decision. Through exhaustion they take a break only to re-enlist further down your path, hoping to change your mind.

As unpredictable as a handful of mixed seeds, the fillings in this section offer no stability yet promise to make regular appearances in your life, offering variety and entertainment along the way. What you 'put out there' and what you 'get back' may involve a little action, romance, suspense or pure comedy. In what order and for how long will be dependent on what seeds you have in your hand at the time and the path you choose.

Words find their way into your 'ideas', onto your 'landscape' and flourish under your 'direction'. I'd like to explore these areas with you first and hope that's OK. The main characters will soon join you, raising the bar, in a philosophical venture to inspire self-discovery.

S*O*M*E*T*I*M*E*S
Taking Ownership

Sometimes we say to ourselves, "If only I did that then" or "I wish I knew that then" or "I knew I should have done this sooner" or "I should have stopped before I did that". The fact is you didn't, you haven't and you stopped when you stopped. Then we consider the word *why* (perish the thought) and give it permission to muscle in on either a bout of self-pity or a simple matter of fact. As it gently pushes its subordinates further down the line, allowing each word to jiggle around until they reform to make sense, a judgement call is made. *Why* is now on a mission to turn the tired clichés into questions. "Why didn't I…?"

Whatever it is you think could have been achieved differently back then – because you have since racked your brains for a compelling reason and discovered a new idea that had you known before would surely have painted a rosier picture – is still speculative and you don't know that to be the case. If it helps you to tie up those emotional loose ends on the basis that you are never really going to know what would have happened had you made a different call, then no one can challenge that and claim to know the answer any more than you do.

Sometimes the hindsight cliché can save the day. It can take the heat out of the coals of events soaked in a reality that over time becomes rather hot, and any residual embers continue to fuel the mind chatter that can drive you mad until you throw that refreshing bucket of water over them, giving them an excuse to stop smouldering. Aha; you are indeed off the hook now because you could argue it wasn't your fault anyway. After all, you only acted on the information and knowledge you had at the time – didn't you? What a game changer already and only three paragraphs in!

Now what are your options? Well, you can either get on with exploring new beginnings now, or you can waste a bit more time wondering what took you so long. And I tend to think this: *'Time is never wasted unless you use it unwisely to wonder why too much!'* Actually, wondering why is OK to do if only to consolidate and close doors that need to be closed, buying you extra time to carry you through the transitional stage. The 'transitional stage' in this case implies that a period of transition now offers you a kind opportunity to move yourself on from somewhere you were to that somewhere you would rather be. If that feels more like a trek through No Man's Land without the lights on, as opposed to a yellow brick road that at least endeavours to add a splash of colour, perhaps something is niggling you about the past that needs attention. In which case, it may be wise to get it sorted. Be prepared to deal with it so you can sow some new seeds and harvest your own crops, getting more out of life or at the very least more out of yourself.

If you need help in doing that, then seek it out; you can only learn so much on your own. Sometimes, you can only ponder so much before confusing yourself and going round in circles, and the reality may be that you don't get the answer you want. The answer you actually want probably isn't going to help anymore or it isn't the same as the 'right' answer. The great thing about dreams or our imagination is that we can make up the answer.

We can make it as right as it needs to be or as creative as we want it to be; or, we can find an answer that satisfies us in order to move on in life. Whether that is actually the right answer sometimes doesn't matter… because sometimes, if it works for you, it is right.

Simply remain grounded, keep your own truth intact and feed it with the odd outside perspective so you don't shrivel up and, *voilà*, there you have it: a good foundation in which to blossom following a cheeky period of hibernation, lying dormant to rest but always with the view to waking up refreshed and prepared to take on another day. OK, so refreshed is debatable but one has to aim for a fresh start as a new day dawns; do you agree?

Sometimes the seed is sown but it seemingly takes ages for it to germinate and appear as something recognisable. Seeds don't always grow into what you thought they would, could or should. It's as if that thought or idea you planted, once out of sight for a while, decidedly shape shifted or became modified as a result of being abducted by aliens and replanted to somehow throw you off track. Sounding a tad extreme, I expect it will still be in its original tamper-proof packaging where you left it but maybe because you changed and also grew along the way, you could no longer recall what the finished product was meant to look like, further outgrowing your original ideas.

Sometimes, your idea begins to grow and you know you must be doing something right. But then, one day it stops! Do you throw it away, abandon your hard work or nurture it, 'wishing' it to develop? I was going to say hope, but does that imply that whatever it is you are trying to achieve is outside of your control, fuelled by an element of desperation thrown in to complete your mission? Similarly, to pray for something to happen is often deemed acceptable and indicative of trusting and believing that something outside of you can bring about a result and appears an acceptable intervention.

Being reliant alone on someone else to repair your broken car, carry out your heart bypass or fly you halfway around the world so you can complete that business deal… and arrive home in time to put the kids to bed, are interventions that require expertise. If you don't have those skills, then it's OK to find someone who does. Sometimes when you hope the car doesn't cost too much, pray the heart pulls through and wish that you didn't have to spend another few hours in the air, but trust that everyone knows what they are doing, it is possible to still take comfort in the belief that you are doing the right thing at the time. Remember, hindsight is something that has a habit of kicking in a little too late anyway!

Remaining in control in order to manage a situation during the development of an idea, connecting the dots that make it both plausible and deliberate, ensures foundations are strong and the choice of direction is owned until the wind changes. Managing your reactions will steer you through storms, test your patience and bring a new meaning to the word *humble*. All this, with the support of inner wisdom, external expertise and knowledge, openness to learning, becoming adaptable to change, taking ownership and responsibility for getting from A to B, will surely be considered by any stretch of the imagination as doing your best. And your best will always be enough. Sometimes, it has to be enough.

Sometimes if your intention is to help this original idea have another growth spurt, get its act together and show you a little more respect for all your hard work then maybe the time is ready – maybe you are ready. The time for both usually needs to be aligned.

I am sure there has been a missed opportunity that I didn't see or I sensed its presence but let it go because I wasn't ready to take it on. Does the same opportunity come around again? I would like to think so if it was just down to a misunderstanding between self and the Universe. Any side effects from a sudden feeling of *déjà vu* would probably subside as the past memories fade as quickly as they snuck in. A second chance presents itself in a mature form that mirrors your own stage of maturity, thereby existing in symbiosis until the relationship moves on, having served its purpose.

So whether you plant a similar seed and try again, or delve into your packet of mixed seeds and try a new one out this time, just lay the old one to rest; break it down and put it back into the land and say thanks. Then get on with a new adventure.

An idea is not your master. It doesn't own you; you own the idea. It doesn't have to be nourished if you have changed your mind; it can wilt like a weed with no water. Don't give it your trellis and it is unlikely to climb. Keep your feet moving and then it won't tie you down. Simply find another garden to walk in, feel empowered to start again and feed your soul and not your head alone. If you let all the 'ought to's' and 'should do's' take a hold every time you try out a new idea, then you've already lost your power. The idea will be off having other ideas of how it wants to develop! How can something truly work for you, if you are making it fit another mould or someone else's dream?

Sometimes you have the right or good intention and you are all fired up, but you've simply planted your dream in the wrong place. So pick it up and move it. Your path caters for all kinds of ideas.

Find the strength and you will find your own way.

P*A*T*H

Appearances Aren't Everything!

Start off by visualising a path and what immediately springs to mind? If I asked you to visualise your own path – the one you are on – would you draw a blank, wonder what planet I have fallen off or would you know exactly what I was talking about?

If you are drawing a blank and the letters P-A-T-H have nothing in common with a winding stretch of rubble, and is only an acronym you use in a text when you've been insulted (**P**lease **A**pologise **T**hat **H**urt!), then I could lose you right here. Incidentally, how would that even appear in a text?

"Hey! P-A-T-H... lol"

"P-A-T-H! :(!"

And I suppose that would be it. Not so impressive, after all, and still miles away from resembling some sort of track.

So, it's a word that has more than one meaning and is certainly open to interpretation. It can be fluffed up with hot air, until you forget it could mean something tangible, sitting beneath your feet. I plan to keep us grounded! Although I wonder, can I introduce this 'Path' concept without taking my own feet off the ground? Thinking about it... this sounds highly unlikely. It wouldn't be my style if I didn't include a couple of those ascending ideas but they are just that: ideas squeezed into balloons that float sky high when you let them go.

I prefer to think of *path* as a non-offensive word that rolls off the tongue as easily as it rolls around the countryside, minding its own business. Indicative of 'taking you somewhere', a path isn't a conveyor belt which promises to move you along without participation. That said, travelators exist at airports. These are moving sidewalks that can take you from one point to another but you are expected to get on and off one by yourself… and carry your own baggage. Your own path will certainly accommodate some of the latter – until you choose to let it go.

By the way, do you have any memories of funfair rides that took you – or rather jolted you forwards – through a pair of deceptively small arched doors where you were immediately plunged into darkness? Sporadic illuminations appeared from nowhere as you began to lose sense of any direction in which you were being taken. You were being carried along, bombarded with noises and other distractions that confused your senses.

Finally, you left a world of madness behind as you were shunted back into the light, back into your own world of entertainment; a reality which still presented you with a set of distractions – only this time, the playground stretched far beyond a blacked-out dome that had only existed to amuse you temporarily (and swallow up your pocket money). Rarely closing its doors to visitors, your path is potentially a big tourist attraction where your imagination can truly interact with your ideas and bring them alive; also, it can sometimes get you into trouble!

Behaving, at first, like children who've been given the freedom to run loose in a chocolate factory, words, too, enjoy the unlimited opportunities to run wild. Hopping in and out of conversations, because they can, doesn't make them invincible, either. They can only be carried so far by linguistic travelators into a sea of context, until they are stopped in mid-sentence to have their boarding passes checked. Sometimes it is simply better for an unhelpful word to leave the conversation and allow the words which are proving to be most valuable to remain on board for the ride. Although, you could argue that those which are open to interpretation do punctuate the conversation with reflective moments. Likewise, others simply need to buckle up and endure the emotional rollercoaster to experience a reflective moment of their own; that is after checking their phone for messages… "P-A-T-H! :(!"

So, back to business; what did you end up visualising? Did you conjure up images of tawny-coloured earth-trodden tracks that either neatly edge the landscape or cut awkwardly through, following the contours of a scenic mass abounding with signposts suggesting there is always more than one way to get to that somewhere you think you want to be?

And breathe…

Alas, what do you decide to do when that piece of scenic mass and its undulating landscape is yours for the taking? With little more than untidy edges and inconsistencies sprawled out as far as the eye can see, a direction is something you could end up 'in', rather than intentionally follow.

When there are no tangible, pretty signposts to blame for feeling totally lost and you have little more to hand than your instinct to save you, what is there left to do? You make a path! (Now, don't go rolling your eyes!) *You* make your own path; *you* take responsibility; *you* shape it – even when the ground beneath is bumpy – fill in the holes and build a few bridges. You can't control the weather along the way, but you can pack an umbrella… Choose your direction and take your ideas forward.

Introducing that little beauty called Instinct into the equation is never too early from my own perspective. Let it remain a thread for now that gently weaves its way through each filling without taking the stage before the production has got into full swing. The word *instinct* is unlikely to play a low-key role along your path, as it is provocative by nature and will keep you on your toes. As for the scientists among us or the equally acclaimed critics who thrive on evidence-based reasoning, it would seem lame for me to use it by default, yet hunches and instincts fuel the hardiest of us to take a leap of faith at times!

We are all different and we are not *all lost* in our lives *all* of the time – otherwise we would be wandering around collectively, looking like something that closely resembles a community of alien-possessed mannequins, that have no idea where they are going but always seem to appear uptight. I suppose, when you are lost or confused and don't know where you are, even if you have your marbles intact, it is easy to see why you may appear uptight, from another person's perspective.

Many of us are quite happy ambling along a path. When the path appears to be going in the right direction and you are feeling in a good place in your life, it may be as simple as following the road ahead, going where it takes you and keeping up the good work. Or, maybe you have begun to master the art of not actually showing anyone you are lost and look cool, calm and collected on the outside. You could be planning your next manoeuvre and don't need to advertise the fact you are thinking things through, showing off a wrinkled forehead for the world to see. You could have just had Botox and quickly discovered that no one has a clue what you are thinking about anyway. If ever you didn't want to look like an alien-possessed mannequin, it would be now. Of course, not everyone will take on this appearance.

We have established so far that metaphorically speaking you are on a path. We have also indicated that you could be lost and may choose to keep that secret to yourself (if you can) or you may not be lost and content with life.

What if you are *not lost*, but in the back of your mind you wonder how long you can keep going along this path before boredom settles in, or you wander aimlessly for so long that you could veer off in the wrong direction because your autopilot switch, at some point in time, turned itself on permanently. Whilst you didn't recall being 'unhappy', there were likely to have been a number of opportunities sited along your path when you could have stopped and chosen an alternative route, if only to experience a change of scenery. You could have missed out on something exciting but you won't know that now because you didn't go and find out. Maybe that bothers you sometimes and maybe it doesn't. Yet, there is nothing wrong with sticking to what you know. It has its advantages and is safe – maybe boring at times, but safe. Why put yourself in a situation that could make your life harder but then again, who said a little hard work now won't make it easier, in the long run? It is another conundrum.

I have found a path that I have aspired to travel along, all of my life, and all the paths I have taken have led me here. The challenges and choices went hand in hand. The challenges gave rise to choices and the choices gave rise to challenges. At times, I made my life harder than it needed to be and my own handful of mixed seeds didn't exactly sprout into magical staircases promising to lead me on the path towards contentment. Several flights later I was often back on the ground floor as quickly as a firefighter slides down their pole in an emergency (do they still do that nowadays?).

How do you know when you've fallen off your path? Unless you felt passionate enough in the first place that you were on a particular path, what then informs you that something has changed? The emotions, thoughts and feelings that are churned up when you know you are not quite going in the right direction surely arise because you are making a comparison. Did you plan to change direction or experience an involuntary deviation? Did something happen along your path that subtly pulled you into another direction or blatantly stopped you in your tracks and changed it for you!

Unfortunately, without a psychic in tow, you are not going to foresee any waterfalls that lay ahead especially if you didn't see a warning sign in your peripheral vision. I don't think the umbrella would save you on this occasion, when you fall off your path, unless you are Mary Poppins. If you had an inkling that the waterfall was there would you have chosen differently before you got caught up in the rapids, or would you have taken a risk, clinging onto Hope during the descent?

If you fell off a path during a fall down the rapids and broke your leg, and this meant you couldn't run for a long time, you may feel you are not on your path anymore because you were training for a marathon and will miss the event. If that was all part of the bigger plan then you are very much still on your path because this experience is the learning curve, the undulating landscape, and once your leg is healed you are going to train for next year's marathon. You took a break from running; you broke your leg, that's all (that's all she says!) but did you really fall off your path? This is definitely a subtle nudge from the Universe prompting you to explore new territory.

If the accident resulted in a leg amputation and you couldn't run again – you couldn't run in next year's marathon without a prosthetic leg – you may have to let go of your dream to become a professional athlete – unless you dream big and are aiming for the Paralympics. Now, have you fallen off your path? Is it the same path that just happens to have Mount Everest slap bang in the middle, as your undulating landscape – a larger hurdle to get over? No matter how this idea is sold – as a 'destined' path to the person who has just lost their leg – the likelihood is that he/she feels they are now on a different path. I would agree that no subtle intervention was at work this time and a blatant diversion comes to mind.

It is not unusual to fall off your path without a dramatic exit needing to be written in to your schedule. Sometimes you can get so wrapped up in everyday life that the bigger picture and its vibrant colours simply begin to fade around the edges, as you focus on the day-to-day jobs that allow you to make ends meet. I suppose, if you can keep one eye on the dream then you could convince yourself that the voluntary detours are necessary and take priority, at that time. Sometimes this is just an excuse. You may be prone to taking detours because you lack confidence to stay on your current path or you don't know if the path ahead is where you really want to venture. There will be many reasons why you stray from the path you thought you wanted to walk and, funnily enough, find yourself back on it when the time is right.

You will no doubt recall a time when you were tempted into taking a side track, partly for the sheer enjoyment of exploring somewhere new and not sticking to the main road or planned route. One day you said, "I can't go along this path anymore, I want to have a look at what's over there". Sometimes it will be worthwhile or it could turn out to be a complete waste of time. When you get a feeling that something is wrong, your sixth sense can kick in and beg you to find your way back to the path you were on! Backtracking isn't always easy and can involve backing out of a situation with a degree of humility and sometimes there will be no going back! Maybe just going forward, ahead of where you stumbled, coming at it from another angle, will allow you to stop and catch your breath. You changed direction and whether you like the new view or not, you made a choice... got the picture?

To give yourself the permission to take a chance, at the risk of having an adventure, is maybe all that is required, unless you are waiting for someone else to approve what you should be doing with your own life. I appreciate that thinking about you, alone, may seem a luxury that modern life and family circles may not afford, but we all make choices. Even if you are caught up with running the house, looking after the children, going to work and all of the other things that do not involve these activities – yet still keep you busy – there may still be a part of you that wants to change direction. You may just want to change something about what you are doing, or the way you are doing it, and a small shift in behaviour ends up being enough to put you onto another path – in an emotional sense. Path doesn't have to be something you physically walk along; you are unlikely to change your path and leave your beloved children behind – you may leave your husband or wife behind, but that is your business.

Well, what prompts you to change direction? A waterfall isn't literally around every corner; you can only imagine the impact that being swept down Niagara Falls could have on you, compared to a slide down the embankment behind the bike sheds, because you had other things on your mind! Both could be life-changing! Falling and getting a little scratch may be enough to prompt you to respond and ask yourself: 'What if…?' You could wrestle with statistics or measure the probability of something else happening, had you fallen further or had the scratch been worse – that's if maths is your strong point. Then again, you could argue that falling down and getting a scratch isn't sufficient to help you change direction, unless you happened to be doing something else behind the bike sheds that resulted in that family circle being formed earlier than planned.

Does a direction imply we are going forwards along our path or do we go backwards along the same path as well? If you went backwards on the same path, then ultimately you would be able to undo all the actions you did, right? This sounds more like time-machine territory! So, when we say, "I feel I am going backwards in my life", what is it you feel is happening? You are moving forward through your day. Even when the clocks go back an hour, you are physically present to witness the artificial hands of time spin anti-clockwise and provide you with another sixty minutes to play around with. Nonetheless, you are cruising along in the same direction – even if you're asleep.

If you happen to be airborne and travelling to a part of the world that is behind your own time zone, the aircraft won't be flying backwards. And let us assume, for now, that time doesn't 'go' backwards, either. So, when you get to your destination, it is only when you come to look at your watch do you get a sense that something has changed, having had no recollection of being dematerialised along the way and transported to an alternate universe! I dare say that if you changed the time on your watch before you took off then your sense of 'time' may not have seemed so alien to you upon landing. After all, time doesn't stop going forwards just because you put your watch back and neither does your life.

On the other hand, if you are thinking of going *backwards* and return to doing something you have done before, maybe you will do it better this time. But if you didn't do it very well before, then what has changed now to make you think it will be good to try it again? Do you need to go back along the same path or can you consider that what is waiting for you ahead could be far more interesting than what you did before. And 'waiting ahead'. What does that even mean? Could it be that something is already positioned on your path, sitting cross-legged and arms folded, waiting patiently for you to arrive before getting up to greet you with open arms and shouting 'hallelujah'? You can't even claim to have stood up the blob of imaginary opportunity, if you didn't know it was waiting for you – just like a blind date that has been set up by your friend, who forgot to tell you when and where! You can be forgiven for not arriving on time.

Adding to this scenario and injustice, assume that you don't arrive on time because you missed a turning on the way there. You end up going *backwards* instead of forwards to take the one that you originally intended and by the time you get to it, you begin to question if it is the same one you passed before. Depending on how much time has elapsed, it will hopefully appear recognisable. But if it doesn't look the same, can you accept this as a sign for you to bypass it altogether and trust that fate has a more attractive path for you to follow, just up the road?

Think of a time you have been on a motorway and missed the turning – so you take the next exit, instead. You go around the roundabout, across the bridge and come back down the other side – you are going backwards along the same motorway you just came up, but forwards because you are not driving in reverse gear, I hope. Finally, you take the next left turning, which is on the opposite side of the road from where you had originally planned to be – once over the bridge you are now in the right direction, *for you*. But what if you kept going forwards on the motorway; would that have still been in the right direction?

Geographically, you could argue that taking the next turning would have got you there eventually. It may have taken you a bit longer and a few extra miles out of your way but what's a few more minutes added on to your journey, and who knows, the adventure may do you good! Maybe what is waiting for you decides to lie down out of boredom and appear as nothing more than a sleeping policeman designed to slow you down in life, as you pass through an equally sleepy village it serves to protect. This is after being intercepted by a herd of cows that choose to cross your path, forcing you to take in the charming scenery that would otherwise be overlooked had you still been bombing along in the fast lane, at whatever speed, on the motorway.

A path takes you from 'A' to 'B' (physically or emotionally). Think of it as a road trip and hopefully you have a destination in mind. If you were told in advance it was going to be an adventure would you want to miss out on all the fun or does that depend upon your approach to life and what 'type of person you are'? Have you always been an adventurous character or has a past experience curtailed any future desire to put adventure before sensibility, ever again! Maybe you would like to be more adventurous, yet cannot fathom out where to begin; after all, what does adventurous mean?

Do you opt for a challenging path, because it will make you stronger and the element of surprise only inspires you to go on, to discover more, fuelled by adrenaline? Or would you prefer to find the short cut; the easier one that could get you 'there' a bit quicker but could land you in a whole lot of trouble along the way and will still present its challenges, whether you are using the motorway or taking a cross-country detour?

It is never just about us. We interact with people on their path and they interact with us, on ours. At what point, and how, they intercept can play a huge part in whether we stay on a path or change direction. We influence each other, even without any contact. We may not know that person on a personal level – we may have never met that someone – but something they said or did prompted us to make a change and initiated a turning point in our lives. This could be about a celebrity or even a character in a fiction book you are reading; something they said inspired you. A newsreader will describe the unseen footage of despair and destruction in a place where you have never been. You watch, you listen, you read and you interpret.

What is happening when all of this is going on? Are we being drawn into what someone else is doing along their path – even from a distance? If you haven't met them they don't know you exist but you know they exist! Did their actions affect you? We may not be aware that another person's actions or opinions have an impact on us at the time, but later they pop up in a conversation and you think, *When did I hear about that?*

Commuters on a train interact with other people visually or vocally. Maybe none of those subliminal or tiny interactions will make a difference to that person on that particular day; but who knows the effects of things seen or heard that day on another situation encountered later in the week, the month or in later life. These experiences are nicely tucked away in the not-for-now part of the mind's database, as something that may never knowingly be tapped into again. How valuable we are and yet we don't even know what we are worth. If we had to download all the information caught on our own mental camera, every day – apart from being dangerous – we could be worth millions!

So how we continue along our path, going forward, may be influenced by how we interpret an opinion or a piece of information, and can change how we may decide to go about something we had planned on doing one way, but now decide to do another way – or not at all.

People's opinions may be signposts in disguise and just when you thought those signposts didn't exist they pop up to offer a little direction! Other people and their positive or negative energies will collide with yours but it is still your path. They have intercepted like a bunch of free radicals moving in and out of your life, bouncing around, leaving their mark, and you don't realise the impact, at the time.

Once the gates are opened, our life-long membership will have an expiry date – we just don't know when that is. Many of us will see our lives as just a period of time that exists, to do as much or as little as can be done, and there doesn't have to be a mysterious hidden meaning behind every decision we make – neither does every experience need to be analysed.

It can also be a chance to exploit as many opportunities as is viable, and some of us prove to do this exceptionally well, leaving others feeling a tad envious. Alas, living a full life doesn't mean it has to be filled with copious amounts of experiences that may not necessarily add up and give rise to any one thing in particular being fulfilled, as you speed down your path, trying to pack as much in to it as possible (remember you have to carry your baggage). All those experiences will have involved their own sacrifices along the way and some can disadvantage your life in one area or another. The upside to living a full life is that it puts you in credit with 'The Bank of Life Lessons'. No, that doesn't mean you will automatically end up becoming wiser than the next person, who didn't task themselves with acquiring credit in this way. A life full of one or two things which satisfy the appetite may be all that is required for some of us, and will bring with it its own set of experiences to last a lifetime.

Be that as it may, someone else's path can often seem more appealing. It can also be an illusion of perfection. We can overlook the fact that we all think and behave differently, and so walking in someone else's shoes may not suit us, in the end, as we realise our approaches to situations are unalike. Our customs and cultures, our diversity and our dissimilarity all present us with different obstacles and delights along our paths. Whether these actualities lie ahead on the main road that keeps us focused, or silently surprise us when we have chosen to take a detour, they will not, alone, allow any two situations to be the same.

Some people have an idea where they want to get to in life but don't know where to start; that sounds like a coach's dream client. Likewise, you can have an epiphany about a desire to get started on something and feel uncertain about where you could end up because you hadn't formulated a clear picture – yet!

If you don't know where the final destination is going to be, can you still get started? Of course you can; don't be put off by anyone that tells you otherwise! Sometimes we find out where we want to be – by accident. How many times have you gone out for the day, not knowing quite which direction to take, and half a mile down the road you think, *Ah yes, how about... that-a-way!* Who knows if you were divinely guided; saw a sign on the way which prompted your brainwave to signal left or right; or suddenly you just knew... because you remembered something that someone said on the train from... months ago!

You could take the view that if you don't know where you want to go then how on earth can you plan a route? No one is saying it is easy to be inspired or indeed get motivated but if you take a few small steps in a direction that feels comfortable then inspiration may be one of those delights that just happen to be sitting on your path ahead – waiting for you! Call it a blind date!

Discovery and exploration is going on all the time, whether we are aware of this or not. It is difficult to avoid it happening but the gap, when observed, between discovering something new and going on to explore it further, will depend on what has been discovered and whether it's of any interest and importance to you, at the time.

For example, discovering after all these years that you like fresh peas may seem interesting because you have only tried mushy peas in the past, which you've always detested. It is not something you are inclined to ponder on for too long, if at all. The emotional distance (the gap), between discovering it is possible to like peas and exploring why, will be wide; the result isn't likely to impact on a great deal as you walk your path!

Now working out what you want to do with the rest of your life could be different. You will be actively discovering and exploring ideas or opportunities in order to 'get somewhere', 'be someone' or 'achieve something'. Discovering and exploring any potential link will become a two-way street and you gain a thirst to explore, once something interesting has been discovered. The distance now, between discovery and exploration, will be less; the gap will be closing in. It is the start of a beautiful friendship and this time you are engaged!

There will be an endless number of things to discover and explore on our own path and all the other characters, which haven't even got a mention yet, will no doubt be influential. They will influence how much we toddle off to do and how we go about doing it. Emotions will get in the way of doing some of those things very well and, thankfully, allow us to achieve others that we thought would be impossible.

Do we agree, in principle, that a path is a journey we go on through life, even if the word *journey* is one of those annoying words that you want to reserve for describing something you start when boarding a bus or train? One life plan is made up of layers of tarmac in the sky but not without its potholes, flyovers, underpasses and neon-coloured picket fences that line your path – so you don't keep falling off. Yet it is multi-layered, multi-faceted and fragmented and the only other way to get off, before the exit hatch opens up, is to jump off – and sadly some of us do.

A path, for some of us, can be a lonely stretch of space; one which we walk alone, even when we are surrounded by people. For others loneliness can feel a remote place and one which sees no visitors. Seeing our own world sitting alongside other people's worlds, which don't connect, can feel isolating but we often have the option to build bridges, if we want to do so. If we can connect with ourselves first and learn to start our discovery from within, we can channel our truth through our thoughts, our voice and our heart.

I realise it is one thing offering up this perspective and another thing working out how to do it in practice. I believe there is a way – a way of throwing this idea around. If it happens to be one of those I stuck in a balloon at the beginning, maybe a few of the characters itching to join us can step in shortly, catch the end and share some of their candyfloss.

After all, your path is a playground to be explored!

C*H*O*I*C*E

Join the Brigade and Get in Line!

"After all, it happened *to* me. It wasn't my fault and if I could change it I would, but naturally – I just didn't have a choice!" she said.

"The funny thing is, I was on this path and a situation bumped into me. I am sure I didn't bump into *it* (the situation) and I found myself taken in by it all and so I went along with it. I didn't have a choice… you know?" he said.

"This path analogy – wow; if I could really make one work for me then I am sure I can choose where I want it to go, and how and where I want it to end! I have heard about the 'Create your dream' speech and 'The like-attracts-like' concept that underpins nearly all the motivational speakers' keynote speeches on the planet! Has anyone heard about it? They say, 'Think it… and it will happen'; 'Feel it… and then you're halfway there' (wherever there is). Then apparently, you let your thoughts go and leave it up to the Universe to deliver – well that's the last bit, I think," said by the one who has now decided to investigate further into this incredible idea that there is a post office situated somewhere in the sky, collecting these thoughts. There must be a postman (or woman) working flat out, capable of either dropping a bombshell on you when you least expect, or bringing you what you asked for without paying the postage.

So, as I am *the one* who continues to be a masochist and exhaust the above concept (as I do think there is something to be said for letting go…), I also recommend having a back-up plan! This is to avoid twiddling your thumbs during the process and do something that doesn't involve over-thinking.

On one particular day, after sending a request, I took my interest to another level – some may say, quite literally, another universe. It was when I began to count the number of Pendolinos that ran through my local train station in my lunch hour, out of the window at work, that I decided I was taking this law of distraction theory too far. This was either an activity that demonstrated I had moved on or was a cry for help, as I was slowly losing the will to live! If you haven't heard of a Pendolino, it is a train that runs at incredibly high speed to get you from A to B faster than you can say, "Law of Attraction"!

I didn't really notice any attachment between my brain and the impending manifestation. Needless to say, I was silently hoping that the latter would happen as soon as possible; you can't help but remain poised, keeping one eye open. I usually left my standby light on and took comfort in believing that communications were at large. I was willing to go along with the idea that the thought I originally had could get transported into another dimension and return looking something close to the original intention.

I believe in the Law of Attraction process although I am not going to be writing a book about it in any detail. I think a couple of lines here and there will suffice. Any intolerance beginning to build up, for those of you who'd prefer to skip ahead, will soon notice it pass. So kindly smile at the point of view, recognise it shapes a space on the page and allow it to walk by – as you would with any stranger in the street. Think of it as one of those extras that appear in a film, in the background, and focus on the main characters that are sneaking in to warm you up.

Suffice it to say that thinking and feeling about something you want will surface eventually – if it is meant to be. Constantly waiting for the result to unveil itself, and feeling consumed with not knowing that your message has been received by the 'Law of Attraction Elves', is highly frustrating, and does nothing but make you yearn for the result even more! Yearning is regarded as non-productive and a form of attachment.

When you send a message to the Universe – all you can do is hope (and believe) it has been received. When you send a letter by recorded delivery, you can at least be reassured that the postage paid will be sufficient to allow you to continue on with your day knowing that something tangible will be passed on. And hopefully arrive at the other end. If you are not planning to become a member of any universal wishing club any time soon, then you will be pleased to know that Hope is a character that will crop up soon and appears to be non-discriminatory – so yearn away if you want to!

*

So do we have choices in everything we do? I mean everything? We go about our business and collide with the army of choices sprawled out on our path every day, and seek to find excuses to avoid making decisions, especially if they are too hard to make, choosing to put them off until tomorrow!

What does choice really mean for you? It isn't really the

definition of 'choice' *per se* that is probably hard to describe. It is more likely to be about how the available options surrounding a situation can make it harder or easier to choose. The number of scenarios you have to traipse through before you can actually make a decision can sometimes be draining – and on top of that, nerve wracking.

It comes back to whether you have made the right decision at the time. Have you explored all the avenues; have you taken into account the consequences of your actions and really thought your options through? Have you taken responsibility; are you a responsible person and do you take your actions seriously? Or do you float from one choice to another, playing a game of multiple choice because you don't really know the answer? You choose randomly and hope for the best.

We are not just talking about whether you bought the right toothpaste, or chose the right wine for dinner; we may be talking about ditching your job, breaking up with your partner or whistleblowing on the next president-to-be! The consequences or risks associated with making a difficult decision have not only taken the choice-making process into another dimension, but have changed your total perception of what choice actually means to you.

It's just another thing to do each day; it's an inevitable act to embrace and you may even take solace in the fact it can be entertaining if you approach it with humour. You wake up and feel like being accountable, and sometimes you want to blame everyone and everything on why the choices you made didn't go as planned – more often than not you know why and you just have to live with it!

If a choice presents itself, it is usually because something needs to be decided but you don't always have to decide to do something; doing nothing can be the right choice! If I asked you whether you wanted to eat chocolate or cheesecake, no one is forcing you into making a decision; and actually, as unbelievable as this may sound to some of you… you don't have to eat either of them anyway and can decide to abstain. There are no choice detectives watching… or are there?!

So, we have established that choices have to be made every day – on so many different levels. The 'choice-making' process itself doesn't accompany your set of choices in a flat-pack box, with a pop-up flow diagram to make it easy for you decide – that would just blow the whole 'free will' theory out of the window! There are no tiny wafer-thin paper guidelines, neatly folded, crying out in a size 4 font (that no one can read), in twelve different languages, that after 'scanning', politely suggests you go to their website. You know, the one that specialises in 'How to make a choice and live with it…' or else call them direct for further information. Direct, of course, means that you call a telephone number that takes you directly to their voicemail and leaves you feeling deflated as you get to option 6 and can't remember what the first one had prompted you to do! What if you make the wrong choice?

I have made a point about the onus being on us to choose wisely, whilst varnishing it with cynicism, but wouldn't it be great if we could press a button and be privy to a bespoke set of instructions to suit the occasion? What about applying for one set that will cater for 'How to make a choice and live with it… *each and every time*'? That would do nicely. Also, '*Live with it…*', in this context, does sound as though the choice we are going to make will be forged with despair for some time to come, when what I really mean is, whatever choice we make, we have to accept the direction it will end up taking us.

It could be an exciting choice to be worrying over – maybe about whether you go to Spain or Italy for your holiday this year. A decision made in a moment of vulnerability, because you have just watched *Under the Tuscan Sun* (this is a fabulous movie, filmed in Italy, that you can watch over and over to cement the ideology that the spur of the moment choices you make in life really can result in a fairytale ending…) that now has you booked on a flight to Italy, choosing pasta over paella!

We cannot delude ourselves that every choice we will ever make in our life will be right but does it have to feel right before we make one? When we're in the midst of toing and froing with ideas, we may feel uncertain that the choice we are making is going to be the right one but we make a decision, for whatever reason, and we live with the consequences – positive or negative.

Right is an interesting word that definitely changes its spots to suit the occasion! We suggested earlier on, that we do what we do at the time, so it must be right in that moment. What follows on from that decision and how you end up feeling is another matter altogether. Most of us pride ourselves with recognising 'a right' from 'a wrong', especially when our moral compass is joined to our hip and propels us forward, encouraging us to 'walk the talk' to demonstrate we have the ability to practise what we preach, and a conscience to keep us morally grounded.

How to make the right choice, when it comes to our own personal affairs, isn't something we can learn on a course. There isn't an Emotional Sandwich that can pretend to know the answer either; there isn't a coach or mentor, a teacher or trainer, a man or woman of the cloth that can claim to know for certain what the right choice is for you – other than you! People can, though, help you to make a right choice.

Everyone can look through their window in their ivory

tower and view your life through their eyes. We can choose to base our decisions on how we want to live our lives or on how we think other people may want us to live our lives. Sometimes we consider both, because we have other people to consider in our lives who may be affected by the decisions we make.

A choice, in practice, may fall on an individual to make or become the basis of a group decision. How long does it take to make the right choice? There is the split-second choice to consider and the 'take all your time in the world' choice; the lengthy consultation period; the laborious change-control process; the hold fire until we have the facts conundrum (that equates to the 'how long is a piece of string' scenario); and, last but not least, the hierarchical approach. This is the one that either involves so many people that even the senior decision-makers have forgotten their remit, in fear of taking accountability, or the inability to agree simply results in a poor decision being made, or not at all. Any form of decision-making that involves a degree of human intervention will come with its usual challenges and will need to be overcome.

Today you woke up and headed to the kitchen to make breakfast, trying to decide if porridge or eggs would fuel your temple through to lunch, or if fruit and toast would suffice. As you juggle the family or simply indulge in your own morning ritual, including high-maintenance activities, you ask yourself, slumping over the worktop half asleep, "Is this really a decision I have to make every day, for the rest of my life?" Yes – more than likely if you want to continue to eat breakfast!

Now take your imagination past breakfast and think of a more challenging set of choices that have a habit of arising on more than one occasion in your life. How about recalling a situation that had you dialling up the past for advice, only to find that the past is now out of date and the circumstances on which you based that choice then have changed. It would be like going back into the past and actually reading a TV manual for a TV that doesn't exist now and expecting it to help you connect your new, shiny, high-tech LED screen, with fifty buttons, to the extra-terrestrial dish that now sits on your roof. I knew aliens were involved from the moment I wrote about 'Sometimes'! It sounded a tad extreme two chapters ago, because we were focusing on how we personally change, and the ideas we had 'once upon a time' may change too.

We may not look at the same idea in the same way each time. Almost like a painting that tells a different story as the colours change in a different light. Therefore, a set of choices, now, can appear similar to those experienced in your past, but 'something this time is different' and now requires a different approach. Even when you know 'you have been here before', this doesn't mean that you will automatically know what to do the next time you find yourself in a similar predicament. How many times do you find yourself in a similar situation and the circumstances are somewhat different? So, how can you make a choice now, based on any past experiences unless an experience is 'identical'? There will be plenty of times you can apply past learnings for a quick win, and feel chuffed that this time you finally got it right and you didn't make the same 'mistake'. Then you have the ones that really need a fresh pair of eyes.

Trying to repeat the past and applying the same strategy, or reinventing it while still using second-hand parts that didn't work the first time, isn't going to bring about a different result. Did you ever bake a cake with plain flour and then found yourself wondering why it didn't rise? Did you put the same cake back in the oven, having injected it with a couple shots of self-raising flour, in the hope that a repair job would somehow counteract any wrongdoing in the first place? Doubtful! Two words come to mind: start over.

Fear not; simply gather the right ingredients, apply past learnings and then the second time around is bound to be digestible. Now, that is a filling which is seeping in earlier than planned: Fear. There is nothing like a little cross-contamination to keep these wordy relationships on fire. Think of 'Fear' as the dab of hot English mustard dotted in your ham roll that is a complementary condiment, but too much of it can tip your taste buds over the edge. 'Fear' is going to have to wait its turn, even though I cannot promise it won't crop up to remind you it is on its way as it tends to interfere.

So, where were we? Yes; it will be through choice that a decision will be made and each decision made will take us either over a step or onto a step, so we can finally reach the place where we want to be – even if that place is not a conventional one that has anything remotely to do with a town or location. It may be a 'feeling' place that you end up in when you have made the right choice between, say, deciding to cook that night or to phone through for a delivery.

Right ends up being the smell of deep-fried pancake rolls which, incidentally, are currently being cooked up in your imagination before you have even dialled the number, as opposed to the smell of dishes pining to be washed, weeping because they are going to suffer neglect overnight, because you didn't want to cook in the first place. Making a voluntary decision to indulge in 'trans fatty acids' and 'hydrogenated fat', avoiding any threat of catching the 'kitchen blues' is a choice you freely made and, whilst unchallenging, will have been highly emotive.

I didn't feel 'well' at work today so my boss gave me three

choices: I could leave the office and work from home, in the peace and quiet; come in at the weekend and make up my hours; or take the time off unpaid. So, I have three choices and none of them really appeal. One of them has to be chosen because I am under a contractual agreement to work! When I get home will I want to go to bed because I feel ill? When I feel better at the weekend, I may not want to work. If I don't work then I won't get paid! I decide not to get paid, draw a line under the situation and start the next week feeling all refreshed. I made a choice. I probably made one that meant I had to postpone my shopping plans; I would have to write a longer to-do list at work on Monday and draft up a few apology emails in the process to appease my customers.

All in all… a choice had to be made. Any residual impact requiring my attention will surface at a later date and this is a chance I was willing to take at the time. I must have carried out an instinctive risk assessment in my head, no doubt based on feeling under the weather at the time, but if there was a sense of urgency to tackle a life-threatening piece of work, I am certain I would have chosen differently.

We do what we do at the time! Whatever those influencing factors turn out to be, appearing on our radar, leading us into temptation, they flaunt themselves momentarily. They may appear as a flash of inspiration or distraction, arriving at an opportune moment, no doubt designed to lead us to behave in one way or another; think in one way or another. Choices must present themselves for a reason or do they present themselves because it is inevitable that there will be more than one option to take in any given situation? There have to be two in the very least: what you choose to do and what you choose not to do!

If we really do have 'free will', and manipulating each step along the way to fit our shoe size is as important as creating the path that will go the distance, then choices are something that can be met with a degree of excitement. After all, we are making history. We are being responsible for our own life and taking ownership. We can view the choice as an opportunity to change direction, make a new plan or walk away and let fate make a choice for us. We may think we have chosen to do nothing but we chose all the same.

Leaving it all to fate could work too – is that what I am doing when I send my request off to the Universe? I like to credit myself with doing some of the hard work too. It takes courage to do something with your dreams and make things happen in your life. I am inclined to add that remaining positive and hopeful are both key players, and even if I am one of those people who has a little faith in that postman in the sky, it doesn't seem to protect me from actually having to still make choices. I just have to choose how big that dream is going to be and then set about making it happen.

Suppose we make a choice, still using our free will, and realise in the seconds that follow that we made a mistake – even though it felt right to us at the time. It may only take a second to come to this conclusion; yet, in some cases, it can take us years to pick up the pieces. But we can end up getting a lot of other things right, later on in life, as a result of making that one poor judgement. It is difficult to see any correlation until the benefits catch you up and put a smile back on your face. Their staggered appearance along your stretch of path proves deceptive but begins to make more sense as you do a few laps on the way. Circular detours can give your other ideas time to develop.

Remember, your handful of mixed seeds is varied and it is only through discovery and exploration that we learn. If you make a poor choice and the opportunity comes around full circle, inviting you to make a similar choice again, you can choose wisely with an added dose of that delightful word: hindsight. Serendipity is around every corner – you just don't know where or when it will strike.

Your choices are interpreted by an audience, at one time or another, every single day. These are the virtual players that have all the answers, but don't actually get the same opportunity to put them into practice, because your world and theirs are not the same. The sports fan that watched the game and confidently told everyone how it should have been played from a comfy spot that didn't necessitate any need for movement – other than the mid-air rise to reflect their anguish or a triumph – *is* the virtual player and observes the choices made in the field.

A jury that has not been privy to all the facts, and is certain to form an opinion about a choice you have made recently, as a result of eavesdropping inappropriately or basing their ideas on hearsay (or evidence), will form part of the silent jury that sit among us. Whether they are watching you buy your spring rolls or eating your cheesecake our choices may be seen from afar and judged.

What you see through your eyes, as being the best way of doing something, may not work in practice for someone else. I suppose in this case, you will choose to agree or disagree. It would be a shame to invest all your energy in making a decision and not expect it to do what you had hoped, wouldn't it?

H*O*P*E

Bridging the Gap

If you go to all the hard work of making something happen in your life, wouldn't you expect it to work out, or do you take the stance that (whilst it would be great if it did) it is unusual for everything to work out – just because you hoped it would?

Surely it is OK to have expectations even though we may run the risk of them letting us down. You start out believing, with all your heart, that the expected something is going to work out or why would you do it? If there was an element of risk being involved, then it would make sense to hang on to Hope – with dear life; although, hoping alone gives me the impression that there could be a lack of confidence lurking behind the scenes. What if you are uncertain that what you are doing will really work out because Expect has clearly lost its nerves, relying on Luck to saunter in and save the day. Alarm bells are ringing – who needs who and why?!

We are exploring what it may mean to be hopeful but at what point do you call in the cavalry? When the plot thickens and the choices you've made suddenly reveal a hidden agenda and you are certain you didn't see that coming… then Hope may be your rock – when there is no more left to do!

Incidentally, if Hope is having an affair with three other

characters, do they all know that they are involved in each other's relationships? *Hope* appears to be dating *Expect,* who commands respect and thrives on being assertive and confident. *Risk* likes to have *Hope* around when it feels like being mischievous and is basically using *Hope* as a bit on the side. *Luck* is the charmer and can be outrageously flirtatious but it is its own boss. You can't make *Luck* do anything it doesn't want to do; don't plan a date with *Luck* and expect it show up – just hope it will. So if *Risk* and *Hope* are colluding one day, *Luck* could show up at the right time.

We all have an idea about what Hope and his friends mean to us. Why have I indicated Hope is a male? I have no idea! Probably, it is because I'm a female and *Hope* is my own personal soulmate whom I welcome as a companion on my own journey; in any case, it sounds protective and I can romanticise. Take the following situation as an example.

If you have chosen to apply for a job, you hope to get an interview. Then you go to the interview with expectations about the job and what you can deliver by remaining positive when you get there, all fired up, expecting to get the job. What you may actually be saying to yourself is, "I hope to get the job". Some of us may not expect to get the job if we haven't applied for a job like this before and have been told that the candidates attending are highly experienced. You are unlikely to know who they are and really, do you need to? Your priority will be to prepare and ensure you know what you are talking about – maybe say what you think they want you to say (that's interviews for you). Also, say something they didn't expect you to say that will give you brownie points. If you go along not expecting to get the job then you took a risk; as luck has it, you get the job!

Hope tends to be thought about with fondness even if we link it to situations that may not share the same level of enthusiasm. We may say the word *hope* in a tone of voice that carries an element of desperation keeping Confidence in the shadows. Alternatively, we may allow it to be spoken with unusual optimism or with a certainty in the voice that is representative of usual. We write it down and trust that the person who reads it will sense our desire for something to happen – either for them or for us! I reckon we tend to think about Hope more than we care to let on and remain unbiased in the way we use it.

So what does Hope think about his relationship to Risk, Luck and Expect? Let's get to know this trio in a little more detail while exploring the different territories that they are likely to inhabit, and where Hope finds itself equally attracted.

Risk and Hope

Risk taking – doesn't that accompany every choice we make? Even when certain that the right decision has been made, have you really got any control over the end result? Have we got any control over what is going to suddenly come along and impact on the choice we made, along the path we are on?

We are accustomed to thinking that a risk implies that something negative could happen – and it could. Equally, you could take a risk and the end result could exceed your expectations. Any concerns you had, when it started out as a threat, have now been relinquished as it becomes an opportunity. Anyone who has learned about project management will tell you that whilst you need to consider what the risks could be and have a back-up plan in business (as in life), a perceived risk may not happen and could be circumstantial. You may back down, if the risk is too high, or take a chance because the odds are for, rather than against. All the influencing factors, which you had time to explore, hoping they wouldn't surface and negatively impact on your project, may change for a number of reasons.

What about when we take a risk that hasn't had any time to build up momentum in your mind? For example, you pull out at a roundabout because, in that moment, you believe you can go around it without the oncoming car colliding into you. It is a risk. Although you chose to take it and instinctively felt it was OK to do so, you could not be certain that the other car wouldn't crash into you or even speed up on purpose as you moved into his/her space with complacency. You cannot control the actions of the other driver – only anticipate that what you are 'about' to do will not impact on either of you. I can't imagine in the moment, before you pulled out, that you had any time to say, "I hope I will make this!"

If a collision occurred and afterwards you were asked why you took a risk, you may reply that you hoped it would be OK. In this instance you made 'Hope' the scapegoat. So, you would have been hoping all along, subconsciously, but the nature of the risk didn't allow you any time to cogitate and spiel out any protective mantras beforehand or during – if you were being that reckless. I would personally hope that if you did have any time spare to think about taking a risk when driving, your instincts would kick in and persuade you otherwise. Maybe it is best you reserve that adrenaline rush for a non-participatory viewing of the TV show, *The Dukes of Hazzard* (feel free to google this, if you don't know what I am talking about).

As we are focusing, for a moment, around the implications of taking a risk, I am going to keep to the driving theme. Incidentally, the other day I witnessed four counts of reckless driving as I was on my way to work – all by one driver! I was travelling at a suitable speed and refrained from insulting each speed sign as I drove past. A car pulled out from a lane on the opposite side of the road to me, just in time to avoid a collision with the car ahead of mine. It was not another slip road and so he needed an invitation to join my lane! I wondered if he was lucky to be able to pull that stunt off or plain stupid for making the attempt in the first place and relied heavily on Hope; it was early in the morning. People make crazy manoeuvres trying to get to work on time. What gave it away was the look of angst that I caught on his face as the swerve of his car flicked the back wheels out and if you have ever seen the film, *Herbie Goes to Monte Carlo*, this was a close impression. It didn't end there. He was speeding up; slowing down; overtaking the other cars, one at a time – even when oncoming traffic had no plans to slow down, making each one a close call. Risk number 2 (or 4, depending if you count each overtake individually) made me wonder if this guy was a consistent risk-taker in his everyday life, or was he hoping he wouldn't get caught out, just for today.

Well, finally, through what appeared to be an act of impatience he winged a right, into a lane that was only supposed to be entered from the same side of the road and not from the opposite direction – cutting across. I can only recall the animated visions that appeared in my head as he zoomed off into the distance, to be seen no more. In what seemed like only five minutes (and at the start of the day, remember), this man took several risks. What does that say about the rest of his day – yet to come – and how many more risks will he take? Is Hope really giving up its generous time to mingle with such unorthodox behaviour? Will he really be thinking about 'Hope' while he is terrorising the community with his dangerous driving antics? Maybe he just expects all his risks to work out – and his over-confident behaviour is in fact his lucky charm!

We all do risky things in life. Some risks we take will be higher or lower than those taken by our peers. If it is something you do not ordinarily do, it will seem risky. If you are used to doing something all the time – and sorry to point out the obvious – it may not seem risky; you may know it is a risk but it isn't emotive.

Expect and Hope

I hope that every time I make a decision it will be the right one. I probably do expect a particular thing to happen – is that logical or plain arrogant? After all, I don't intentionally make a choice and plan on it not being the right one! (Do I?) Do you?

If we make a decision based on a limited number of options and hope that one of them will be the best out of a bad bunch, will Hope act as a bridge to allow 'what we chose and what we expected to achieve' to safely cross together? If we don't have any hope to glue the building blocks together, will the choices made and the expected outcomes have an opportunity to meet all on their own?

Do you expend your energy, consciously being aware that you are being hopeful, or is it just a 'business as usual' mindset that doesn't need reassessing all the time? Some of the happiest people I have met are those who manage their own expectations and don't need to keep checking in to see if these are being met every five minutes. Hope is an integral part of their lives that doesn't need a voice and is quite capable of delivering against priorities and requires a little faith on your part to trust it to get on and do its job.

Hope just sat quietly and did what you wanted it to do. It silently travelled through space and time and cast its spell, sprinkling its magic dust on the decisions you made. It allowed you to take a back seat and watch patiently to see what worked out and what didn't; it did its best. Hope did its best to meet your expectations. It cannot deliver every time.

Some decisions made during the choice-making process were flawed and not quite up to scratch. Sometimes, what we hope for will not turn up trumps and no matter how much hope gets splashed about, it will simply never be enough. You can't blame Hope for not delivering and maybe you relied too heavily on fate to twist and turn. If you doubt in your own ability to make the right decisions and pull in the resource – *Hope* – every time, then that is maybe where you are going wrong. You have to have confidence in your own decision-making process. Stilting the process with a desperate plea to Hope to step in is not empowering.

That said, even I am hard pushed to not misuse the word, allowing it to slide in through the back door and mark its territory, giving it automatic membership to sit aside the rest of my vocabulary. I even use it first thing in the morning before I get out of bed saying, "I hope it is going to be a good day today!" There isn't anything wrong with that sentence. It isn't offensive and sounds quite innocent. OK, so I could sound more empowered: "*It is going to be a good day today...*" Any better? (Who's convincing who here?) OK... how about this: "*It is a good day!*" I am still keeping the door open to the Universe and it can contribute if it feels up to it; I am not summoning it to interfere as it will anyway. I believe myself!

I know, I know; it is probably 6am when the word *good* has already breezed in to your life, for a fleeting moment, and then left your vocabulary by 7.30am, due to an alien invasion of one kind or another. This may appear in the form of a toddler or two; traffic lights that seriously didn't agree upon each other's schedule that morning, on the way to work; or running out of coffee meant that 'Good' had no right to enter your vocabulary in the first place.

Nonetheless, when you call on Hope (as you may have resorted back to doing) do you expect it to be a magician? Do you expect a day to run smoothly, with no effort? This is not an unthinkable notion. Why does everything have to be an effort, anyway? When I wake up, of course I hope it will be a good day; who doesn't? I will do my best to make it a good day regardless of whether Hope makes an active contribution. I inject a little bit of passion into everything I do and it's a fantastic feeling to end a day knowing I have done my best; I aim to pull it off without exhausting Hope, keeping it as a third party intervention – the same can be said for Luck.

Luck and Hope

Luck is something we aspire to meet in our lives with open arms and a humbleness to reflect a limitless amount of appreciation because it comes into our life as a gift. It crosses our path and charms us into thinking we may have made it all by ourselves, asking for nothing in return. We hope to attract Luck but I don't know if we make Luck. If we could make Luck, just imagine what we could do with it; alas, it is the bonus ball and we all hope to be thrown one of those from time to time.

We create opportunities in our lives and hope that Luck will find us, more often than not out of the blue. We may assume that if we strive to create a clear path ahead, then Luck will hone in on us better. It finds us when we are not looking and also when we have had no luck in finding it, when we do choose to look! Are we looking too hard, relying once again on something else to improve our own lives? We hope it will find us amidst our own confusion, holding our hand when we reach out in the dark. Luck can find us when we think we are managing quite well on our own, thank you very much. Maybe we were doing OK because Luck kept us buoyant and we didn't realise how many events in our lives were held up by bubbles of Luck that rolled around us, emulating our own curves, and looking back we were never alone – we had Luck on our side.

I don't mean to be contradictory. I am toying with the idea that we must aspire to be mindful of what we are doing, where we are heading and how we plan to get from A to B during our lives, on our own and with the help of other people. I am also aware that some of us believe in being guided along by the silent visitors that walk our every step and we live in a world where spiritual intervention is present. Having said that, some of us do not buy in to this myth.

If Luck has anything to do with divine intervention, I am very happy to consider this as a little freebie in my life. If it has nothing to do with fairies, and an invisible force is reserved for a rendition of *Star Wars*, then so be it. If we cannot make luck *per se*, I would be keen to know why some of us have more of it, or so we lead ourselves to believe. Some of us are just down on our luck and have a tendency to think that the grass must be greener in everyone else's lives.

The off-the-cuff comments, made by people who think everyone must be luckier, are reflective of their own relationship with the word *luck*. You just have to forgive any ignorance, when they direct one at you – we don't all have the opportunity to tell our story and set them straight.

Sometimes a person is not lucky and created their own opportunities, making their own sacrifices along the way in exchange for the goods. They hoped that whatever sacrifices and choices they made on their path would, at some stage, give rise to a positive outcome which is perceived as being lucky. If you clearly have an audit trail to challenge this accusation and have the worn-out shoes as evidence, then Luck is unlikely to have carried you all the way. If you took a wrong set of steps, can you say you were unlucky or should you own up to the fact that Luck's darker side didn't have anything to do with your own poor judgement? If you took the right steps, but the eventualities along the way meant you didn't have a hope in hell's chance of getting through unscathed, this is unlucky! We all know when we have been lucky or unlucky – don't we?

This brings me to the end of a section that I trust has got you thinking about your own relationship to Hope and whether it is just an acquaintanceship or the love of your life that you can't live without. You may decide to stop being reliant on a supernatural force to direct you (or save you) *before* putting in some degree of effort yourself. You may choose to do both.

You may feel inclined to review how you approach those innocent ideas that start out as mere dreams. The ideas suddenly burst into life one day and as a result they fire off a round of choices in all directions landing in pieces on your path. Then you round them all up so you can make a few comparisons and a final decision but they often sit confused, still in pieces, suffering from concussion. They each appeal to your better nature, hoping to be chosen while you are also feeling equally confused. Hope will have your back – just ask for guidance.

As a result of discovering and exploring our path, and even experimenting with the choices available, we are given hope that there is room for improvement in all aspects of our lives. Sometimes we hope for no other reason, other than: because we can. For some of us – living in a challenging world – we simply need to have hope in our lives. Hope will be embedded in the first thought of the day and it will never stray throughout each waking hour.

Hope may be accused of adultery at times but it can be your friend for life.

Course 2

Fillings Experienced in Moderation

Balance and Management

'Confidence is a prerequisite for finding the courage to feel normal.'

Our sanity is reliant on how we manage our emotions. Experiencing different levels of emotion is healthy until their extremes are met with adulation or fear. Knowing that neither can be maintained without the help of an external influence volunteering its support, or our own internal dialogue leading us decidedly astray, is at least some consolation when we are striving to find a balance in our lives. In other words, there will be something we can improve.

Whilst moderating our behaviour may be a sign of maturity in an orderly world, I question if orderly is representative of the world we really live in or a life we aspire to live, knowing full well that individuality will soon put a spanner in any argument coming close to implying that orderly would be in some way the answer to remaining sane. It would most likely drive me round the bend.

Exploring the essence of normality is deserving of a red carpet introduction because it underpins everything we crave yet everything we oppose. Quietly reflecting a confidence that is endearing yet well managed, it ensures that 'different' is synonymous with 'normal' until darkness seeps in and forces safety to come first.

How you define too much or too little of anything may depend on your own experiences and I'm certain the next character will provide you with a lucid illustration.

C*O*N*F*I*D*E*N*C*E

The Waiting Room

A beautiful sight to see! The mysterious cloud envelops the space around her delicate form, providing invisible armour that allows her to manipulate the air with grace, reflective of a practised craft. The confidence that keeps a ballerina on her toes is the same confidence that can lead her to fall. Too much or too little will affect her balance and anyone who watches a ballerina perform, at one with her surroundings, will see a seamless, yet well-managed flow of movements that may have you thinking that she was born with it.

Are we born with it? Confidence may have been passed down through the generations within your family. A question of 'Where does he get all that confidence?' often remains rhetorical, as the links are eventually made. I am not sure if we enter this world with a ready-made supply, passed over from the other side for good behaviour in a past life. Although, we could arrive along with a well-equipped backpack of emotional toolkits in readiness for an adventure ahead, and confidence just happens to be one of them. If you are fortunate, it could have been packed on the top so you can place your hands on it straight away or it could be at the bottom, making it inaccessible as you have to push the other emotions out of the way first.

If we are not born with it, then where can we find it? We may acquire it as a result of our experiences throughout our lives, which could explain why it comes and goes and why we build it up – only to find it gets knocked down and we lose our confidence.

The teenager who doesn't seem to bat an eyelid at school but has a twinkle shining in his eyes leaves his peers in awe as he swans around with an air of confidence and has the girls flocking. Whether this has anything to do with his looks or his innate ability to charm the teachers, remaining top of his class – who knows? Is it the stability he thrives on at home, living with a family that encourages him to excel, which allows confidence to grow faster and stick around? Maybe his family had absolutely nothing to do with the start of this beautiful relationship and were never around. It is quite possible that Confidence found him first!

This young man may lose his confidence one day. He may become over-confident and end up annoying people who cross his path, because they are still trying to find theirs. If his levels of confidence are not well managed he is likely to fall down if he doesn't connect with his surroundings; maybe he could practise ballet and become more present in each moment. We know he is on his own path but he is interacting with other people who will be impacted by his behaviour and he has to find a balance, without doing himself a disservice at the same time. Insecurities can rise up from within and snatch the darn thing away at any time, and over-confident people are not immune to these invasions, no matter how hard they try to hide the fact they are taking place.

Confidence is an admirable quality and it shouldn't be compromised unnecessarily. If we want more of it, we need to attract it into our lives instead of allowing envy to create a distance between those who have it and those of us who don't. Confidence can rub off on each other. When you surround yourself with confident people it can leave you feeling empowered and lift your spirits – you feel that anything is possible and the process starts from within.

You can choose to learn from other people's positive behaviour whilst admiring the way they present themselves and how they communicate, speaking with confidence. Even the way they walk into a room, commanding its attention with warmth and sincerity, gets you thinking, *I would like a bit more of what they have.* Next time, see if you can drum up enough confidence to ask them to share their secret. Who knows if in that moment, a speckle of confidence is spared and aborts its mothership, beaming itself across to you in readiness to replicate as like attracts like. It's worth a shot and seems a healthy and humble approach to take.

Of course, it is not unusual for Confidence to sneak off, take a last-minute holiday and forget to tell us, leaving us stranded until it returns, wondering what all the fuss was about, as if it hadn't even gone away! You can get your confidence back; it just depends on whether you are prepared to go and find it or expect Confidence to find you each time. When we lose our confidence, it implies we had it once upon a time and we owe it to ourselves to go and find it again, especially if its absence is having a negative impact on our own lives.

Confidence is only misplaced even if you don't remember putting it down anywhere in particular. Maybe you left it on the back of a chair in a waiting room while you were collecting your thoughts before embarking on a new challenge. As you waited for the right opportunity to come along, hoping that Confidence would sit wide awake throughout while you mentally prepared, it probably fell asleep. By the time you left the waiting room, having pondered for too long, you had forgotten beforehand that you even had it on you!

When you lose your self-confidence the world can seem smaller – the room can feel smaller. Whether you are taking up dancing again, returning to studying or going out on a new date, you trust that your old friend, Confidence, will return before you give up and head back to the waiting room. If you do find that a positive part of you is missing and returning to your comfort zone is the easy option, then you may as well just put a comfy chair in that waiting room because you are going to need it.

Confidence likes to know that if it enters into a partnership with you, you will do your best to help it develop and you can feed off each other. It will meet you halfway and even pick you up when you trip over, but it doesn't support you. It really is a symbiotic relationship and it needs to know you want to make it work; then it is more likely to put in the effort.

Once upon a time you enjoyed dancing; you were improving all the time and for one reason or another you stopped. When you return to the dance floor some years later, your feet won't move, your heart beats faster and you feel like a lemon. You have lost your confidence. You know that you want to dance and you know that you can. The more you try and summon Confidence back into your life – at that very moment – the more it refuses to help. Why does it abandon you when you need it the most?

You go home to reflect, trying to understand what it is that keeps happening every time you have an opportunity to dance and the feelings of inadequacy become more intense until you give up trying to dance, in fear of humiliation. It is at this point that you realise that maybe it isn't just about dancing.

It is becoming a pattern that you have excused for too long. Focusing on one activity was just the distraction and when you looked at the bigger picture, it was going on in other areas of your life. Confidence was running out on you and it was time to understand why!

Looking for Confidence to accompany you, as and when it takes your fancy, is far too confusing for it to get its head around. If Confidence was restricted to dipping in and out of your activities, just because you couldn't work out how to build up a reserve, then there will be a lack of connection between the two of you. It likes to see a little consistency, in terms of how you approach your life. Confidence realises that just because it exists in one area of your life, it doesn't mean it will inhabit every one with the same degree of tenacity. Confidence doesn't take a one-size-fits-all approach to everything you do in your life and it will feel just as challenged in new territory as you do; it prefers you to take charge. Confidence *is* your dance partner so learn to lead and it will follow.

It will identify with your patterns of behaviour and mirror whichever one is going on at the time. Positive patterns will have it running towards you for dear life but it will run a mile in the other direction if it senses too much negativity. If you are calling out for Confidence to save you on the dance floor, in the office, in your relationship or in other aspects of your daily life, without understanding why you are lacking it in the first place, it can have a naughty habit of not showing up at all.

It is almost as if it is saying to you, "Look, I'm over here but you can't see me because you can't see past the mountain of despair you have right in front of you. How can I come and help you, if you don't make a shift and get rid of some of the darkness that's lurking around? Lighten up for goodness' sake!"

Let's hold fire and think about this for a moment, before we go on. Is it a possibility that you may have to have a smidgen of confidence before you can attract more of it? I mean, if Confidence doesn't gravitate towards negativity and your own lack of confidence puts you into negative equity, so it doesn't come running, then how can you actually get more of it – without having a little bit put aside in the first place? The issue here, though, is you don't have it to start off with; you want it; you don't know how to get it. If it only comes running, when you have it, why do you need more of it? If it runs a mile when you don't have any, then what are you supposed to do?

So, what if you don't know why you don't have it (yet)? Clearly you are asking for help, which is positivity performing at its best. It is quite plausible that Confidence could task you at a later date to complete some reflective practice, as a token of appreciation, and put on its sneakers now to save the day! It doesn't have to leave you in the lurch until you have figured out, on the spot, why you don't have it; but then again will you really reflect later? After all, who likes homework?! Is it not possible that your lack of confidence, in a particular area of your life, is one of those lessons that you are destined to repeat until you have addressed it, head on, and understood its meaning – no matter how painful or unreasonable the reflection turns out to be?

We don't always start out being negative but, for some reason, the subtle energies at work seem to be rather influential and find a weak spot. What if you simply need some reassurance now that you can be rescued in time to change your mindset, before the darker side lures you in and cynicism becomes easy to practise? Crikey, this sounds more like purgatory! You are at a point called the 'in between place', having been greeted with an opportunity to wallow for a moment. This is the place in which you dwell just before picking a side; just before choosing to be Positive or Negative. The '*I can*' versus the '*I can't*' mantras talk over each other. As the word *can't* squeezes itself into more and more of your lazier flung-together mantras, you begin to find it increasingly difficult to escape a downward spiral of doom and gloom.

The positive picture you once had in your mind of dancing the tango or dating DiCaprio quickly fades into the background and becomes encrypted. Now your image only bears a mythical resemblance to a colourful legacy left behind by the equally famous 'da Vinci', and who happens to share the first same name, Leonardo (both are artists in their own right). Confidence is beginning to get worn out and unable to cope with all the uncertainty… It is certain, though, that a conspiracy is going on behind the scenes, and it is fast entering purgatory to join you! I think Dan Brown, the author of *The Da Vinci Code*, would have something to say on this subject as he has written a thing or two about cryptology.

Confidence quickly conducted a thematic analysis on the qualitative data thus far and decided that the number one theme had to be all about 'hidden messages'. This was probably accounting for the confused state that preceded any decision making. What else could sway anyone to travel blindly into the abyss, taking them on a journey from positivity to negativity, riding back and forth, until they settled for a side through exhaustion or anxiety?! Was Confidence about to fall too? And what or who could finally bring you both back from the edge…?

*

"Wake up, wake up! Give me strength… It's just a bad dream. It doesn't have to be this way… 3-2-1." I thought I had better throw in some actual dialogue and count you back into the room. You are not falling down on my watch!

Hidden messages or not, I am sure that on such occasions it wouldn't hurt for Confidence to sit tight, be patient and offer a little bit more support each time you both meet. This will give you a chance to build up those reserves, instead of it cowardly running out on you when it gets too much like hard work, leaving you to slide down the next slippery slope alone. Even Confidence can't turn its back on a cry for help, can it? There is good news to follow!

By remaining positive, Confidence will already have knocked on your door – it will do so by default. Sometimes we don't listen to our own words of kindness tapping away in Morse code internally, informing us that Confidence is, indeed, on its way as a response to our distress signals. It was coming to our rescue after all and impatience was our only distraction. We got caught up in the avalanche of despair that became louder and louder until we literally became snowed under and the Morse code stopped. Confidence will hopefully wait somewhere until you are ready and recall it for duty.

Confidence has to move through that expanse of separation between *what is and what could be* – the void in the middle is the exact place where Confidence usually gets lost in the first place. It is also the place where you will find it waiting – if indeed it waits for you.

I suggested it could run a mile if it is confronted with your negative patterns of behaviour, although Confidence doesn't discriminate between positive and negative situations in your life. The behaviour and the situation are two different things.

Confidence needs to be attracted to you and not the situation. A negative or positive situation may exist but it is up to you how you choose to engage. If you are dealing with a negative situation with contempt and fuel it with your own negativity, *it is this negativity* that is forming the barrier. Confidence is unlikely to interfere, at this stage, and is probably watching in frustration. I am sorry to say that it may be witnessing your less than attractive side so you can hardly blame it for not sprinting towards you! You are frightening the life out of Confidence. I feel sorry for this character whose heart is in the right place as it is simply protecting itself, keeping you at arm's length, and saying, "If you want my help, you need to help yourself as well."

Once you have learned to befriend Confidence it is a jolly good companion to have around and life can be a lot more fun. Allowing it to youthfully leap in and out of your footsteps along your path ensures that a connection exists at all times and you are both on the ball. Maybe some of you have memories of jumping in and out of oversized footsteps, made by other people, along the beach as a child. You wondered at the time whose shoes you would fill when you grew up. It hadn't crossed your mind that you'd need to fill your own shoes first. Even now (if you're all grown up), you may still be prone to window shopping and wondering if you have enough confidence to try another pair on!

What does the ideal amount of confidence look like, so you know when you have just enough? If Confidence has feet twice the size of yours, turning your imprints in the sand into cavities, then this may indicate it could be growing too fast – but can you really have too much of it? Interesting question, because I think it is relative to what it is you are trying to do or even become. There is no doubt that confidence will be high on your list if you want to become an excellent brain surgeon or indeed any other surgeon; that is if taking a scalpel to another human being for healing purposes is the path you have chosen. This is when I would encourage Hope to work with Risk, Expect and Luck; let them integrate to their heart's content, supported by every ounce of confidence you could muster.

Confidence gets a hard time, because it is often mistaken for arrogance. We have considered the grace that Confidence can humbly reflect and this is the lovely, softer side that has my permission to rub off on me anytime! I reckon arrogance is the tougher side of Confidence. And if I had to have brain surgery one day, I'd probably be OK with allowing an arrogant surgeon to save my life – as long as Luck wasn't running the entire operation!

Unfortunately, confident people can pose a threat to our own little world and stir up emotions within us when we meet. We don't even have to speak to each other and still sense that the space in between contains something contagious. You may just feel cautious about this person because they are appearing flamboyant and wearing confidence with the buttons undone, showing off their true colours. You would rather they didn't display so much of their natural resources even though they probably had no intention of offending you either.

I suggest that Confidence has to be fit for purpose, making allies and not enemies! If there is any surplus floating around once the job is done, then we have a duty of care to rein it in so it doesn't get up everyone's nose. On the other hand, it is hard enough to multi-task emotionally to manage our own expectations without the worry of sparing everyone else from their own darker side that they could do with exploring, once in a while. It is about getting the balance right and you will find it, one way or another, if you take the time to practise.

Suffering from a lack of confidence can be debilitating in your life. I'm sure we have all witnessed a person confess to this injustice at one time or another saying, "I don't have the confidence to stand up for myself" or "I need to gain a little more confidence first…" At some point in your life, you may have said something similar. It is not important to exude confidence in every part of your life, as we mentioned earlier. It is, surely, about finding the confidence to do the things you would like to do because the lack of it is holding you back.

When you don't have the confidence to act upon some of the things in life which appear to be holding you back, the doorways to opportunities you only dream about may remain closed. The door could be ajar as you witness the light enveloping the frame, on the other side, like a fresh layer of golden treacle spread seductively over a bronzed piece of toast, but you don't have the confidence to push it open. It even smells good, yet you feel undeserving of a taste. Our confidence is challenged by chunks of different emotions, rising up from nowhere, each bringing with them a unique flavour to confuse the taste buds.

The impact of worrying about 'not having enough confidence' can consume your energy and in the quest to find it you can end up with tunnel vision. You wake up and you are on a mission to find it; you go to work and you search harder; you read more books; join more clubs… or you don't do any of these and you stop doing anything other than worry. The lack of Confidence in your life has you toing and froing from one extreme to another; the scales are frantically tipping back and forth and there is no respite. Do you do nothing and go back to the waiting room and give up all hope of finding it, watching life dance around you and never asking Confidence to dance? No! You ask Confidence to fill the void. Get it back on its feet. Let it see those footprints in the sand and make it run towards you and get your Latino moves flowing freely again!

Suppose someone else takes your confidence away from you; wouldn't that be considered stealing? "He took my confidence away, when he said that"; "She won't have any confidence left if you keep doing that to her"; "By the time she finished with them, their confidence was gone". Any of these examples can apply to a multitude of scenarios and each one indicates that someone else did something to someone to take the confidence away from them. If someone broke into your house and took your valued possessions, they would be stealing something from you and possibly, a part of you emotionally. You may never get your valuables back, but in time you find the confidence to leave your home again, without checking the doors are locked… half a dozen times.

Confidence is not something tangible that was directly taken so it is impossible to dial 999 and put a call-out for the police to look for a missing… well, what exactly…? It is, alas, something now missing from within you and you let it go. You look for a solution and a quick fix as you send out a search party to find Confidence, which took a leave of absence again. It probably went off to do some of its own soul searching, on sunny shores, under the influence of an ice cold Martini. Partial to enjoying its company on occasions, Confidence always clung on to the notion that it could be found anytime as well. I like to believe it can.

I believe we can all make remarkable changes in our lives when we break old habits and patterns of thinking that are simply not working for us. As a first step, I suggest that you become more self-aware and realise that you can *'choose change'* and choose change when it matters. Have a think about this idea and see how you get on. There is a lot to be said for learning to respect our emotions. Acknowledge they exist and then allow them the freedom to move around (in your head) with an element of fluidity, without causing havoc. If someone tells you that you can't do something or it could be a tad difficult to change your life (or something about it), then if you are inclined to do so, you have the option to go and find Confidence and choose to change.

Everywhere we go, we are surrounded by people who outwardly reflect a lack of confidence. We will meet people who may not have an abundance of confidence but you wouldn't have known that, unless they explained. We don't know what mysteries lie within each other's past unless they tell us. Then, sometimes, all we can do is to help each other to move on to our next step and boost our confidence as we interact. It is no coincidence that we meet people at points along our path for this very reason.

We have touched on having too much and too little confidence; we just need to consider that what you currently have may be just the right amount! If you are reading this section for interest and are in a great place in your life or, at the very least, have enough confidence to go ahead and do all those things you want to do, then you will be one of those people that others may look to for inspiration. When you have enough confidence and you don't have to check into a toll booth each day, paying a price in order to access your path ahead, it frees up your energies for other matters.

Remember, Confidence doesn't differentiate between a good or bad situation as it is just the backbone required to make something happen or not happen. Even a burglar needs an element of confidence to ransack houses. Confidence really isn't biased and seems willing to help anyone who is positive. In this case, it is a shame that it can't break that rule and override the perpetrator's level of enthusiasm in such a situation. Alas Confidence cannot get in the way of free will.

How about you make this a rule: find the confidence to be you and not what someone else wants you to be. They may want you to be the person you want to be anyway! And let us not forget that we can also enjoy having approval. It is a lovely milestone to reach, when you have a friend or relative acknowledge your tribulations in life. At work, it is good to be appreciated as this just takes your confidence that little bit further on the dial and you clock up a few smiles that sit somewhere between your third eye and your solar plexus and it feels great.

You give Confidence a 'high-five' and tell it, "Thanks for keeping awake this time, matey".

Confidence replies, without hesitation, "Thanks for not buying that comfy chair!"

N*O*R*M*A*L

The Puppeteer

Let's start with the bottom line: is it about being OK with who we are and being comfortable in our own skin? This is your outer layer of protection that can be worn with pride and no one else is going to wear the same design – you are unique! Your skin has 'designer label' stamped all over it with your own DNA taking most of the credit. Even when it gently breaks at the seams it has a tendency to repair itself – the wonder of nature!

There is a key difference between physical damage to the body and emotional damage. It is hard to repair what you cannot easily see, becoming heavily reliant on exploring your feelings instead of looking for something tangible to fix. This is often why some of us find 'emotional territory' a less comfortable space to explore because it is easier to compute someone's physical discomfort than it is to sit beside another who appears *perfectly normal* but is suffering in silence. We don't always award them both the same degree of empathy and this could be an innocent oversight because you cannot see their pain. It is also a great excuse when you want to practise the art of emotional avoidance (you may not see their pain, even if you sense their pain) but you prefer to keep your emotions tucked under a rug! The issue with continually avoiding your emotions and refraining from getting too close to other people's (heaven forbid you may learn something from sailing into uncharted territory), is that it starts to become your normal pattern of behaviour and the rug eventually becomes a trip hazard.

OK, so what does Normal look like? The word *normal* is reflective of everything but… normal. The word has such a positive undertone that we could convince ourselves of doing anything or saying anything – if we considered it to be normal for us to practise in the first place. If we keep doing 'it' or saying 'it' – for long enough – Normal will pay us a visit and accredit our efforts with a stamp of approval. A new 'norm' is born!

We want to feel normal in our lives, and we don't want our own idea of 'normal' to be unduly influenced by what another person considers being normal – if we don't actually agree. This is exactly why normal underpins everything we crave for yet everything we oppose. We want 'normal' to be right for us. We crave a silent space that sits peacefully in its rightful place, within us, extending Normal an open invitation to return at any time. Normal doesn't always find its way peacefully into our hearts and minds, facing adversity as it stands up for itself, battling its way through the undergrowth to reach us, alone in the wilderness.

We oppose 'normal' when it is just another 'get-out' clause used in society to overcome our differences practised by a majority to make two wrongs a right! What has become usual for us to practise or say may have been influenced by an event or what someone did or said at one time or another. Alternatively, we could settle with the notion that we are born a certain way and it must be in our genes. Now the latter concept really can get you off the hook: "It's just the way I am, sir," he said, as he sat in detention for the umpteenth time.

Normal is involved in: what you do and how you do it; what you say and how you say it; what you wear; what you eat; how you live… and by now you are getting the gist. We are talking about what normal is for you. We really have to work towards getting this bit right as quickly as possible in life, so we can aim to live life to the full and with fewer complications. Call it 'finding yourself', for now, but the funny thing is that once you think you've found yourself, *you are not sure how to be yourself*, all of the time. The irony is that being *you* or *true to yourself*, is often saddled with the complications you had planned to avoid. When you get to the point in your life when you can look Normal in the eye and say, "At last, I have met you face to face…", the next question tends to be, "How long are you planning to stick around for?" This is when you need your friend Confidence by your side, to give you the courage to feel normal.

Let us assume you have reached this point and you are getting to know more about what makes you tick. As you start to put a few more jigsaw pieces together you will begin to see the bigger picture, reflective of your personality. You start to recognise your likes and dislikes popping up in different areas of your life on a regular basis. Then you notice your opinions are subtly dotted throughout as you begin to join them up, recognising pattern forms. It is this sense of familiarity that gives you the confidence to create your own recognisable brand and keep adding to your collection, securing your identity over time.

You identify with pockets of ideas and concepts that hide in the grooves of each shapeless piece of puzzle until you fuse them together to provide clarity. Our values and norms come in all shapes and sizes. One person's idea of a circle is more oval in appearance, but when you are drawing freehand it is unlikely that the circumference you drew will match an off-the-shelf template. Normal is a guideline. Once you have found the confidence to parade your entourage of differences in public, giving them artistic licence to stray from the guidelines and develop a style that you can adopt and call your own, then it is time to make your tick go tock!

Just be yourself; you found the 'tick', so all you need to do now is build up momentum until you get the tock to kick in – all of the time. Maybe you are overcoming stage fright before going out to give the performance of your life and you are a little intimidated by the stronger characters on stage, with more courage in their emotional toolbox. You haven't quite plucked up the right amount yet to give them a run for their money. Although you do have Confidence running behind in your footsteps, slightly out of breath, desperately trying to catch up with you in order to protect you from the emotional conflict it was predicting could lie ahead. It was right, as you resorted to sitting back down in a seat among the crowd, just as Confidence was finishing a 200-metre sprint on your behalf. It would seem you felt unready to showcase your version of the latest production of normality, until you rehearsed again. What a shame it can be such hard work to make 'normal' an everyday life practice!

All of a sudden, you meet some of those alien-possessed mannequins. You may remember they were lost a while ago but have decided to crash-land on your path and pay a visit. Overnight, you say to them all with conviction, "Enough is enough. I don't want to be like you". Realising how tired you have become from fitting into one of those tiny theatrical seats, day after day, that look equally as tired and antiquated, your quest to finally stand out from the crowd moves up a gear – how liberating for you!

When your ideas are constantly being challenged, do you feel you are being asked to prove something? It is natural to discuss ideas and perspectives as it can be a lovely and inspiring thing to do; after all we are doing this right now. It is an opportunity to share ideas, whether they directly relate to your own life experiences or not. It may happen to be one of those quirky moments that stop you in your tracks, during a conversation, because *nonsense* and *psycho-babble* collide with Einstein's theory of relativity and somewhere in the middle you found room to consider another point of view! Hah! I don't think everyone believed in Einstein at first, and some folk will have dismissed his ideas as just an overactive imagination.

The world gets used to change whether it is as a result of a movement led by one man or one woman's passion to make a change for the better, giving rise to a new meaning to the word *normal*. Are we evolving as a race so fast that we struggle as a society to keep up with changes at the same time as one another? Some of us oppose change, even if we cannot do an awful lot about it because the majority vote was cast; it can lead to an imbalance in how we go on to manage our emotions, once the change is made. Maybe normal is something you protect or hide, for fear of exposing yourself to ridicule until the desire to be normal, for you, starts to uncoil from within as you free yourself from suppression. At last you are beginning to get the balance right.

Alas, at times, discussions surrounding our opposing ideas of what normal looks and feels like are safer to avoid. It doesn't make you a coward. This is just for your emotional protection and may preserve your sanity as a result. It is more likely that you can end up walking into a one-sided interview that requires a correct answer and a compromise of emotional integrity before leaving completely drained, having had the life sucked out of you by a panel of emotional vampires.

Sometimes we feel the need to explain our behaviours or reiterate our values, and on other occasions it really is just a waste of our energy. Does the act of explanation really do ourselves any favours, as we hope to feel more understood and accepted by society? And do we do it to make someone else feel more comfortable about *who we are* or *what we are doing*? Did someone ask you to explain or did you simply feel the need to justify your actions? Maybe you are still finding your tock and haven't fully given yourself the consent to be the person you really want to be.

If you feel like a puppet in someone else's life it is invariably because you are acting like a puppet in your own! You learn to move your own strings in a certain direction until it becomes a natural movement – restrictive – but you set these limitations. Maybe when one of your strings snaps and you free yourself from your own restrictions you will find that your fear of being different will fizzle out, too. Your insecurities will become yesterday's news. You have to find Confidence and break free together. Once again, it is all about giving yourself permission to feel normal; it will thank you one day.

What was the point in finding Confidence on the dance floor when you continue to dance to someone else's music without giving it a thought as to whether you like it anyway? You own the stage and you don't keep sitting in the audience wondering when it is your turn to perform. Get up there and show them all what you're made of – just be you. This is what *tocking* is all about!

Whatever it is you start to do, and keep on doing, will end up forming a habit. Natural reflects a habit which is replaced by a norm and all your norms put together become your normal; whether it is the normal you planned on being is another story altogether and I will leave you to reflect on that thought.

When darker behaviour crosses a line in society that was drawn to morally protect and keep civilised and uncivilised participants at arm's length, Normal is called upon in an emergency to play referee. Normal, in this instance, will side with the majority vote and its good conscience will normally deliver a final and agreeable verdict. A majority vote in other instances may not reflect 'normal' behaviour, especially to the minority remaining who do not share their commonality of interest. If a majority vote was made up of any form of darker behaviour which put the minority in harm's way, then this would be a good time to question when normal becomes OK to practise.

Politics and religion attempt to keep to their own side of the seesaw in the playground of world affairs but they both throw their weight around so the balance is continually tipping from one side to the other. A little bit like one of those pendulum thingummyjigs that have a number of balls attached, all being more than capable of bi-directional movement as they pick up momentum. Each one shouts across to the other to 'move on to their side', taking it in turns to voice their opinion. They both may as well just sit in their own rocking chair and talk to themselves, getting the same rhythmical effect as they go back and forth as neither party tends to find that middle ground.

It doesn't even have to be about politics or religion. You could quite easily be sitting in a meeting at work, debating a family dilemma or haggling over your business plan with your bank manager. When one set of rules conflicts with another, you may have to add a bit of choice into this sandwich as a condiment and choose to agree or disagree. I didn't say I was going to have the answers; I am still working those out for myself!

A negative point of view doesn't go hand in hand with a negative person. When you talk to someone who has a different point of view and who doesn't understand why you choose to do what you do or the way you do it, this is a normal side effect experienced from interacting with people along your path. There are benefits of mixing with negative opinions from time to time. I don't suggest you intentionally seek out people who are negative, though, but if you come across them (and you will) then use the opportunity to find out something positive about them or about yourself to make the experience less… empty!

A negative encounter can keep you focused. It can behave as a benchmark, so you can see how far you have actually come along your own path in life. It can put the zest back into what you are doing if you lost it or it can remind you exactly why you are doing what you are doing. We can endeavour to meet likeminded people but it isn't about avoiding people who don't necessarily share your vision; you are going to meet them every day, somewhere. Is it about making 'your normal' a life practice so that you feel more able to cope with being challenged? I reckon that is a good place to start.

Talking passionately to someone else about your ideas and dreams and then noticing part way through that none of what you are saying is sinking in, you quickly come to the conclusion that you are not on the same wavelength. Whether it is their inability to envisage your end goal or it doesn't appear to be interesting enough to them to warrant any further interpretation makes you wonder if what is represented on the X and Y axis on your normality graph doesn't even show up on theirs.

You decide at this point if their reactions are going to

demotivate you or spur you on to excel beyond your wildest dreams. If they belittle your approach and impose a drop of scepticism onto your dreams, because their sonar equipment hasn't picked up on any soundwaves yet, you could lose your confidence and the courage to keep your 'normal' insight. Two silent submarines submersed in the depths of the ocean and one of you hasn't detected the other's full capabilities but you know each other's vessel exists.

By now I am hoping you have oodles of confidence and courage to feel normal. It is time to take a printout of that normality graph, where X marks the spot, and put it in a frame. A certificate of achievement is awarded in recognition for perseverance, stamina, self-respect and quite frankly for not sitting back down when you felt those sea legs wobble once you reached dry land.

Whether you are in the theatre or on a submarine, you are your own ticket master. Buy a ticket, punch your own holes and keep that ticket with you for life. Don't get to the end of your life and look at your ticket and think, "I haven't got many holes in my ticket". Imagine all of the things you could have done, places you could have been and events you could have influenced, all because you had the courage to be you.

Go ahead and have *normal* tattooed all over your body. It is, after all, your skin. Paint it, pinch it or parade it – but love it all the same.

C*O*N*T*R*O*L

The Double Acts

Is Control responsible for precision? A painter's brush or a tradesman's tool will, after practice, be used with precision to bring about a quality result, with a certainty that Control has been behind it all the time. When you see something being made or performed with precision, you can admire the amount of control which that person has had to maintain throughout.

If a baker is icing a cake using one of those piping bags, filled up to the brim with sugary gunge, that has to be held carefully at one end whilst keeping it elegantly poised at the other, I would expect them to have control over where they plan to squeeze! We hope that the surgeons who performed incisions with Confidence by their side would agree that an element of control was instrumental in using sharp equipment! They must each learn to have self-control even if these two occupations couldn't be further apart from each other; although, surgical glue used to close wounds will need to be squeezed in the right direction to avoid a sticky situation.

Increasingly, it has come to my own attention that people don't always handle the word *control* particularly well, especially when they hear it being thrown around at work. It can be open to interpretation and liven up a conversation. A conversation overheard in a corridor that includes the misunderstood word being batted around will lead to earwiggers wanting to know more about who is controlling whom or what is controlling what and Control is already under suspicion.

A lack of confidence in how to use and interpret the word *control* often explains why it can be a cause for contention. People tend to have selective hearing at the best of times and if we don't listen properly to what is being said, we can miss the important bit of context in a sentence that gives the word the permission it needs to be used, without Guilt or Fear echoing in the background and having a field day.

There is a wider belief that it carries a negative connotation. I would argue that it isn't the word itself that holds a negative connotation under its arm, swinging it from side to side simply to antagonise its hecklers in the front row. Although, I wouldn't blame it for wearing a safety helmet everywhere it goes as it comes under attack. Control is another one of those words that can get a hard time! If it abandoned the English language because it was getting bullied off stage by political correctness, it would most likely end up being accused of going AWOL.

Control, in most contexts, can be good to have in moderation and, you could argue, at all times if we think back to that surgical procedure! Control is a reliable ally to have around until it gets forced to become part of a double act that pulls it in the wrong direction, for one reason or another. It is easily influenced. What do I mean by double act?

Well, Control is a balanced character until it is tipped over the edge by a partner in crime. It ambles along keeping the status quo, all by itself, until something or someone comes along and pushes it sideways and it has to react. The clutch fails and the car proves difficult to control; the extra glass of wine had her feeling 'out of control'; he couldn't control his temper once he found out the truth. Control is guided and can be easily led astray. When the clutch works fine the car is controllable; when she limited her wine intake she felt in control; when he was none the wiser, his temper was under control.

I am certain I didn't have to spell out the explanation for you but I wanted to be clear. It will be great if you give thought to your own ideas. What or who is your partner in crime? We've all had those moments when we have experienced something or someone impacting on our ability to remain in control. This could be about self-control or about anything, really. Control generally misbehaves when it isn't managed. I guess that's why management control systems exist!

Control can be kind and confident. It can offer direction and be protective. It can give you the reassurance that someone knows what they are doing and when they take control of a situation they are able to lead. A person with self-control can often keep their emotions under control. Control doesn't have to be a darker force that lurks around every corner, riddled with ulterior motives that can only imply that a hidden agenda lays dormant, waiting to jump out.

I like to see someone in control of their own person and I find it reassuring to know that Control can adapt. It works well when it is diluted with the softer side of Confidence to give rise to a charm, coated in just the right amount of authority that reflects a well-rounded personality that remains non-offensive and presentable. I think I have just described a personal advert for an internet dating site: 'down to earth and dapper'! Where has he been all my life?

Using control to suit your own advantage, without disadvantaging other people, is an ideal balance. You look at that confident person walking into the room we spoke about a couple of sandwiches ago. The same person can enter a room feeling confident that he can manage the environment and his audience, yet is influential – if that is what he is expected to be. Let us assume it is a 'he' for now; the dapper gentleman is going to run a training course and needs to deliver a syllabus from start to finish. This uncanny James Bond lookalike that has swanned into the auditorium needs to remain in control of his session plan, deliver the activities in a calm and controlled fashion, and manage the different dynamics within the group. He needs to do all of this to bring about the desired result: a successful training session which is ultimately under his control.

If he didn't stop talking and dictated every aspect of the session without allowing people to speak or have the time to explore their own learnings, in their own way, then it would be a controlling environment. The trainer would have too much control and may appear over-confident. Then the delegates are unlikely to enjoy the session or enjoy interacting with the trainer. In this case, the trainer may come under fire for reflecting a controlling behaviour mixed with arrogance. That's a double act to avoid.

*

Control and manage are two separate words, although the word *manage* is heavily appraised in the business world and often replaces the word *control*. Both words have an assertive personality, keeping them upright and standing to attention. They both have expectations of themselves and other people. Control likes to be in charge and is commanding; it commands your respect, even if it is undeserving. Manage sounds affable and engaging, and you want to get on the right side of it, just to make everyone's life easier, but it has a warmer persona and invites you to challenge – even if you don't end up getting your own way.

If you hold a managerial position, then how you manage a state of being in control is an art because you want to demonstrate a fluid and empathetic approach towards your team players, but they are usually aware that ultimately, you are the one in control. You may not be able to fully control the end result, especially in the project arena, but the desired result will have been clarified from the start.

When we cannot manage things ourselves, do we look to someone else to take control of the situation or are we just looking for someone to help us, so we can manage a situation better? Depending upon what level of responsibility you have at work, I believe that the latter is encouraged, otherwise how do you learn to become a better manager? To manage doesn't mean you are always in control as you may not be able to control all the variables that exist but influence other people to meet the collective set of objectives. This will be the plan, in order to bring about that desired result, as identified at the beginning.

Controlling other people won't actually help you to achieve your goals at work either, unless you are totally happy with losing respect from your peers and go to bed each night with your ears burning. OK, so you met your target and will get the bonus. It is preferable to learn how to master a balance in our relationships at work and acquire a good set of management skills along the way, even if what you are really doing is learning to master self-control.

Micro-managing people to the extent they don't perform so well will resonate with controlling behaviour. The idea that performing under pressure is good for you simply doesn't work for everyone; it is usually only good for the person putting the pressure on, as they hope to manage a situation using control. Micro-managing is not attractive when you are shadowing an employee's every move and breathing down their neck, although some people are not particularly good at managing themselves and find this quite helpful!

Learning a soft skill at work, in theory, is one thing but executing it in practice is completely different. Learning about leadership and then going on to become a good leader may take time. Saturating an atmosphere with learning interventions, and then expecting everyone to wear the same uniform upon completion, just gives the illusion that everyone knows what they are doing and talking about. "It's alright… I've got it all under control!" are the cries frequently heard from the most recent graduates who are still finding their feet.

Control often sits behind closed doors and sometimes the 'normal' you have strived to attain is asked to be boxed during working hours. For some people it may be when they get home, after a day of freedom, that a controlling situation unfolds; their safe haven happened to be at work!

*

When does Control get too big for its boots and become too heavy handed? If it set out to underpin leadership and turns the task into a dictatorship, I think Control needs to take some time out. Along our path we meet 'controlling people' and we find ourselves in situations that 'feel controlling' but often it is the situation itself that houses the control. We either allow ourselves to be controlled in a situation or we can end up taking control of a situation.

We use our free will to control and to challenge. Remember, we can snap the same strings that allowed Normal to break free from its constraints; it is possible to do the same with Control, when it is holding us back. This may not sound like an easy approach, although I believe it is the right one to explore, and requires a range of techniques and life practice to pull off. Sometimes we are aware that Control is bossing us around; yet, we don't always know how to get that boot onto the other foot. This is the one that uses reverse psychology and can get you in a muddle if you are not particularly good at it!

Control can involve making demands that are not understood at the time, and some of us are expected to endure their repetition, even when they are not acceptable. One way to stay in control would be to assert power over another powerful individual and fight power with power but it isn't a healthy approach. Just take a look at society as a whole. There is enough evidence lying around the globe to demonstrate that this doesn't really work. If it is between two people, it doesn't tend to make either of you feel better. Most likely, it is only one of you that would appear to be better at doing it.

Bullying is a form of control and influences people to do all manner of things that they don't want to do. The power between two people or two groups of people is unbalanced and Control is having the upper hand. The power shifts and allows Control to thrive in one corner. The other corner begins to lose their confidence and as they become less empowered, they begin to withdraw and feel controlled emotionally.

These Emotional Sandwiches just offer perspectives; they don't tell you how to get the food stains out when you spill the sauce after each bite, as everyone has a different idea of what it takes to do that. Bullies are like stubborn sauces; you know they have something in common with each other but need to be tackled slightly differently.

The impact of being repeatedly bullied and mentally tormented equates to nothing less than an emotional tumour moving in and taking up residence. Bullying can be equally as life-threatening as tumours that reside in a physical form, neither of which have been invited. Emotional squatters test your patience, push you to the edge and take up an exhausting amount of energy and the unsigned tenancy agreement just allows them to feed off your emotions, free of charge, as you strive to gain control. Those who don't regain control may be tipped over the edge. They may find that exit hatch prematurely.

All forms of illness eventually hold hands with your emotions. You walk together on the rest of your journey, becoming better acquainted, wishing you had paid closer attention to some of those emotions before. If a parasite does take control over your body, you seek to remain in control of your emotions and challenge its arrogance every step of the way, fighting it with its own medicine, hoping it will back down into remission.

*

Apart from making attempts to improve your carbon footprint with the view that future generations will thank you one day, controlling the weather (throughout the world) remains a fictional idea. The concept is reserved for film and TV where the bad guys are able to press a button to start or stop a hurricane.

You could find yourself in the midst of a tornado in real life and unless you are in a safe place, you will undoubtedly be swept away into the spiral of destruction which you cannot control. An uncontrollable situation took place, regardless of whether you could have chosen differently, had you heeded the warning to avoid stormy territory at that time of year. You were there and you were unable to control the events that unfolded.

Tsunamis and volcanic activity may find their way to your doorstep uninvited, and for the people living in these regions they may be unable to evacuate for emotional or physical reasons; or time wasn't on their side. The residents will have been unable to control the arrival of a tsunami and when it does arrive, it can't usually stop itself. Even the tsunami doesn't have control of its own ability to engineer such catastrophe, as it is triggered off the back of other planetary factors. I expect it was building up momentum, probably feeling quite guilty of any outcome that was about to unfold.

A tidal wave was out of control. It will no doubt have been asking for forgiveness in advance, as it was surging towards shore, hoping you would manage your reactions when it finally hit. Alas, those it affected will be unlikely to have any sympathy, especially as its uncontrollable behaviour will have destroyed life and land. Only unconditional love for life and land will help people to make sense of their emotions and manage their reactions. Some people will feel out of control and others will find the strength to manage their reactions in order to help those who can't. Grief will go about its job to start off the healing process. The sea will go back to being calm and the sun will come out. The events of the aftermath of *force majeure* and its uncontrollable behaviour will go on to restore balance.

As people, with the ability to think and feel, we have to be accountable and take responsibility, unlike our weathered companions. Our own self-control simply cannot go around losing its sense of control whenever it feels like it; otherwise it will find company and enter into one of those double acts! The untrained coach within says, "Get a grip of yourself and find some self-control"; "Take back control of your life"; "Don't give your power away and feel out of control". I hear you, coach… it is all about control-control-control!

We talked about Control requiring a partner in crime in order to form a double act but not every co-worker is trespassing. Self-control is a discipline. When you have self-control and either manage yourself well in a situation or refrain from doing something you prefer not to do, then discipline has jumped on board. Control and Discipline forge a worthwhile partnership and self-discipline is formed as a result. If Control can be sedated and remain under the influence of something more favourable, that doesn't involve being negative, then it can become victorious.

A productive double act can behave at its best when you surround yourself with people who are good for you. There is nothing more grounding for the soul than finding your natural state of happiness in the company of a good friend, colleague or family member, and Control performs well under the influence of your soulmates. When the two get together (unless you plan to behave out of control together) you are more likely to feel in good spirits. People can energise you and good people in your life can help to prevent you from spiralling out of control when darker days pipe up and drain your energy. Weary emotions and mood swings are reduced to a corner of the playground where no one wants to play and in time they move on as they become despondent.

It is interesting when you start to play around with this concept and look at your own reactions as you form a double act with the different fillings along your path; you can feel more or less in control of your life depending on the amount of each that is present.

The Double Acts

Confidence can be part of a great double act... as can Time, when it is on your side, and you can feel in control. When you work with Patience, you may feel more able to cope. However, when you have to be more patient – than you would like to be – Patience could be misconstrued as a partner in crime and you could actually feel less in control. On this occasion look for another inspiring partner to double up with and take the pressure off Patience. How about Hope or Trust, and relax into the moment and regain self-control?

So, it seems to me that Control can be influenced both ways and it appears to work with you on a personal level! Are you in control of the path you walk along? Ooh, I have just experienced goosebumps. All of a sudden, after everything we have explored, seeing the word *control* in this context has left me feeling slightly intimidated – by my own question. I think it is because, just like the weather, there are bigger things at large which can influence us to take those detours and fall off our path. Would it be more appropriate to suggest, then, that with the help of our emotional toolkit, we focus on controlling (and managing) our own behaviours and train ourselves to practise the art of self-control, in readiness for the journey ahead? How strict you want to be with yourselves – along your path – is entirely up to you, unless Normal has had to step in and play referee.

If we and everything in our lives could run like clockwork it would take precision engineering to pull it off. Therefore, would such precision help us to control our path or simply remove any need for us to maintain control, because it will be built in already?

As we are about to head off into darkness (not literally), it is worth mentioning that Control functions regardless of whether the lights are on or off. It can work in the light and it can work in the dark. We as a society cannot control natural light outdoors (I don't think?!). We can create artificial light. We can build walls around the daylight to stop it from flooding in so that darkness exists and then tap into any artificial intelligence that will turn the light on!

So what has darkness got to say for itself now?

D*A*R*K*N*E*S*S

The Rainbow Effect

We all get stage fright but we learn to love the limelight occasionally. Some of us thrive in the spotlight and find the darkness off stage unsettling. How many actors do you read or hear about who suffer from depression or have inferiority complexes off camera; maybe they preferred being in character which they could hide behind. Maybe life off stage really isn't as much fun as the life they live on the stage or on set and reality is darker behind the scenes.

The light for other people either has them reaching for the dimmer switch to deflect from any difficulties going on in their own lives, or because their life is just fine the way it is, they don't need every aspect of their lives lit up for the world to see. Attention to detail is all very well but bright lights can take away the curiosity and can leave nothing to the imagination.

If light was a true colour then Darkness would just be a light with a different colour running through that takes the shine off what we see sometimes, making things look a bit blurry – that's all! When the lights are on at night they can keep us awake and Darkness is equally responsible for a restless mind when it hides the familiarities that usually make us feel safe.

The transition from darkness to light is a natural

phenomenon because it happens every day and we are familiar with seeing the darkness; sometimes we simply don't like it! Is it the darkness itself we don't like or what we sense is sitting in the dark when the lights are off? I am not necessarily talking about unknown entities – which are there whether it is light or dark, I expect – I am talking about something far closer to home.

It is often when we are in the dark that things can appear illuminated because we start to see everything we had hidden in the daylight, which is surely the time you would expect to see everything on display. Darkness doesn't always equate to night; anywhere that light doesn't shine, Darkness will take its place. And, if that's not enough to keep it happy, it can even find you in the light!

Darkness can exist inside you even when you are sitting in broad daylight. When it is time for Darkness to descend outside it can still choose to sit with you when your table lamp is on, sprawled out, hands behind its head, wiggling its toes and craving attention. It takes a sneaky peek at you from under its arm to see if you are looking and if you are beginning to get wound up by its constant presence. It is capable of sitting silently but because you know it is hovering, it disturbs your peace and quiet as it encroaches upon your space.

Alternatively it chatters away and turns all those thoughts upside down. Everything you had nicely tidied up before going to bed to sleep has now been rudely disarranged. Retiring to the living room to switch off (in hope of watching a film through to the end for once) is a plan that you've frequently thought about yet rarely executed. Darkness behaves like a child who has been asked to go to bed but has other ideas to empty its toy box again. As it pulls out each chord on the dancing dolls, nudging them to play along to a master plan, Darkness has another agenda.

The bottom line is you would prefer Darkness to go and mingle with its equals outside or in another room when it misbehaves. However, if it can bring itself to lie down beside you without fidgeting, just to complement the light in your life so you can rest, balance is restored and Darkness can be more easily managed.

Darkness isn't the enemy. We are often our own worst enemy, as Darkness doesn't tend to care too much for boundaries unless you define them and set a few clear rules. It really is up to us to learn to manage Darkness in our lives and get to know it better. If we keep rejecting it, without finding out what useful message it has to deliver, this will only encourage it to hang around and drive you mad. Dare I say it… on this occasion: take control!

We are not exploring the definition of a 'darker side' to a person, here in this sandwich. We are exploring what 'Darkness' as a word can mean and how best to greet it, when it shows itself to you – on your path. It is up to you, individually, to explore what Darkness means to you and how it can make you feel *and* if you want to make it a shade lighter. Darkness can be well meaning and we will seek to understand why, shortly.

Firstly, when we are looking for something to see, we can't always see it with our eyes alone. We visualise in our mind's eye what we perceive to exist, using our imagination to add colour; we also visualise what we know exists, as we recall images of what we have once seen. Unless you are in a position to daydream and allow your thoughts to wander momentarily, the night (or your night-time, should you be working shift patterns or have a hectic social life) is a time for sleeping. Night-time does have a habit of waking up our gremlins which prompt us to see what either isn't 'there' or distort whatever 'is', and should leave us well alone.

On the other side of the coin, Darkness can bring us peace. I am not talking about when you have a migraine (which is a good enough reason for wanting to immerse yourself in the black mist of tranquillity). Darkness, especially at the end of the day, can be a haven for relaxation. It provides an ambience conducive to healing (if noise is omitted) and a time to collect your thoughts and put them safely out of sight – without the thoughts themselves collectively getting ready for a night out in your head, partying until goodness knows what time!

A colour chart in your local DIY store will give you an appreciation of the shades that exist in between black and white. White reflects light and black reflects darkness. Although, as you hold the laminated chart up in front of a light, darkness can still shine, as the angle it is held at captures its layers of depth and brings out a beauty. We become attracted to the richness and the authority it reflects and we begin to feel comfortable with its magic. So many things in our lives are black: our cars, our TVs, clothes, furniture, bedding, mobile phones, crockery, hair (yawn-yawn-yawn) – the list is endless. We are attracted to black because we are more comfortable with this colour than we care to believe.

When we experience the extremes associated with light and darkness, we begin to notice the pull they have on one another; they are entwined with Yin and Yang which are also deserving of understanding and respect. Darkness may also be sprinkled into those four sandwiches that sit on the 'Limitations and Acceptance' table that you will dine at later. This is because it takes time to understand your own relationship with Darkness and there tends to be a mutual respect, when you have finally stopped avoiding each other.

Is there a connection between Happiness and Darkness? I

believe there is. A cloud of darkness hovers over us, when we haven't quite made up our minds about what happiness really is! Spending your time thinking you should be this way or that way because you are still muddled up with your tick and your tock reminds us that *Normal* is still not feeling quite itself. This puts a strain on your emotions and your ability to find true happiness. I question if finding fun is the answer to happiness or if happiness within comes first and fun just finds you once the cloud of darkness lifts (maybe fun can lift the cloud of darkness, too).

When people say to you, "Lighten up, have some fun", and you think to yourself, *I am actually, OK*, is this because their idea of fun is different from yours? There will always be someone who will question your interpretation of fun or happiness and offer you free advice on how to find more or forget to put the constructiveness bit into their critique.

Sadly, we don't all find the strength to open our eyes and see the rainbow sitting between the clouds of darkness under a spotlight on a rainy day. Although for some of us, short-term happiness may be achieved by standing beneath the colourful arc and soaking up its positive energies in order to shut out Darkness, temporarily. On the other hand, if Happiness could occupy a space in your mind, long term, and claim it as a new independent state, then the quest to shut Darkness out completely and put an end to its military-style occupation of those borders would be an attractive proposition.

The mission, as always, will be to find safe passage to cross over into your happiness zone, especially if you feel like you're still in a war zone or coming through the other side. Many of us manage to slip back into the state of happiness, relatively quickly, at a flick of a switch. And then there are those of us who have seemingly acquired full citizenship and can't imagine being anywhere else. Now that's an achievement!

Outside influences just have a habit of affecting us all differently and some of us are more susceptible to falling prey to an unwelcome visit from Darkness. I only suggest that when you next encounter a darker moment in your life – apart from asking it to move on in the kindest way you can to suit you – notice any little triggers that may have attracted it in to your life in the first place. These are the ones to befriend and have a little chat to. Darkness just occupies space because you felt vulnerable. It is when you can identify the triggers and overcome them (or at least manage them when they appear) that Darkness will look at you and say, "What a waste of time it will be, hanging out with you today – you are far too happy and positive". Yay! Mission accomplished!

If you ask Darkness, "What is it about your visits anyway, that give you permission to hold me back from becoming truly happy?", Darkness is likely to reply, "I only come along from time to time because you let me in when I think you need some company. You give me permission to stay." In order to keep Darkness at bay, even when you don't want to smile, I would suggest that you do smile and see how it feels. I bet you will feel better. Even if you end up laughing at how unimaginably hard it was to do. You will nark Darkness off anyway!

Darkness tends to prey on sadness and doesn't take kindly to you being excited about the prospect of feeling happy most of the time, making this your norm (tickety-tock!). When a sad moment or a disappointment in life starts to become the novelty and a bad mood is an acceptable part of an occasional 'bad day', irritation is just a side effect of being human.

Darkness can be painful when you see the grimness in a

sunny day that leaves you unable to make head nor tail of why you feel so numb as you stand witness to the beauty that the day is offering but with which you cannot emotionally connect. Instead, treating it like an unwanted gift that was born out of kindness, you can only acknowledge that the kindness exists but cannot appreciate the gift itself.

When the light goes out – inside of you – the emptiness and the numbness is indescribable, and it becomes hard to explain this feeling along with many other feelings that have sunk to the bottom of your emotional toolkit. You slowly begin to feel your higher self detaching from your own body, as if it is withering inside of you, disconnecting with your human lifeline, like an alien that is incompatible with the air you breathe. If the past has had anything to do with this, and thinks it can shadow you through to your exit hatch, it needs to be flattened!

The past has gone. Some of the reasons that gave rise to the pain in your past may have left the dock many years ago; that ship sailed, but you may still feel stranded and abandoned with a shell of memories. They tend to resurface when you collide with other ships that appear similar and the few emotional triggers you have not yet conquered remain on board your own vessel, nestled between the floorboards. Darkness can come out of hibernation even when you begin to find your north and south again after years of island hopping, to keep the pain hidden. Darkness can misunderstand your distress signals and navigate past memories back to you, mistaking your current bout of light reflection for some sort of unfinished business but the sat nav just needs calibrating – that's all. You didn't intend for Darkness to get back on the bandwagon and start singing along, whistling the old songs that have seen their day.

Finally you choose another path in life and it may awake a

few ghosts but if the *Pirates of the Caribbean* movies are anything to go by, they can usually be dealt with by a dashing young man and an alliance of friendships. Take them back out to sea and throw them overboard and let them sink into the abyss. Let the memories rest and also find peace. They must be equally as tired of being resurrected. Incidentally they are now making their way to the captain's quarters looking like a confused crew of Chinese whispers whose visas have expired and are not wishing to be judged anymore. They don't even know the truth anymore about how they came to be on board the ship and ask for forgiveness. If they had a chance to run a ship again, they may choose to do it differently and the message now would be very different. You can give Darkness permission to leave.

At times we all need something, maybe outside of ourselves, to help bring the light back into our lives when it has been a bit dull. Spirits can lift when you give them some space to fall in love with life, all over again, after what may have seemed a lengthy period of emotional hibernation.

A space in time can be created between the old and the new – the past and the future. It is a space that allows change to take place if it needs to. It opens up an opportunity for solitude to step in and say, "Just be". It embraces feelings of all types and allows expressions to unfold and be revealed. It offers a space for innocence to develop and be revelled in; naivety will be forgiven and tantrums are part of the healing process. Darkness will come full circle and become eclipsed by the light; all but a crescent of Darkness will remain to remind you it is still there so you respect their differences and strive to find balance in your life.

Course 3

Fillings Enriched with Good Nutrition

Understanding and Respect

> *'Patience takes time to master and good judgement requires trust.'*

Understanding what makes you tick, as has already been mentioned, is well worth investigating. Respect your entitlement to be you; after all, who else are you trying to be?

I trust by now you have come to terms with the idea that you are on a path, the one you chose even if you don't think you did, as it appeared at the time to have chosen you. Then you considered whether your own thoughts and behaviours could be moderated, whilst remaining true to yourself. You may have found this a challenging experience but you're here now – well done!

Firstly, what do you do when you find yourself feeling under the weather; do you plan to do something else to make you feel worse? Ideally no, so you fill up on good nutrition, feed your soul and do what you can to feel better. So why, when things in your life don't go as well as expected or everything feels out of kilter, do you reach out and do something that invariably makes it worse? It isn't just your body that needs a health check – it's your life too!

Is time really that limited because we booked it all out in advance, forgetting to allow any contingency for reflection, plastering over the cracks instead of understanding how they appeared in the first place? Whilst accepting that hindsight cannot change the past, it may come in handy now; take the time to listen when you hear its words of wisdom.

Be patient, trust your instincts and judge yourself kindly.

T*I*M*E

Speed Limits Apply

We say that time is not on our side but surely we have to create the space around us for Time to move in – just as we keep a spare room free for a sudden guest appearance. As we hold onto a pocketful of space lined with a magnetism that seduces Time, and encourages it to occupy, then we can stop treating Time as something lost which needs to be found.

Thinking about this logically, before we ensconce ourselves in excuses as to why Time is, on the face of it, off playing away when we need it the most, Time is actually around us all the time – right under our noses. The fact that we are too busy to draw breath and increasingly blame Time for being conspicuous by its absence is simply a reflection on the way we are choosing to live.

Time isn't in one space and not in another. It doesn't pick and choose when or where to exist; it just does – doesn't it? After all we cannot buy more of it off the shelf in a '24/7', open-all-hours supermarket, choosing a larger quantity to last longer, as if it were a box of washing powder with the added bonus of buying one and getting one free, because it is already free. Time itself is fundamentally free as it wafts throughout the Universe, twenty-four hours each day, seven days each week.

Arguably, it is the space in which Time can exist that has been around for billions of years and long before time measurement existed. Therefore, it isn't too far-reaching to suggest that Time could exist in 'one place' and 'not another', because we haven't explored every dimension to find out if that is true. Time could well be represented in a completely different way, somewhere! And even when we get there, into another dimension, we may still be looking at our old watch having listened to its 'tick and tock' for as long as we can remember. It would seem ironic after everything I've been impressing onto you thus far, to have to then change the beat you've been accustomed to hearing – just when it began to sound 'normal'!

Over the centuries, mankind has made unethical decisions about how another person uses their time. Examples are evident throughout history and continue to be embedded in the array of dysfunctional activities seen in society today. We don't always use our time wisely and sometimes we are told what to do with our time. Time probably doesn't realise how much trouble it causes; then again, is Time at fault or is the human race trying to find yet another misfit to blame for its lack of accountability?

Now, if you have freedom and are fortunate enough to be able to exercise your rights to live freely, you are within your rights to off-charge your time. You may be offering a product or service that will either take up your time to provide or will have already taken up your time to produce. So time is free until you need someone else's time and then the bartering begins! You cannot transfer any of their time to your world to stockpile, because it will slip through your fingers as soon as you try to catch it. Although you can, with good time management, use your own time more efficiently by opting to use or purchase someone else's resources. In this case you have looked to achieve more in double the time and hopefully feel half as tired in the process!

Do you remember when we discussed the word *sometimes* in the first section? We discovered that it is OK to trust in someone else's expertise to help you in life, because you don't have to do everything on your own. The division of labour represents the diverse experience available and makes the world go around. It includes everything from having your hair cut to paying a mechanic to fix your car that was in the garage seven chapters ago! Both experts are capable of improving the colour (thank goodness) when the paintwork looks a bit rusty around those edges. Maybe you paid a landscaper to erect your garden fence; you know, the one that kept falling down because you either couldn't do it properly or didn't have the time.

Saving the time you would take trying to do something yourself, which would take another person half the time to do (because they are trained in that field), is a sensible thing to do. You may decide you would rather use your time to do something else. The cost incurred for completing some of those activities will of course influence your decision to either pay someone else or take on the challenge of doing it yourself. Although I cannot help you make that decision I can encourage you to bring your awareness back to your perception of time as it is never too late to do so, and in doing so, you may be able to put some balance back in to your life.

We are most familiar with using a quantifiable reflection of time during our day-to-day conversation, for example using the expression '24/7'. We further organise our diaries in the hope that we can tag a few extra minutes on to the end of an hour – when no one is looking. Can you imagine the knock-on effect globally if we all did that; how would you know who was running late?!

Well, I wouldn't tend to say, "I wish I had a few more years to do that", but I may say, "I wish I had a few more hours in the day". But do I really want a longer week? To be honest, I am not sure if another day or two in practice would solve the issues that appear to arise through not having enough time. If we did have more time, would we use it wisely and appreciate the excess time on our hands to simply do nothing, as opposed to the 'nothing' that needs something doing to it – just for once?

Wisdom may be perceived as something we tap into as a last resort in times of need, rather than accumulating it throughout our lives, keeping it accessible and on tap. On tap would be my own preference, using it to pre-empt an outcome so I can at least prepare, rather than simply react to the outcome when it arrived. Either way, it is never too late to wise up and appreciate the time we have – and respect the fact it can be gone in a flash.

In other words, if we cannot manage the time we have now then what leads us to believe that having more of it would be useful? On the flip side, what if we had more time to go back and finish that something off, because it will serve us or others well upon completion? If we had more time to find answers to cure all ills and more time to negotiate our way out of battles, even though the latter may only provide more time to endure its conflict, would this be a good thing?

On a lighter note, if you had twenty-seven hours in a day and enjoyed an eight-day week, would you find more time to complain that you now have to work harder and pay more tax as a result? Would you despair at the long winter nights that were already too long and seek out a new hobby, because the thought of doing nothing in the world we live in sounds far less appealing than suffering the exhaustion that accompanies doing too much? Doing too much in a short space of time is why you were wishing for more time in the first place.

No doubt many of us would fill each day with more of the same. So, the idea of having more time would make little difference to our overall wellbeing if we didn't look to change our patterns of behaviour and consider whether we actually ran out of time, or simply tried to do too much in the time we had available.

I wanted to buy a new pair of shoes last night but I ran out of time. I ran out of time because the shop closed shortly after I left work. I left work later than I planned, but just as I was driving up to the shopping centre, the car stalled as I didn't have time this morning to stop and get petrol as I was running late because I had to get some milk which ran out as I was making breakfast. If only I had more time I could have organised myself better and none of these delays would have happened.

The reality that I would *never* have had enough time to choose a decent pair of shoes after work in the first place is totally irrelevant (as shoe shopping is a time-consuming affair) but do you think, hypothetically speaking, I was trying to do too much in a short space of time and blaming everything going wrong that day on the lack of time?

If the answer is yes and I am looking to excuse myself from all responsibility for what may seem to be a set of trivial issues in the whole scheme of things (compared to seeking world peace) then I can pretty much assume that if I continued with this pattern of behaviour, then the likelihood is that nothing is ever going to be my fault! This would be an ideal time to think about what it is I keep doing that brings about a ripple of complications in my life.

Everyone will have their own example! I made this one up – except the part about shoe shopping taking so long – but take a look at a few of your own 'out of sync' days, that resonate with one red traffic light after another! Also, recall the days that you leave home, maybe to go to work, and you sail through one green light on to the next, as if the thoroughfare had been designed just for you. Do you ever think how unusual that is or simply accept that occurrence as being the start of a great day ahead? Would something like that engage your senses or would you not even blink an eyelid? Is green your norm in life and red, well, just the colour that inhabits an off day from time to time? Which is your norm?

Sometimes you can be a positive – cup half full – sort of person and still hit the road blocks and traffic jams, finding it difficult to manoeuvre successfully from A to B without feeling dishevelled and in need of breathing apparatus by the time you get past the front door at work. And why, when all you have done is to have been positive and enthusiastic to please, is this your reward?

It must be something to do with having 'High Expectations'! Surely we set the bar too high? Clearly, we are just not managing them very well, that's all. No one said how high to set them in the first place when it relates to our own life. Nonetheless someone somewhere says, "Jump", and if you are on the ball you reply, "How high?" How high to jump isn't really the issue! How much time you have in order to jump that high and return to the ground unscathed is where you could do with focusing your attentions.

Running out of time is something we fear. We are more likely to set ourselves up for a fall that will not promise a comfortable landing, when we turn our attention to getting as much done as possible without anticipating how the end will pan out. This is especially true if we continue to sprint through life at such speed. Speed limits need to be enforced!

Instincts can pull us back when we are going too fast but that in no way infers that we listen to them. We frequently ignore the signs they have to offer, which is what they are, but whether we don't want to believe they exist, feel embarrassed to think outside the box or have become arrogant and think we can beat time, only you will know your own mind. Your experiences in life will speak volumes.

It would be interesting to see if you are one of those people who choose to accumulate wisdom *en route*, developing it over time so its culmination becomes your guide so that your intuition serves you well. Maybe you choose to dial it up when a threat is imminent and hope it will answer favourably, knowing full well that you haven't taken the time to keep in touch but still expect the same level of service!

Deciding whether you are that red or green type of person isn't a clear reflection on your desire or ability to be positive at all. It is a reflection on your relationship with the word *time* and what you expect from yourself as well as what you expect Time to be able to deliver. You could be positive that you will have enough time – but that doesn't mean that you will!

Surely Time isn't going to deliver anything for you on its own. Time is the resource. You allocate the time you need to fulfil your quest: a minute to think, an hour to exercise, a day to shop, a week to study, a month to land a new job, a year to grieve, a decade to run your car into the ground before you can afford a new one… and a lifetime dedicated to understanding and respecting the silent and unseen laws that hold us all together by a thread of divine intervention. If you continually abuse Time and expect it to deliver the impending results at the same speed that your brain or imagination drums them up in the first place, you are not taking this 'Time' thing seriously.

Speed Limits Apply

We have established there is no time to borrow. Money will buy you someone else's time for a task to be carried out to save you considerable time to put to better use elsewhere. This is just business as usual. This isn't anything to get excited about but how many of us are prepared to share the credit? Not everything comes at a cost and if you actually ask for help, you may find that it doesn't always come with a set of terms and conditions, just a token of appreciation will suffice.

Avoid squeezing all the energy out of yourself in one go. The precious life energy inherent in all of us either lies dormant or quite frankly runs out too fast. Then you struggle to top it up again to that minimum line that allows you to function efficiently running the risk of burn-out. Try not to focus all your energy each day on just getting by and, instead, make your life your own individual thoroughfare with your own set of traffic light controls – now wouldn't that be the icing on the cake!

The quantity versus quality conundrum is an integral part of everyday learning. Let's face it, it happens to all of us. Packing so much into each day may give rise to nothing being achieved as well as it could. You may not even recall the moments or the feelings you had with your encounters. You may have missed out on beautiful moments with people by not fully listening to what they had to say, missed the point, said you will come back to them but never do, promised something you couldn't deliver and all because you thought you had to go faster so that you packed more in to the time you had.

Something has to give eventually, don't you think? I am not implying it always does and someone somewhere will prove this concept wrong. Then I will be there to say, "Well done", asking, "What do you know that millions of us around the world do not?" Then in the next breath, I would suggest he or she bottles the advice and sets up a multi-level marketing company. Naturally, I would implore that person to take me on as the first distributor! However, compromising on quality may lead to compromising on your health, happiness, contentment in life, relationships and financial stability.

I think the message I am aiming to convey here is to simply be mindful about your own capability to achieve something in a suitable timeframe, without constantly draining your battery beyond repair. Otherwise you could find yourself falling into a wormhole. Apart from that being something that could involve insect larvae, and goodness knows what else, it is also thought to be something that connects sections of spacetime together. And I think it is synonymous with what is happening with your train of thought as you are temporarily stuck in the middle of red and green, and amber is colouring your day.

Establish yourself as a positive, pragmatic individual who is actively visualising green as the new you. It was all go-go-go but you got caught up in the excitement and fell into the trap of trying to do too much; then the go-go-go went to slow-slow-slow and the slow turned into a stop and created a traffic jam. The red, apart from resembling a seething colour of despair causing vascular constriction and your blood pressure to rocket sky high, is now reflective of a warning light that has indicated that things have not gone quite as planned. It is just like an oil indicator light flashing in the car, shouting "Hello, hello" in Morse code. It quietly offers you protection but only you can heed its advice, if you are not too busy. It is likely to be telling you to recharge your batteries and stop pushing on the accelerator!

Well, we have come to the end of this sandwich with no more left than a crumb trail for you to refer back to, once you've digested this filling enriched with goodness. Time is precious but every day you get another opportunity to have more of it, so don't beat yourself up if you didn't meet all of your expectations today. Look on the bright side: tomorrow you can start the clock, all over again, to see if the next twenty-four hours will be any more productive…

P*A*T*I*E*N*C*E

It's Not the Speed That Counts!

Patience sat quietly and meditated in the garden, appearing to have all the time in the world – even when it didn't. It only needed a moment of silence to realign and feel composed before being recalled for duty.

Sometimes, keeping up with the demands that came in from every direction felt like hard work. This wasn't because Patience couldn't cope with the volume of requests; it was happy when its pager was going off, taking that as a sign of a world becoming more attuned. Either that or people didn't know what they were letting themselves in for when asking for Patience to turn up. No, the more challenging part for Patience was sensing the person's expectations and then witnessing their disappointment when it couldn't deliver. And there are reasons why Patience is not always enough. It cannot always transcend your own limitations.

There were people, nearby, who genuinely seemed desperate for Patience to show up and help them through troubled times. Caught up in the realisation that they didn't possess any, and coupled with a longing to locate some as fast as possible (as if it was something that could appear instantaneously), demonstrated to Patience that they were becoming more self-aware. Actually, there was no reason why Patience couldn't suddenly enter into their realm of consciousness and begin its usefulness without a person having to undertake months of training and practice first. Just by tapping into their emotional toolkit to look for a source of guidance to help them cope with the events going on, while Time spun around dancing to distract, was being proactive. It only takes a tiny spark of effort to turn on the ignition and keep Patience in the hot seat until Time ceases to give its attention to whatever it was that needed support.

Then there were those who expected Patience to surface unconditionally, or so it appeared, while not really understanding what it means to be patient and often defining the word *desperation* less accurately. They imagined that Patience would 'arrive', 'perform' and 'exit', having fixed or changed something all by itself. This could suggest that Patience is seen as an external resource rather than one which is internally accessed and developed as nature intended. Then again, if it was something external we could probably buy it. Just like everything else we buy, to fix us, when we don't have the patience to do it ourselves. Anyway, it wasn't up to Patience to judge if desperation alone was the driving force behind one's desire to make its acquaintance or if desperation could even be defined. It is an elastic word that can be stretched in all directions. It means something different to each of us when it is attached to changing situations which the eye can barely see and the heart may only feel.

Patience cannot be biased. It is only too pleased to work with you, not caring how you bring it into your consciousness but only that you do. We can all learn to welcome Patience on board while we sail and surf the waves of time, allowing any one of our experiences in life to further teach us something new about this respectful character in relation to ourselves.

*

Patience unravelled itself from the lotus position and looked around in wonderment. It always sensed that nature knew more than it was letting on about the mysteries of life, never giving away all its secrets easily. Knowing this meant that Patience was more than happy to work overtime, in exchange for a glimpse of wisdom – especially when Nature was being expected to produce.

Nature doesn't promise any 'quick fixes' but can surprise you when you stop, for just a moment, and smell the roses. Nature has the power to heal as much as it has the power to destroy and it cannot be underestimated. It is no wonder that Patience feels at home in Nature's presence, sharing the constraints and limitations that Time can pose, but doesn't necessarily manifest. A mutual understanding has to exist between Patience and Nature, even if they work at different speeds.

Patience is frequently asked to deliver more than it can in the time it has available. The person asking can invariably run into trouble, thinking that Time can provide all the answers or Time *is* the answer. You see, being patient doesn't necessarily go hand in hand with 'having to wait longer' to accomplish something. It is not so much about requiring *more time* (every time) in order to achieve a goal, as needing to become more tolerant in the quest to reach it – using whatever time you have available, more wisely. Is it simply about managing your reactions and emotions in order to feel less… impatient?

When a person is willing to embark on a working relationship with Patience, then it makes for a much healthier and successful journey ahead. Recognising that Patience is something that will serve them well may not be the hard part to figure out.

Invariably people tend to find it difficult to apply, each and every time putting up a struggle which breaks the connection and the spark fizzles out. This is when you can find yourself back in the hot seat! Your respect for Patience goes up a notch, as you finally come to realise all the benefits to be had from working together. Sensing the extra weight back on your shoulders, which had been previously carried by Patience, now leaves you wishing that the connection remained unbroken. Fortunately you can re-engage with Patience at any time, albeit perhaps on a different task if time had run out for you, on this occasion!

Patience tends to be left out in the rain on many occasions and has learned to pack a waterproof jacket in readiness for one of those rainy days. It knows full well that it can be hard to work with round the clock. Is having patience a part of a lifestyle practice? I think it is something we all strive to have – as one of our five a day! After all, it is a filling that is packed with good nutrition! Even eating healthily, all of the time, requires a level of commitment too! It is difficult to deny that with practice, many things can be achieved. Even the process that leads up to refining your skills could turn out to be enjoyable, once any negative attitude subsides. Bear in mind there is a wide range of situations to consider, each one requiring a lesser or greater amount of patience.

I remember when I was a youngster learning to thread a needle, being told to have more patience! What did that actually mean? The task involved lining the eye of the needle up with the end of a piece of thread that always seemed to be frayed no matter how many times the end got snipped. I don't think Patience required an 'amount of time' to perform at its best. All the time in the world wasn't going to get a strand of cotton to do what it didn't want to do. It was, however, about the amount of times I practised this task in order to become better at guiding it through the hole – and keeping it on the other side long enough to bring my hand around to catch the end before it slid back out!

Often, as I squinted one eye, whilst quietly smiling with joy at my impending achievement, I learnt that moving too fast – in haste to catch the so and so – was detrimental. The speed in which I moved invariably caused it to fall out. Moving a little more slowly actually got me to the end result far quicker. Therefore, you could argue that it would appear, in this instance, I took a little more time. Yes, more time because I moved slowly (after all it takes time to move slowly). Yet, less time was spent overall as I didn't have to keep starting over and over again once I changed my pattern of behaviour.

I don't think Time is always a prerequisite in order for Patience to work to its full potential. Patience will always be accompanied by Time but not always dictated by Time. Nevertheless, something can take time to achieve and it is quite possible that it simply cannot be achieved any faster. You may need Patience to accompany you while you wait or while you do what needs to be done. This is because there will be other influencing factors involved and Time is not prescriptive. When I became successful at threading needles, I think I simply became accustomed to doing it with an element of patience and it began to take less time than it did before. So, as a result of practising patience I became more tolerant. Out of necessity, I even went on to make my own duvet covers, curtains and clothing; this is when Time played a different part, as I had freed it up (wisely) to save me a few pennies. Remember, our time is valuable in more ways than one!

It would be a good idea to consider something else that requires an amount of time to complete and one which invites

It's Not the Speed That Counts!

Patience to tag along, to accompany Time during the process. If we know, in advance, that we will have to wait for something to work out, then we will know how much patience is required along the way – right? It's doubtful we will know how much exactly as we have learned that Patience doesn't equate its existence to that of time! It isn't unreasonable to assume that once we have practised something several times we could probably gauge how much Patience was involved at the time, and would need to be involved again, were the same circumstances to arise.

Start with a simple analogy to whet the appetite and imagine you are taking a one-hour maths exam or, say, an art exam. You are already anticipating that a little patience will be required while you face up to and overcome the odd difficulty in either finding the solution or creating a new design. How much you will need isn't known just yet, because you've never taken the 'real' exam before. You only hope that you can keep calm and rational whilst tuning in to a meditative state long enough to reach the right conclusion and come back out of it again in time to hand the work in completed – all within fifty-nine minutes, having one to spare!

Using a negative situation to illustrate a point, assume that you didn't pass first time and now have an opportunity to do it all over again. You undergo a bout of self-evaluation and come to the conclusion that you ran out of patience as you attempted to draw the silhouette, in the art exam, without first drafting up a sketch. The result looked more like a splodge of shadows, about to pull their next victim into the afterlife, underground, as they appeared to fall off the bottom of the page one by one. The decision to practise a few more times and allow Patience to entertain along the way meant that during the retake the amount of patience required could be more predictable. The exact quantity is still debateable but hindsight comes into play. On this occasion, whilst you may not know how much you will need next time, you know it's a darn sight more than you had before.

When we practise the art of being patient in our everyday lives, we will become familiar with our own practices and recognise what makes us tick. When we look at what our 'normal' approaches are to executing our goals, handling difficult situations or making a lifestyle change – which turns our world upside down temporarily – we will have an idea about our potential to remain patient throughout. We may have an idea in advance how much we will need.

How much is required is unlikely to be measurable. Often, you will hear yourself say, "I need more patience" or "I don't have enough". Neither statement represents an amount in kilos. You can't bag it up and pack it in your toolkit in exact quantities, but you will have a sense of how much patience you have already or are going to need. Equally, you may embark on a new adventure and find, part way through, that you just don't have enough of the magic stuff to help you reach your destination. Maybe it wasn't about Patience after all, and it was simply because your mission was too challenging – all the patience in the world would not have been sufficient to carry you through to the finishing line. This is OK. The key here is to recognise what it is that held you back. Get that bit right first and then you can think about your next steps. Understand what else you need to learn. If the decision to stop doing what doesn't work is the lesson to be learned, then you can move on and put Patience back in the ring with something else that feels a little more up your street.

Supposing Patience is as generous as Time, it still doesn't (just like Time) do anything all on its own. Although, having said that, I am certain we like to think that it does. When we say, "Just have patience and give it time", what do we mean? Does that mean we simply do nothing? After all, Patience will look after us – won't it? If we are putting so much emphasis on being patient then why doesn't Patience appear to be doing anything? Oh right… it all goes on behind the scenes. Patience is part of an illusive act which draws us in when we find ourselves gallantly marching towards each goal and we trust it will also be our saviour in times of need. Are we getting confused with Hope? Nope! I reckon when we are being hopeful, we require Patience to hang around as well. When we are being patient, Hope may sneak in and offer moral support. These two characters are different. I don't think either one can be the other's replacement. They just happen to complement each other, especially when Time and an element of uncertainty are involved.

*

Patience adores Time; she is a humble and delightful character to get to know and have around. I promised myself, initially, that I wouldn't be gender specific when I wrote about the characters that gently emerge throughout this book. I am finding it hard not to at times but if a gender comes to mind then I will go with that first instinct. In fact, feel free to change the gender; whatever works for you. If I had characterised Time in much the same way, I bet it would have been a masculine entity and on reflection Time had such a presence that it now makes complete sense. Patience is attracted to Time and they get on very well. They are made for each other.

Naturally, these two characters cannot be entirely responsible for what happens to everything they oversee. It's like saying to them both, "Will you watch my bag?", as you go and get a coffee, then expecting them to be fully responsible when it goes missing in your absence. They both saw what was happening but couldn't actually do anything about it. Once it does go missing, though, they both come into play but they didn't do anything on their own, so why make either of them responsible?

In this next point, did Time or Patience actually do anything on their own? If you put a vegetable seed in the ground then it will take time to germinate and grow, so you will need to be patient if you are planning to use the produce in a future recipe. You can't plan to uproot it the next day and throw, let's say, a carrot into the pot; it isn't a realistic proposition. It's going to need water and a few nutrients to swim up the old xylem first, in order for it to grow. The xylem is the transport system, for those of you who have left your biology days behind. Then, it will be kissed goodnight by both Patience and Time and watched over with kindness. Gosh, if only all things were this simple.

Watching is often the operative word! Watching the slugs come along and disfigure the leafy carrot tops that protect the roots, which we go on to eat, doesn't mean Patience actually achieved anything by hovering around, doing nothing to intervene. It doesn't alert the pest control service on your behalf, so what role does it play? So far it has offered little tangible support in your endeavours to grow a carrot. So, to prevent any slug invasion from happening it is worthwhile taking the time, first, to prepare the ground; this is when Patience will probably flirt a little with its suitor. Preparation requires Time and so invites Patience along to keep it company.

Often in life, there are plenty of things that need to be present in order for something else to happen. We usually have to get involved, somehow, in order for a desired result to surface. The postman in the sky can put in the overtime but it takes a degree of patience on our part to leave him to deliver our intentions when he is good and ready. This is unlikely to happen (in our time zone) if we keep on clock-watching.

Even I'm wondering, *how does Patience operate?*, as it is beginning to sound more and more mysterious as I play with analogies. If Patience came with an instruction label it would possibly say something like, "Use on a regular basis: to assist you in making difficult decisions; while waiting for long-term plans to unfold; helpful in cases where uncertainty can still be unproven, given time; when your mind is constipated – you can't think straight – and you've nearly given up all hope."

Phew! And this would just be the initial paragraph that could be found occupying the outer layer of packaging, if indeed Patience was obtainable in a little box for convenience and sourced over the counter. It would clearly come with a caveat, telling you to read the full set of instructions inside as they may contain additional and important information.

There will be side effects from adding Patience to your existing portfolio of emotions, and whilst it isn't an emotion *per se* it can certainly make you feel emotional. Emotions can be experienced when you either haven't enough patience left to cope with the task in hand, or you can boast about having so much of it to begin with that you end up feeling a little too laid back. An excess can be a hindrance if it stops you from finishing a job you started; you can fall prey to developing a form of apathy that mutates the longer it is left ignored. You thought at first you could manage your time. Yet, from previous experience, many of us know that Time runs out. Time is deceptive, although it is probably ourselves who work on this pretence.

Can you really be too patient? Is it rendered useless when it canoodles with Time, forgetting that it had a remit to support you rather than inadvertently slow down your efforts? Wasn't Patience supposed to help you get through something instead of keeping you time-bound? Firstly, we tend to slow ourselves down when we take our eye off the ball or divert our attention elsewhere. I am not saying that we don't have cause to do so on many occasions. We can be excellent at justifying our actions! Secondly, being time-bound isn't such a bad idea. Sometimes this serves a purpose because, while something is going on over there, something else can be going on over here; eventually the two events marry up and hey presto: result! You get mail delivered to two postcodes; the law of attraction gets to prove itself when left to operate in the peace and quiet and, interestingly, Patience stops being something you have to search for and occurs as one of your natural resources.

What are the consequences associated with waiting too long for something to come to fruition in our lives? Well, it may be useful for you to start thinking about the things that hold you back before deciding if it has anything to do with Patience and if using it as a scapegoat is appropriate. What if Patience was the victim here and leaning on her was just an excuse to avoid dealing with something else that was stopping you from moving forward? I am quite certain that a range of positive and negative consequences will be indicative of your past experiences and some may start with an 'if' or a 'but', or a phrase that caveats the reason why something hasn't been achieved yet. Equally, the consequences may just be the side effects that you had envisaged all along, and Patience happily saw you through to the finishing line in one piece.

A common phrase, 'Patience is a virtue', would be fitting if we knew for certain that good things are always waiting around the corner as a result of actually waiting. No doubt they will be – somewhere – it's just the case of us finding them or them finding us! They are bound to be twiddling their thumbs or hinting for us to head in their direction as they play a game of charades, squashed up against a one-way mirror looking persuasive, yet we can't see them. We hope to catch sight of them in our dreams and as we go into a trance, daydreaming to bring them into our own reality just for a moment. Other times, they just happen to turn their backs on us, unaware that we can see them from a distance, as we frantically try to get their attention – but alas our eyes don't meet. And so we wait again! Each time we bridge the gap with optimism until the time is right to shake hands.

I would like you simply to consider an idea that we can either hide behind this humbling character, Patience, to convince ourselves that waiting is a polite way of demonstrating our ability to connect with Nature (and all good things come to those that wait), or, we can go jump the queue, dial up Nature direct and boldly ask it to reveal its secrets to success and that you won't tell a soul… Nature will surely admire your audacity.

The laws that exist behind Nature's existence are like puzzles. Just when you think you have them sussed they reveal another layer of mystery. You can feel a tad impatient. Incidentally, this isn't always a sign of weakness, as it can encourage you to take the initiative to go and get better acquainted with Nature and take action. Patience has a beautiful knack for getting away with being 'appropriately' arrogant and may only appear impatient when it acts alongside Confidence, believing that everything is a possibility (which isn't always a bad thing). I think you have to learn from past experience and decide for yourselves when impatience has been unhelpful. Then you can begin to master the art of being patient and enjoy the benefits.

Patience is aware that sometimes it can take a long time to help you work through one of your plans and witness a dream unfold through your eyes, in the way that you imagine. When things take time, we can be prone to becoming disheartened. We go between feeling positive and negative but it is important to understand and respect that these two words are not synonymous with success and failure respectively. Feeling one or the other does not, on its own, determine the end goal. When you feel negative for a while, it doesn't mean that the end goal is doomed to fail. On the other hand, remaining positive doesn't guarantee its success either.

You could be one of the most positive people in the world. But is being positive just a thought process that doesn't amount to anything until you decide to 'do' something too? For years, I was positive that I was going to write a book one day; I knew it wasn't going to write itself and I employed Patience on a full-time basis!

What you set out to accomplish may not have transpired, because the sheer idea of being positive and talking about being positive was supposed to be enough to drum up the desired result. Did you immerse yourself in the vision, or did you become weary of thinking so positively that by the time you got around to putting some actions behind your intentions, you mentally fizzled out and the dream remained just that: a dream? A dream remains a dream if you have no intention of making it your reality. It is the intention with the inspired action that will make it the reality. Remove the intention and it is but a dream – an idea that remains an idea.

So, first and foremost, have patience with yourself as you learn to be you, as you learn to dream and as you begin to understand that dreaming is not only for the faint hearted!

Dreaming is our soul's way of communicating with the human part of us that has a responsibility to take action – in this world. As we learn to be ourselves and not a reflection of someone else's dream, we go on to reap the benefits that go hand in hand with Patience.

Often in life, we don't always find it easy to do something we don't understand. If we cannot see how something will work out for us, we may not attempt to do it or to do it well. We all learn differently and then apply those learnings differently. If I understand why I am doing something, I am far more likely to do it better and then the dots in my peripheral vision tend to appear less threatening. The bigger picture can accommodate my confusion and frustrations, allowing nature to also run its course, as later on I begin to realise that some things are simply meant to be.

So thinking about your own events in life, for a moment, when does patience come naturally and when is it a struggle to maintain a connection? At what point are you even aware that you have been patient, because you had developed an equally valuable relationship with Tolerance and tuned into Nature's rhythms? And at what point did the partnership break down? In other words, when did the spark go out and why? Was it anything to do with Time misbehaving or did you not manage that fellow to the best of your ability? Was something supposed to take a set time to do and you got bored part way through and gave up? Maybe it wasn't so much about boredom, and Confidence scooted off on its travels again as you lost faith in whatever it was you were doing.

We can plan and prepare, though it is challenging to see past a certain point in time and know 'exactly' what's in store. Patience may have felt natural at the beginning and then became a little more demanding; and then a little bit more testing… pushing you beyond your usual threshold in order to achieve an alternate state of mind. Finally, the penny drops! Eventually, hanging around with Patience feels like a walk in the park; you get to wear Patience like a comfy jacket you reach out to and put on each morning as you both morph into one. The habit becomes natural and natural becomes your norm. In the very least it is now becoming a familiar aspect to you that you can benchmark.

I suppose it goes without saying that based on the idea that we all practise patience on one level or another, it wouldn't hurt to be patient with other people when it comes to accepting and even coping with their lack of patience, insecurities and insensitivities. Practise tolerance. It is most likely that all of those shortcomings we spot in other people so easily are reflected in each and every one of us, as we are not immune to periods of self-doubt or rebellious tendencies. We simply handle them and project them back out into the world differently.

Patience holds your hand through the darkness. It carries your weary soul through time when it struggles to cope with man-made pressures and responds to Nature's distress calls. Go ahead and take the time to listen to your inner voice that resonates in your dreams, speaking to you in a language that is effortlessly understood by Nature, most often while you sleep. Dreaming may allow you an insight into some of the biggest mysteries known to Humankind… have you ever thought about practising meditation?

T*R*U*S*T

Emotional Contracts

Imagine living in a world where nothing you heard was the truth; where nothing you saw was believable and nothing you felt was real. Can you imagine never being able to trust anyone, ever again? Not only would this provide for a lonely and primitive existence, it would more than likely cause you to suffer from extreme paranoia whereby even your own survival instincts would become untrustworthy.

The human race thrives on social interaction and we rely on people in one way or another, every single day. We may not even realise how reliant we are on anyone or anything in particular because we have become accustomed to trusting that certain jobs will get done, by certain people at a certain time. Somebody somewhere is doing a job for you and you won't even realise until they stop doing it, and only then are you likely to notice the impact that it has on your own little world.

I wonder if all the small things you take for granted, from having mail delivered or rubbish collected to having the roads swept, would soon impact negatively on your life if no one did them anymore. If you couldn't make that all-important call, send your emails and watch live TV because technology no longer worked or satellites were orbiting around another planet instead of our own – I am sure these malfunctions would impact on business and general life.

There are people all over the world getting up each day or night, working hard to provide a service to another industry which makes a product that eventually finds its way onto your doorstep. The supermarket shelves will display the fruits of someone's labour; the emergency services remain on standby; charities work tirelessly worldwide; governments multi-task and armed forces are either on guard or in battle. Someone somewhere is being saved from something that has happened or is about to happen. What if no one was helping anyone anymore because we didn't trust ourselves to help out in the first place or we didn't trust someone to help us? I think we would be in a pickle!

We naturally trust because if we gave all of these examples our energy and worried about who was doing what and when, all of the time, we wouldn't be able to focus on our own individual purpose in life and find our own path (you may be involved in one of these professions). Personally, I don't want to live a life that is based on mistrust and I like to trust people until I am given a reason not to trust. I need to trust so I am not consumed with doubts which can keep me in a less than comfortable place and emotionally drained.

Trust between two people (or two groups) creates a bond. Initially, you enter into an emotional contract and the relationship formed is not reliant upon any particular emotion being on display in order for it to work. Emotions may not reveal themselves unless the contract is broken and come out of hiding to indicate that either side is not too pleased with the outcome. Alternatively, emotions may remain conservative and contained, behaving with dignity during any further exchange of communication, symbolic of each other's trust towards one another; this may involve signing an agreement. At the end of a contract, once the terms are successfully fulfilled, emotions can run free and depending on what you put your trust into at the time, these could be tears of joy as your satisfaction is theatrically expressed.

Trust has been leaving its fingerprints whilst silently turning each page, interrupting at times but appropriately. Trust will be an integral part of your journey in life, as you have to trust yourself and put trust in other people, most of the time. It is agonising to think, looking back, that Trust wanted to partner up with Choices, as they are like childhood buddies that need to remain close at all times. However, I needed to be sure that Choice could withstand the line of questioning it was expected to undergo without Trust becoming overpowering, before allowing the two to reunite. Trust underpins every choice we make but once one is made, Trust doesn't put its feet up. Whatever it is you choose to do may need planning, executing and involve other people. Trust is in demand and is pulled in many directions.

If you find yourself in the unfortunate situation whereby you require an operation, you trust – before you consider anything else – that you actually need to have one (unless in an emergency and you were unconscious). After considering your options you trust yourself to make the right choice and when uncertain, you trust someone else to help you make a decision. You will go on to trust the surgeon, who you know from your research has the confidence to do the job and a reputation that has given you the confidence to trust in his/her abilities. The people around you can hopefully be trusted to help out and get you back on your feet post-op. So, throughout this event, Trust is playing a huge role and everyone is counting on it.

It is clear from the outset through to your recovery that you will have developed a personal relationship with Trust. You will literally *trust* Trust to look after you because you cannot be certain how this event will unfold and whether people will actually do what they said they would do or set out to achieve. The fact that you are *trusting* now means you hold a firm belief in what you are doing, in what other people are going to do and in what is going to be done (the operation). Hope will probably hover around again on the operating table, which is great, but everything has been based on Trust up until now and influenced by logical facts and gut instinct.

We often trust until we are given a reason not to trust. This basic approach is healthy, realistic, empowering and goes hand in hand with the idea that we treat people the way we would like to be treated.

If you say you are going to do something for someone and then you change your mind, will that person trust you the next time you offer to help? It may depend on your reason. Did you tell them you couldn't do it or *just didn't do it*, leaving them bewildered and wondering what happened? Are you given a second chance but let that same person down again?! Do you innocently procrastinate without taking into account the impact of your actions on other people or are you simply untrustworthy and don't mean a word you say?

Some of us have an admirable ability to laugh off other people's excuses, having sussed out that there are simply people in life who cannot be relied upon. At work you may have heard the forewarnings floating around about the woman who always means well, but don't ask her to do anything as she will end up letting you down. In the pub one guy says to another, "He's a nice bloke and is always volunteering to help out, but if you want the job done sooner rather than later it may be best to hire someone reliable". You may have been on the other end of one of these remarks having let someone down. If it resulted in any negative consequences you may have felt terrible about it afterwards, and if you are not used to letting someone down, it isn't a pleasant experience.

Of course it is nice to be trusted! It enriches the soul and keeps us moving in the right direction as a human being, spiritually or otherwise depending on your beliefs. You may decide that there are enough down-to-earth influences that can cloud your own judgement, never mind trying to engage in the idea that spiritual guidance could exist and would require an element of interpretation before becoming at all useful. Alternatively, give it a go and trust the Universe to deliver; you may surprise yourself as you start to get a few more sensible answers coming through, when you ask the right questions. And then listen!

On the other hand, others may suggest it is wiser *not to trust at first*, until you are sure that a person or idea can be trusted. There is logic to having this point of view and it may be based on the situation.

When you are romantically inclined to get involved with someone who you have just met, you may be cautious. They may need to give you a clear indication of why they can be trusted but it is unlikely to be something tangible or a test they can take (unless you have a particular one up your sleeve that works well for you) and it may take time for you to trust the person completely. Surely, you will still trust up to a point in order to move the relationship on to the next level and trust until you have any reason not to trust. You will be the judge of where that point is, for you. Everyone will have different standards and levels of confidence in other people, either marked by a former experience or as a result of following their instincts. If danger felt close by, it stops being about trusting that person alone and more about trusting yourself to do what feels right – scarper comes to mind!

If trusting in other people is not the easiest of things for you to master, it can take up your emotional energy. The energy can feel negative and you spend most of your day on tenterhooks, anticipating a disaster or failure to unfold, instead of allowing Trust to be present unconditionally until you need to decide otherwise.

Trusting that we are only given as much as we can handle in life is a tough idea for many of us to get our head around. Maybe this theory works when life is playing ball but when it all gets too much it can seem a little far-fetched. Taking comfort in the fact that it is 'all meant to be' and we will be more resilient for having had 'an awkward experience' probably doesn't work for half the population. On the other hand, if this concept gives you faith that you are not alone, even though you are not entirely sure what is accompanying you either, you may trust that a master plan will unfold and handling the here and now is as logical as it is going to get. Regardless of what you believe in, we all believe that Trust exists in one form or another; we just have different ideas about it, that's all.

What does 'trusting in you' actually mean? I imagine it depends on the context. Trusting in you to do *something* and feeling certain that you can do it is ultimately believing in yourself: "I trust myself to drive a car without crashing each time I go down the road" or "I trust myself to keep a promise". When you *feel* it is right – to trust in taking action – you are also trusting in a positive feeling that accompanies the act of trusting. (Not to be confused with having to be in a positive situation for Trust to work; kindly read on and then have a think about this. Here goes…)

Trust seeks your approval to get to work and responds to your feelings. If you don't feel that an action is the 'right' thing to do, then Trust will feel apprehensive about carrying out any tasks it is being assigned. If you don't believe in what you are about to do, then Trust will probably ask to step down and let Hope take its place because you are not reflecting the level of confidence it needs to see in order to work efficiently. A firm belief must exist which authorises Trust to jump on its surfboard and ride the waves off the back of your confidence.

You trust in yourself to do something or you don't (boom!). It is a bold statement to make but is it really that simple? Maybe you are nervous about acting on an idea because you are lacking self-confidence and confine yourself to a limited set of thoughts! Trust is sitting on the substitute's bench, like a player waiting to be brought on in a game of football – it is on your side and wants to play. In fact, this is the bench where all the emotional substitutes and reserve players sit, waiting a turn. It's a busy place to visit with all the comings and goings, and sometimes an emotion sits down for a moment only to find it is being asked to get back up; this may be to support another player or help tame the other ones out in the field.

Interestingly, I think that Trust is an extremely reasonable character and understands that you may take time to build on your current levels of trust or to find it in the first place. This is why it is always running around after you at short notice. It senses an uncertainty can exist – especially when you are making a decision – and once you have made up your mind it will need to wait close by. It realises you can be fragile until any uncertainty has disappeared and your vision is clear.

However, Trust is equally clear on its own role and doesn't like wishy-washy situations. It accepts it will be involved in situations that don't turn out as well as you had planned but it expects you to believe from the start that they will. Its role is not to pick up the pieces when it all goes wrong or revel in your successes. Trust has no ego; it only asks for respect and then you can both enjoy an understanding relationship. Trust loves to work with Honest, which we shall meet later.

I stated, "You trust in yourself to do something or you don't", because I don't know if you can partially trust in yourself. After all, what does trusting yourself 'a bit' mean? If you said meagrely, "Well, I sort of trust myself", this suggests to me that you don't... more than you do! I understand why Trust is saying to you, "Make up your mind – and then you will have my full support". Hence this is the reason I am inclined to believe that a positive feeling accompanies Trust, in order for it to exist. What are your thoughts about this now?

Trust won't influence you one way or the other and simply does as it is told once you have made up your mind. Logic and instincts will do all the influencing, offering up a selection of mixed messages that you will have to interpret. They will both impact on how you think and feel, and Trust will go along with your final choice. Trust will expect the same level of confidence to be attributed to the small things you do in life as well as the larger, more complex, situations that pop up along your path.

If you are setting up a business, Trust will be involved in various aspects from start-up through to implementation and delivery, but I bet it will stick by its word and maintain that its own role still needs to be clear. Trust will say that you cannot trust yourself 'a bit' in any one aspect of the business. It will ask you to trust yourself completely to do any 'one bit' and ensure you do it well. It would expect you to learn to trust someone else to do 'another bit'; excellent – so this would be 'two bits' that are going very well now! Learn to do the things you can't do yet and work out how you are going to do the things that neither one of you is ever likely to be any good at doing. If you are someone who is fabulous at doing everything, then consider the time involved and if you've got plenty stashed away!

When we explored the Time Sandwich we suggested we could buy someone else's time to do a job for us. You may have to work with contractors and you will trust them to provide a successful service or product. We would need to trust the person or we wouldn't invest our money – we have to be confident that he/she could do the job. When you don't trust yourself completely, it is OK to ask for help and this may be the resolution.

I don't believe we can *partially* trust ourselves. I do feel that if you are at the stages where you are 'sitting on the fence' then you are also at a stage which is inviting you to jump over and meet Trust head-on in full costume on the other side. Although, it is actually no less logical to trust in yourself to make a decision to turn back, as this could end up being the best course of action at the time. But is Trust greeted on the fence itself in order to make the decision or on either side once the decision is made? Actually, I am inclined to say, 'on the fence'; this is because that is where the decision is being made and that is exactly the point where Trust is being asked to engage.

On another note altogether, when someone beside you is itching to help and you say, "Go on then, you do it, I don't trust myself", maybe it is because they were watching you and made you feel nervous at the time. You didn't demonstrate to Trust that you had enough confidence to gain its full support so it will be sitting on the bench on standby. So what is it that encourages us to trust another person to do a job, better than you can do it yourself? Hopefully you will have a few ideas of your own.

I can recall a time when I was younger and was frequenting yet another one of those phases that found me searching for Confidence in what felt at the time like an alpha male environment. I asked the mechanic in a garage to reverse out of the bay so I could drive out with both of my eyes facing in the right direction, as opposed to compromising my cervical spine because I was trying to look in two places at once. This was ultimately to avoid driving under the influence of – or rather under the gaze of – half a dozen men in crumpled boiler suits held together by brake fluid and goodness knows what else, lined up in readiness for their morning break and some entertainment. Never mind the car having been stripped down to its bare essentials in order to find the original fault; I think the heat from my own internal operating system would have been enough to indicate that if I didn't scoot off and cool down, I too would have needed rescuing from sheer embarrassment! As a confident driver now, many moons on, I trust myself to get out of a space in a garage forecourt – all by myself.

Learning to trust other people can come easily to some of us and prove quite difficult for others. When you don't trust other people because something may have happened in your life that has made it harder to trust, steps need to be taken to overcome any previous cause for mistrust. Once you recognise your own signs, representative of trusting yourself, you will be able to recognise similar signs more easily from other people, who are saying, "You can trust me too". If someone asks you to trust them, do you follow your instincts which may be telling you to trust implicitly or do you weigh up all the facts and get back to them once you are happy to proceed with an emotional contract?

You may have fallen off your path and want to get back into the same saddle you were in before you fell, but do you need to trust anything in particular before you can? Do you climb back up in an attempt to conquer your fears, putting trust into yourself not to fall off again? Trust can work in stages and remember, it likes to be trusted completely during each one and you may have to go through various stages before reaching your final destination.

Once I was in a car crash caused by my own lack of peripheral vision. I was following another car and its driver knew the route. I overlooked the junction ahead and focused on the number plate of the other car so I wouldn't get lost. With hindsight, I would rather have stopped and asked for directions than experience what happened next. I lost control of the car as I engaged with a truck. My car had two windows taken out and a nice big indent in the side. The truck was OK – so was the man behind the wheel. I learned never to follow anyone ever again – I didn't trust myself. I was told to get back in the car and drive home. I am not sure if this would be allowed nowadays but I did get back in the 'saddle' and I conquered my fears relatively quickly. I think this advice worked on the basis that my choices were limited and I had little time to reflect in the moment. Am I positive, looking back, that my feelings were positive? I certainly wouldn't have got back into that car if they weren't! Would you?

We have to use our own 'good judgement' which relies upon Trust to support it when we have to make a choice. Trust issues have to be broken down to avoid indigestion – when you find it difficult to trust, you can find it difficult to swallow. The thought of never trusting again sounds as painful as the thought of being unable to swallow ever again… and why? Because I love my food too much!

Judgement, which follows, has been waiting patiently and I have a feeling that it is going to reveal a couple of different sides to its character. So let us explore why it has been left to last in this section.

J*U*D*G*E*M*E*N*T

Reading Between the Lines

Fancy a chuckle? How many times do you think you've applied a healthy dose of good judgement within a decision-making process only to find that the result made no sense at all! A belated surprise simply got in your way, after the deed was done. Sense did a U-turn, knocking itself out in the process, never to come around to your original way of thinking – ever again. Well… in this instance anyway.

Judgement is passed around in life like a parcel is thrown around in a game of musical chairs, moving from one person to another until the music stops and then Judgement becomes personal. A parcel can be wrapped up in suspicion and insecurities; anticipation is written all over each layer. This reminds me of playing musical chairs as a child. I remember everything was wrapped up in newspaper back then and none of the words made any sense; nothing has changed for me now: it is still a case of reading between the lines! When it comes to our turn to hold Judgement in the palm of our hands we take a good look and shake it around, hoping that what is about to unfold will not lead to disappointment. The music has stopped and we will shortly find out if Judgement is in a good or bad mood!

*

'Good Judgement' and 'Poor Judgement' keep each other on their toes! They keep us on our toes too! We make judgements prior to and following a decision and in doing so, the result may reflect on whether it was indeed based on good judgement or a lack of it! The consequences to the actions of both these characters may be open to interpretation.

The opening paragraph brought us back down to earth with a bump, reminding us that our first decision, whilst favourable at the time, may have left us with a stream of unintended events to attend to. The judgement hat, previously set aside, now goes back on with an air of authority! As the events undergo further developments Poor Judgement becomes restless and, like a predator on the look out for its next adrenaline rush, it can confuse our senses, clouding our ability to make more of the right decisions. While some loose ends are securely tied, presenting us with no imminent threat of separation, others are rearranged artistically and unravel as they are pulled in another direction.

Sometimes it is down to our own poor judgement, and we cannot incriminate any other excuses that get in the way. At other times, we make a good decision (or so we think) which we later find out is unable to withstand the pressures that we originally imposed, though would remain in place for some time to come as we sign our life away. Naivety and Optimism are both stripped naked and left to account for their behaviour. Then again, outside influences can play their part too as they are fired across enemy lines to simply distract us from our purpose or hold us back from achieving it – in the way we intended. Other people catapult their own poor judgement and if you are caught in the crossfire or happened to be their intended target, then the consequences of catching that parcel may well impact on your own direction.

Is our impish friend Poor Judgement (who we can nickname PJ for now) actually involved, from the beginning, even when a situation was seemingly going very well? Does PJ hover around on the sidelines like an understudy who has learned the lines – just in case the leading character took a turn for the worse – hoping that it can step in and put its own twist on the situation? Is it really that mischievous? PJ is the adolescent that is constantly suffering from growing pains which justifies its behaviour but does not excuse any consequences. It is as innocent as a child who is learning and as naïve as an adult who doesn't want to grow up.

What if the main actor was played by Good Judgement and appeared to be on top form having been right for the part all along? After all, it auditioned well and evidently prepared. It was about to be swept away by its audience and a standing ovation was on the cards! What, on earth can take one of our own performances to such dizzy heights and then bring it to its knees, defacing all innocence, tainting the landscape with true disappointment? Did you self-destruct, fall into enemy hands or did the master plan simply not turn out to be the all-inclusive package deal you had bargained for?

Luxury points you in a direction that sees a contingency plan tucked up your sleeve; another ingenious idea that can be accredited to having good judgement, yet can be difficult to attain. Although it takes vision to create an original plan, we need to put a back-up plan together – just in case. We tend to think of the latter as an afterthought, while knowing full well that it is a sensible thing to do. It may appear self-indulgent to have both plans in place, ahead of time, especially when the construction of the master plan took all of your time up and patience to prepare. Your idea of being sensible, and giving it a role to play, may also depend on whether you are anticipating any misfortune ahead, as a result of PJ or any other entity tripping you over. Plan 'B' may not even sit on your radar because Confidence just happens, this time, to be working with you flat out… on plan 'A', following in your footsteps and leaving only crystals of sand behind as evidence.

Finally, the exit strategy you do have in place to move from one plan to the other, if ever such an occasion arose, may never need to be put into effect. Finding one of these strategies in the first place, wedged between cells of grey matter, can be exhausting and potentially distracting. The idea still needs to be extracted from the brain and repositioned somewhere along the arm, under that 'all-important sleeve', to allow Failure to abate, should it make any attempts to arrive and instil fear. The overall aim is to put Sense back on the map, leave PJ speechless for a while (which is a tricky thing to do) and bring harmony back to an otherwise inharmonious situation, while judging yourself kindly along the way!

*

There will be many reasons why PJ will appear on your path and run riot, attacking from whichever direction it happens to be sent. Neither forms of Judgement can exist without undergoing an element of self-reflection. More often, the two will get their heads together at the same time to understand what went wrong; or to learn what could have been done better to keep their energies from clashing. You could argue that Good Judgement keeps an eye on PJ far more closely than the other way around. Although, when PJ is keeping a watchful eye on its competition, it may have ulterior motives. Dressed up in its little investigator's outfit (beige Mac and dark shades), it resonates more with a PI character (private eye) out of a seventies or eighties cop show, than a villain which I may have possibly portrayed. Shrouding PJ with darkness and treating it as though its only mission in life is to overturn any good judgements is probably unfair. I think PJ is just sloppy at times but not vindictive, and so we can explore this point of view later on.

So far, we have discovered that our own judgement can wander off into the wrong direction and we have to catch up with it before it gets us into trouble or simply applaud it for being right in the first place! We base our judgements on logic and instincts in order to bring about a suitable conclusion and I think this area of debate is worth exploring first as they are both rather influential.

*

Instincts don't kick you continuously in the pit of your stomach for fun, chatting endlessly and distracting you throughout the day for no good reason. You may notice your instincts nudge you at a point in time, when you are about to make a decision. When an instinct kicks in, it could be asking you to trust the fact it has got your attention for a reason and it would like you to listen and not be too judgemental. We all have instincts and some may prefer to label these as a gut feeling instead. As a human race, we are instinctive people.

The use of logic, when you are in a quandary, can be just as daunting to rely upon as using your instincts – we tend to question both at the time. Logic isn't always right or as interesting to follow compared to its more mysterious ally, Instinct, which gets a hard time for being less – how shall we put it? – scientific!

Logic is the more scientific character out of the two and it may be perceived as a less risky and acceptable process tool to use to problem solve. It is easier to explain how you came to a conclusion by using logic than it is to declare that you followed your instinct because the latter felt right. Logic doesn't always feel right but the use of logic is often considered a sensible and responsible approach to take when making a decision (especially in times of doubt). Logic can get you off the hook and it can also be used to avoid doing something. Logic is a slightly more controlling character and when it takes over, you may end up not doing what you really wanted to do!

Instincts are confident and are very happy to be 'a normal part of your life'. It isn't the instinct that has the issue when it pops up out of the blue, coming through to you naturally. It is the person who experiences their wake-up calls that tend to assign them a justification as they themselves endure a line of questioning about their decision-making process. Oddly enough we question our instincts, so it shouldn't be any surprise to us when other people start to do the same and pass judgement!

Instincts don't give up on you – but you may give up on following your instincts. Logic may be your safety net even if it doesn't lead you to where you want to be. The idea that we are all where we are supposed to be in life is not an easy concept for humans to digest but whether logic got you here, or instincts got you here, you are here! Congratulations.

Plenty of things in life are based on logic and they need to be. I only suggest that some of us may naturally side with logic before considering the value of our instincts when it comes to making decisions. Logic may be broken down more easily while instinct behaves like our personal compass that guides, rather than explains. You can put your finger on how logic has been used but you can't always pinpoint the reasoning behind your instincts – you just know!

If you are choosing a colour of a dress, a shirt or let's say a car, your instincts may direct you to choose a colour that 'feels right'. When you are at a crossroads and debating on whether to turn left or right, an instinct will rise up from within and make a suggestion. You decide to take a left and go back to the shop to buy the red dress but if it doesn't fit, you don't buy it – that's logic for you! Your instincts may tell you it will fit in two months' time although it may forget to tell you what to do to make that happen. Sometimes we don't listen to the entire message and PJ finds your weak spot, cutting it off in mid-flow, and tells you to buy it anyway. The little monkey! If you went ahead and bought a red car because you passed the Ferrari garage as you turned right instead, I wonder if two sets of messages drove you on to the forecourt and made an impression.

Logic and Instinct are definitely allies that may conflict at times yet have respect for each other. Your instincts have no ego and have no issue in telling you to use your logic on certain occasions. This is probably why it is well suited to mingling with our friend Trust, which you may recall has no ego either. When you trust your instincts you are drawn back into one of those emotional contracts which requires nothing more than a silent handshake to secure the bond.

So why are some instinctive people often happy to be humble and use logic, judging the two concepts on their own merits, while some logical people dismiss the idea of using instincts as a 'nice-to-have feeling' and prefer to stick to the facts. Facts have their place. Facts can be used in isolation and thank goodness they can stand on their own two feet but sometimes they need to be put into perspective and be joined together by a little intuition.

When making a decision, if you don't know whether to use logic or your instinct you may end up tossing a coin in the air as a last resort and hope for the best. Instincts don't mind being used as a last resort but your first instinct is usually right. Instincts are often undervalued. They run around free and they are an integral part of our internal operating system. Some may say that they belong to our spirit that is hosted by our human body, and others may say that that is just an excuse to let us off the hook!

We don't always judge our instincts with the respect they deserve. If we had to pay for an instinct maybe we would value them more in the same way we often heed advice when we have paid for it, trusting an expert's opinion (even if we choose not to take the advice in the long run). It is hard to judge what the outcome will be when we use our instincts and this is why we revert back to good old logic: safe, reliable and somewhat boring at times. When we explored Path it was clear that sometimes people avoid taking detours because Logic got in the way before their Instincts could get a word across. We could also consider that Instincts may have prompted you to use Logic rather than take an adventure and you didn't realise at the time it was walking in your shadow to protect (sounds like a natural bodyguard to me!).

*

When PJ slips up and causes mayhem along your path all of your other emotions will start jumping up and down, competing for attention as some of them will become defensive and have a lot to say on the subject. Any lessons you are about to learn from the experience will already be lining up in readiness for a one-to-one review session with PJ. I can imagine them appearing like children gathered in an assembly hall, whispering to each other as they await their call to assume a role as a prefect. Their role, should they be chosen, will be to coach PJ back to good health!

Good Judgement will step in as a mentor and demonstrate how easy it is – when you know how – to bring about a successful end result, teaming up with Trust and Confidence. PJ gets to consider what it could do differently next time. Good Judgement can't always sit smug on its pedestal and do nothing as it isn't immune to learning, either. We saw earlier that it has a tendency to fall off on occasions, blindsided by its own horizon.

Sometimes PJ will exist to serve a higher purpose, although it may not feel like it at the time! If you have made a poor judgement then the negative outcome may help you to learn an important lesson that you will be reminded of in the future. You will be responsible for the way it is behaving and if you are making it a habit you will have a duty of care to understand what it is that allows PJ to behave in such a disorderly fashion. If you are not careful, you will land yourself with an 'anti-social behaviour order' (an ASBO for short). It is at this point that PJ will undergo one of those one-to-one reviews and even if it is not harming other people, it could be hurting you in the long run as you are allowing yourself to pursue a pattern of destructive behaviour. If someone else's poor judgement is hurting you, because they are not making wise choices or speaking out of turn, then you will need to learn to challenge this behaviour.

We judge ourselves, other people and situations with varying degrees of kindness and sometimes Judgement can overstep the mark. Judgement sits in this lovely section, which is all about Understanding and Respect, for a jolly good reason. This is not because it has either of them unconditionally but because it is important to learn to judge with an element of understanding and respect. The idea that it is not what we say but how we say it can be applied to what we judge and how we judge it! No matter how well you intended to pass judgement if you simply throw it across, with little thought about what obstacles may lie in between, then you can't expect the other person to catch it particularly well!

Imagine you are out walking with a friend and one of you happens to be on a constant diet – the type that never sees an inch being lost from any obvious place. As you both reach a pond you accidentally split off, whilst chatting away. You both go around it in opposite directions but with a view to coming back together to climb over a stile that leads on to the next bridleway.

You tell your friend as you shout out across the pond, obscured by reeds and overhanging branches, that there may be something worth changing about the way they currently diet, though using words that have been immediately misconstrued. Perceived more like an accusation that implied they secretly ate, their blood pressure has risen and triggered a reaction.

As you both fall into the murky waters, drowning in different emotions, it is time to call in the lifeguard. Hopefully you can both recover from any ill feelings and reconcile any differences that arose when little PJ got in the way of you passing on your advice which clouded your good judgement. As the judge, you may have tied yourself in knots because what you said 'came out all wrong' and backtracking felt more like catching an anchor than a life jacket, as you continued to get yourself into deeper water the more you talked!

The one being judged will probably consider if they actually overreacted, although it may be too early to swallow any pride at this stage because they too are swallowing enough pond fluids to keep them infected for a few hours to follow. Or, they may not have overreacted, having due cause to be upset and take offence. It may have been about how you spoke to them rather than what you said and the positives will have been filtered out and automatically bypassed. The only thing left to do now, for both of you, is to wring out any residual water remaining from the splash attack and catch the lessons that have already taken off. They are about to land in both your directions which are unlikely to be the same.

I hope you can relate to the idea that none of us is able to control the reactions that are owned by another person in response to what we say or do. We can learn to manage the delivery of what we say and be mindful about what else we do.

*

The darker side of Judgement naturally brings about a degree of emotional pain when experienced. It spreads an emotional infection as it is passed around. Anyone who believes that they have come into contact with a potent level of judgement is encouraged to take a period of recovery, even just for a moment, to ensure that no lasting damage will result and symptoms can be dealt with imminently. As with all viruses, there are different strains and they may impact on us differently. Whilst Judgement is not a disease, it can bring an element of dis-ease into our lives and we have a remarkable ability to self-infect!

We learned earlier that we can judge each other, vocalising our own opinions and making them known, which can have a negative impact on levels of confidence. Let's be honest now: it doesn't do much for your own confidence if you are putting yourself down and succumbing to a form of masochistic behaviour that isn't attractive. We may hurt people intentionally or unintentionally when we express ourselves inappropriately or with a certainty that somehow suggests that we know better about someone else's life than they do! A judgement made is often better received when it is backed up with sound advice or a non-offensive suggestion for improvement.

As a dance teacher, you may judge someone on how they perform during rehearsals and feedback; call this a judgemental intervention. Once judgement is passed, the interventions that follow will range from offering kind support and constructive criticism through to delivering unacceptable levels of intimidation, humiliation and bullying. A teacher's role is to teach, imparting knowledge and expertise; a student will trust the teacher – it is an emotional contract. If the balance of emotional power is tipped the wrong way, then regardless of whether the judgement passed by the teacher is fundamentally right, the way it is packaged can have a detrimental effect. If you find yourself holding his/her judgement in the palm of your hand, having been passed the parcel and feel somewhat disappointed, simply put it down, say "thank you" and find yourself a new teacher!

Not only are we responsible for how we judge but we need to take responsibility for how we react to different forms of judgement, when we are on the wrong end of it. Sometimes a window of opportunity appears during a less than comfortable experience, with a judgemental intervention that can allow us to escape just in time. We begin to change the way we react to the darker side of Judgement and we simply say, "This isn't acceptable", and begin to do something about how it makes us feel. Good Judgement will carry you through the window until you learn how to use the front door and face the world with confidence and stop being afraid.

Judgement has multiple personalities. They can each play a part and could win an Oscar for playing each role. Judgement can play the good guy and the bad guy. You can hear it now: "And, the winning title goes to… Judgement, for an outstanding performance in 'What on earth did you do that for?'" Judgement is also good at playing a role in a soap drama that goes on and on and usually equates to someone in the show beating themselves up with an emotional stick, judging themselves unkindly and becoming a victim that can support a storyline of self-deprecation in each episode!

We go through life becoming entangled in other people's stories and through these interactions, on what may seem like a treacherous path at times, we feel vulnerable – we let our guard down and we let the judges in. We either find the strength to say, "Thanks but no thanks", or we crumble and seek to cover our eyes so we don't have to see our accusers while listening to their accusations.

This can pose a difficulty if the person you are trying to ignore happens to be yourself! Unless you are looking in the mirror – which is often a time we can judge ourselves unkindly – we cannot actually see ourselves completely. We forever have to listen to ourselves when we speak and we hear our thoughts, passing judgement on these as they go by. If only we could let them go by instead of analysing their every move, because half of the time they don't require any attention. Then, we may be less inclined to allow PJ another opportunity to misbehave.

It is extraordinary really, when you think about it, that we judge ourselves poorly and find this an acceptable intervention but can't abide it when it attacks us from another direction. Good

Judgement must be having a laugh at our expense, watching us talking to ourselves while feeling somewhat irritated.

So, Good Judgement and Poor Judgement are learning from each other. We started off by putting Good Judgement on a pedestal for its mentoring skills but let us not forget that PJ has equally been teaching it a thing or two. Whilst Good Judgement does not rely upon an act of poor judgement to exist, as it does not thrive on a symbiotic relationship with PJ, it does observe. As it reflects on the actions and consequences of its misguided buddy and takes an opportunity to self-reflect, Good Judgement will ultimately become stronger and less likely to fall off its pedestal. Therefore, it has to behave with a degree of humbleness and not get too big for its boots.

Each sandwich in this section has contained some very good nutrients that will feed our soul. As with all good food, we don't always appreciate how good it tastes until we slow down and savour the moment. We gulp our food down as if Time is going to sneak up and steal the plate away before we have finished, but we forget that Patience is keeping its eye on Time all along, encouraging it to slow down once in a while.

We don't always understand how to tame our emotions but Trust will help us to harness the power that is required from within that will help us to learn. If we can keep on the right side of Judgement and learn to use our instincts so they can dance with logic without stepping on its toes, then I have some good news for you, my friends: I think we are ready to face up to visiting the next table. They are a little intimidating at first, but once we get to know them I am certain that in time, we will appreciate their points of view.

Firstly, what has Failure truly got to say about itself? We have already suggested that in the event you have no plan B up your sleeve, and plan A didn't quite meet your expectations, then your upper limb may appear to be a perfect landing strip for Failure to make an appearance. What does the word *failure* even mean, anyway? Go ahead, turn the page and see what ideas I have concocted up to now…

Course 4

Fillings Containing
Anti-Nutrients

Limitations and Acceptance

'Negative perceptions of yourself only seek your permission to change.'

Aspiring to be the best you can be is acceptable. Aspiring to be someone you are unlikely to be is limiting – not to mention draining! Treading water all the time and then wondering why that very same practice every day is getting you nowhere, because surely practice makes perfect, is saying to the world right there that you are placing limitations on yourself for one reason or another.

Anti-nutrients are known to negatively impact on the absorption of nutrients and affect your health. Similarly, too much emphasis on these fillings which ooze failure, fear, guilt and need can impinge on your ability to live a happier life in the here and now, using up energy that could be welcome elsewhere.

Whether they are born from your own weak spots or influenced by someone else's, unfortunately they found their way to your door. Be open to the fact that they came to visit for a reason; it took a while for you to realise that their company was becoming intrusive, and they have overstayed their welcome. Now you know that, it will be easier to send them packing; only you can ask them to leave.

The irony is that whilst we know they don't do us a great deal of good, we may have justified their existence but eventually, they are not so much missed as noticeably absent and it is at that point we can have a healthier relationship with ourselves and other people.

F*A*I*L*U*R*E

Sugar Isn't Always the Enemy!

As the spacecraft landed safely on Earth the visiting alien carried out a quick sense check of the planet and confirmed back to base that its first mission could be recorded as **F-A-I-L-U-R-E**: Found An Inspirational Lifeform Using Ridiculous Excuses. News travelled fast as the hive of elders back home huddled together to watch from afar and learn about the excuses that the extra-terrestrials on Earth relied upon within their everyday life.

They later found out that *failure* meant something different to everyone and it was influenced by expectations. By the time they finished their planetary assessment they came to the conclusion that human beings could be forgiven for creating excuses. This was because they seemingly lived in a world of emotional conflict, pulling them in so many directions that they frequently lost perspective on what was truly important and ridiculous excuses were a by-product.

They were setting themselves so many limitations that when humans did analyse Failure they found it hard to accept that it could even exist. So consequently Failure was something to be ashamed of and people were becoming embarrassed to say its name in public. Stringing alternative letters together, in the hope that a new word will eventually replace the 'F' word and sound more acceptable, gradually sounded the right thing to do. They couldn't avoid Failure so they were beginning to avoid using the word *failure*, almost believing that if they didn't say it too loudly, then it would be unlikely to be overheard. If they could practise selective hearing and silence their own listening devices this would ensure that Failure didn't have to be discussed and a lack of success would be a temporary period of time that existed until success finally showed up.

The alien decided to create its own interpretation for the word *failure* and advised its elders that from hereon it would mean: **F**orever **A**m **I** **L**iving **U**nder **R**elentless **E**xpectations.

Its mission was to observe why the word *failure* was interpreted differently among the people and what impact Failure had on the people when it was experienced. Aliens know that life evolves and universally we are all at different stages in our own development. It wasn't a surprise to learn that words are interpreted differently either. Nonetheless, the investigative alien was intrigued as to why a word had to be changed simply because people couldn't learn to use it correctly in the first place. The word *correct* was always under scrutiny; the definition varied depending on which committee was doing the scrutinising.

If the word *failure* could be better understood, taken at face value and explored within context, then would this approach reduce the emotional attachment that accompanies Failure? An emotion will exist when failure is experienced; this is inevitable – emotions are just dressed up differently from one human being to another. It is not the fact that an emotion unnecessarily supports an act of failure at the time it has occurred; it is the fact that emotions hover around for far too long after Failure has finished its business, washed the dishes and is thinking of its next meal! Failure is given far too much attention and this is why coping with an act of failure becomes difficult and can end up being more complicated than it needs to be. Failure has to develop its own 'coping strategies' when it lacks support.

The alien also wrote in its report that it found that words themselves could represent **W**isdom **OR D**isease, and provoke emotions and feelings. It found it odd that wisdom was often associated with positivity and disease could be prolonged by negativity. Failure was construed as an underachiever attracting negativity and, when it was held accountable in conversation, it was considered a disease. The alien went on to argue that Failure was innocent and was no more of a disease than the negative emotions stored in the mindset of a human that kept Failure in an unhealthy state. Failure is admittedly an attention seeker but it can teach you so much.

Failure is a character that is simply doing its job. Don't dress it up to be something it isn't but, at the same time, you don't have to punish it and vocally condemn it as something to fear the next time it happens. Failure will step in again and be equally as annoying or embarrassing (even when you have attempted the same thing twice) but you have to keep trying – when you believe something is worth 'fighting' for. If you keep on failing, then maybe you really are hitting your head against a brick wall and it is time to go around the wall and see if success can greet you on the other side without getting a headache. Dealing with a failure is another area for consideration, but for now we need to come to terms with its existence and see if together we can approach it differently and not succumb to intimidation.

If something hasn't worked out the way you planned you may conclude that you have failed. If you tried to do something and it went completely wrong, let's face it, you have failed and on this occasion you were not successful. If it worked out, then (guess what?) you didn't fail; your plan worked and it was considered a success. Failure is as it is; you don't have to protect Failure, hiding it away as if your lack of accomplishment needs to be disguised. You may want to disguise the fact you failed but what is this really saying about you?! You didn't want to fail; no one wants to fail intentionally. You may feel embarrassed because other people are now aware that you failed; so what?! Don't they fail as well? Is everyone else so perfect that their acts of failure look prettier than yours? Is it how you react to Failure, when it shows up, that is the difference between being a good or a bad loser?

Wisdom insinuates that something positive has been woven into the contours of the word that gives it the respect it deserves. We forget that wisdom has been on more adventures than Aladdin and his magic carpet and is born out of negative experiences that have learned the error of their ways. OK, so it may have inherited its experiences from one life to the next, but even wisdom had to start somewhere.

Failure may carry a negative connotation (if you want to perceive failure as negative), but the way you react does not have to mirror that darker side. Failure can give rise to a positive experience that can even protect. How many times have you attempted to do something that failed and afterwards you were inclined to agree that had it worked out you may not be on the right path or doing something you truly aspired to do. You end up thanking Failure for getting in the way and so the outcome was rather positive! The act of failure itself is considered negative; upon reflection the result of failure can go on to have a positive impact in your life. Isn't this exciting to know?!

When Failure is looked upon as a disease, then naturally we are going to want to avoid being in its presence. We will try our utmost to avoid failing and we may even avoid doing things that could lead to disappointment and give rise to failure. This will be closely linked to Risk and if we don't want to leave ourselves wide open to the possibility of meeting up with Failure, we may not take a risk. We may choose differently because one option is less achievable than another and we don't want to consider failure as an option. We avoid Failure as best we can and in doing so we may miss out on opportunities and adventures. We don't know that we will go on to fail. We are setting ourselves limitations so that we don't have to experience the emotions that accompany Failure. If we learn to accept that failure doesn't have to equate to the end of the world or a life-threatening disease and that failure may be a learning curve that will stop us walking in a straight line forever, then we could enjoy the detours.

During these evaluations the elders were trying to keep up with the ambiguity that their appointed alien down on earth was uncovering. They could see how Failure was something to be avoided but felt saddened by the fact that Failure wasn't, in one form or another, going to be avoidable and humans were desperately going out of their way to find reasons it could be. Excuses surfaced when failure was experienced, but they were not entirely understood. Whilst an excuse was also a justification, it didn't mean it was misplaced. The excuses seemed to be coloured with Fear, Guilt and Need. All of these limiting emotions kept the impact of failure in a negative place and stopped its own emotions from moving on; instead failure was becoming a sole reason not to try something again.

Confidence was surrounding it, hoping that Failure would stop replaying the scene of the crime over and over but it was up to the human to pick itself back up, take the negative and positive feedback, and choose wisdom over disease. Negativity eats away at the weaknesses. Failure is only a weakness if you choose to let it be your weakness. Have you actually stopped to think about the positive sides to Failure? So adopting the idea that failure is an acceptable part of life, why do we tend to beat around the bush and call it all the names under the sun when it occurs?

The alien made a few bullet points, to summarise how three words in particular were able to influence Failure to feel less than adequate, but if people understood what Fear, Guilt and Need meant to them – in relation to their own shortcomings – then maybe they would stop bullying Failure and be more empathetic.

Failure tends to get emotional; the following contains three extracts taken from the notes made by the alien during its observations:

Fear

Humans have a tendency to fear Failure. When they fail they feel as if they have let themselves or other people down and fear how people may react. They fear the consequences of their failure. Different levels of failure exist and the lack of success can be detrimental to a lifeform. Fear supports avoidance; when a human fears that failure will result, they may avoid an action altogether. Fear of failure can be triggered by past experiences and negative encounters with other humans, or a previous act of failure can inhibit their confidence to try again. Fear can hold a human back in their quest to live a happier life, placing limitations on their own abilities, and these insecurities can be transmitted onto another human.

Guilt

When a human fails to achieve a goal they can either feel guilty or be influenced by another person to feel guilt. Humans create their own emotions and cannot be given these by another person. However, humans tend to display emotions easily and when they fail they usually exhibit guilt in one form or another. This may pass quickly as humans are a supportive lifeform having found that different methods can be used to help someone deal with any guilt associated with failure. Some humans have poor communication skills and have not learned how to vocalise their thoughts and feelings. The younger generation would benefit from understanding that failure is an acceptable part of life but the mature lifeform has a duty of care to prepare them for failure in case it happens. This has become a bespoke practice and may require a sensitive approach because all lifeforms have different personality traits. Therefore each act of failure should be addressed on a case-by-case basis.

Need

Humans often identify a need to do something before they can complete another task. If they fail in their quest and become unsuccessful they can exhibit signs of distress which accompany failure because expectations have not been met. Human cultures vary across the planet and use a form of assessment that defines failure or success. If humans need to pass a test in order to practise a profession, then Failure could intercept and stop them from proceeding until they resit the test and finally pass. Sometimes the need to pass an assessment is not a necessity. When humans experience failure, some are more able to accept that it was not meant to be (it wasn't their calling). Rather than limit their own thought patterns, they often demonstrate the ability to move on to another project. A healthy approach to failure may still involve using excuses but these are more on a par with reasons.

*

Deferred success is real. Success is often deferred until Failure gets its act together and stops wasting your time. I am happy to hear people say, "It isn't failure, it is only deferred success", as long as they are not hiding behind Failure and treating it like it didn't exist. Failure can exist and it can still be deferred success; it doesn't have to be one or the other. Failure, in this instance, may have existed to simply slow down the journey that will finally stop at the station of success.

Sometimes we board a slow train that costs less but takes a little bit longer. It seems at the time to stop at every location along the line, but it doesn't really. It stops occasionally so you can reflect and remind yourself that places do exist in between. Whilst the final destination has been planned all along – and will be reached if it is meant to be reached – the momentary lapses of reasons are just that. They are moments that have taken a tea break and switched the radio on to drown out your impatience. If you don't appreciate the journey then you can be slowed down, one way or another. This may not happen every time, hence the enviousness that you experience when you witness someone else getting to their destination faster, but (and I don't know why) we all get different lessons thrown at us. Maybe we are supposed to see something that we wouldn't otherwise see if we got on the fast train. We should treat Failure as a gift or in the very least consider why it has come into our lives.

Why do we have to pretend Failure doesn't exist? Who are we protecting and what is the reason? Why can't we let people use the experience as an opportunity to learn or is it the additional emotional mess that accompanies Failure that will take up more of our energy and only require more from Patience and Time? If we mollycoddle everyone – adults or children – then how do we create a society that is open to having honest conversations about their feelings which will enable them to respect Failure and not see it as an enemy every time it appears? If we wrap it up in shiny paper and throw it around in a game of Pass the Parcel, the problem is that no matter how shiny the paper, once it is opened, the truth still reveals itself. Good Judgement and PJ will still be waiting. If you have failed, PJ may let you know how it misjudged the situation (probably apologising profusely) and Good Judgement may be on hand to help you get back on track.

Preparing for failure in the event that it happens is not a bad thing! You put a smoke detector in your kitchen as a preventative measure; you take out home insurance in case a fire breaks out and causes damage. You have a house alarm to detect intruders and you have an immobiliser on your car in case they break into it and try to get away – not sure how they arrived but they failed in their attempt to leave; the alarm notified the police and fortunately they are on their way!

It is also about being sensitive to the fact that Failure can knock your confidence and thrive on your trust issues. You can feel like the bottom of your world has fallen through. What if the fear of trying again is an emotion that will paralyse your thoughts? The notion that you will feel guilty, should you try again and subsequently fail, will result in Need running around like a headless chicken because it doesn't differentiate between a desire and a necessity.

There is a time and place to protect people by being economical with the truth. Even children don't want to be lied to but they are clever little beings and will respond well if you coat Failure in a dab of sugar, wave a wand and turn it into a deferred success. Sugar coating the truth once in a while will help anyone to manage their reactions when Failure pays a visit – even adults, who are just big kids too!

It was becoming obvious to the alien visitor that there was a strong movement beginning to form and although the word *failure* had a literal meaning in the human dictionary it was becoming a cause for contention among 'The People'. The alien could not be certain whether this was as a result of the planet becoming overly sensitive and less able to deal with conflict. It noticed that there was a motto in circulation that encouraged people to challenge and not collude, but it wondered if humans were less able to put this theory into practice. Were they still at a stage in their human lifecycle that was far better at coming up with ideas than implementing them? They react too quickly and don't always put a negative outcome into perspective; when one thing doesn't work, they tend to change the whole system. When something doesn't work for one person they go about meeting the needs of that person at the expense of upsetting an entire community.

The alien came to the conclusion that there wasn't enough time on this particular mission to analyse what failure individually meant to the humans and the word wasn't as straightforward to interpret as it had initially imagined. The elders on its own planet had banned rose-tinted glasses when they realised that excuses were interfering with the learning and development stages of their own kind. They didn't condone bullying and ruled this out many light years ago, but advocated that all lifeforms on their planet aspire to taking ownership of their actions and feelings.

If failure is truly success turned inside out, then you could live with the idea that failure isn't the end but a turning point in your life. Success doesn't necessarily sit at the opposite end to failure. What you consider has been a complete failure in one aspect of your life will give rise to a new adventure that will bring with it an opportunity for success to transpire in a different area altogether.

As the alien boarded its spacecraft it turned around to offer a final piece of advice to the human race. Coming from 'one who knows', it said, "Make your own life fit for purpose because if the skies have no limits then why should you?!"

F*E*A*R

The Holiday Complex

If you had an opportunity to jump out of an aeroplane would you fear the fall or fear the landing? Would the end result be your biggest concern or is it what could happen on the way down? In a split second, adrenaline could pull you out of the aeroplane freezing Fear's assets long enough to allow you to free fall and taste emotional freedom. Alternatively, Fear can keep you in your seat as you tell the pilot it is just a little setback and you will find the courage to jump, but it is just a matter of time.

As we know, Time will just follow you around but it won't make anything in particular happen for you all by itself. When you attempt to do a parachute jump for a charity, with the view to conquering your fear of heights on the way down, it isn't Time that will take any credit. Quite often, the more time you have to think about doing something Fear will simply spend that time talking you out of it.

Talking yourself into feeling fearful and talking yourself back out of this unpleasant emotional state is a practice that comes more easily to some of us. We allocate Fear extra playing time, like a football game that has resulted in a tie during a cup match; the ball has been kicked back and forth consecutively and up until now has presented no winner. Fear wins you over when you give up, watching the ball roll into the net because your own goalkeeper got bored and took off. Maybe you could give up playing emotional games that waste your time and consider inviting Fear out for a friendly drink after the next game and find out where it gets its energy from!

Think of a couple of your own experiences that keep you on the edge of making a decision because Fear cannot make up its mind if it wants to be involved. Perhaps you have got used to Fear being present when you have to make a choice. Tune into your gut instincts and ask yourself if you are worrying over the end result or have an aversion to climbing the steps that will lead you there. Do you fear taking the first step and this is why you don't even tie your shoe laces and get past the front door?!

When fear sets in, overcoming the first hurdle will distort your eyesight and you will convince yourself that a mountain ahead is blocking your vision. If the first step posed no problem and you did in fact manage to push your way through the front door without Fear seeing you, then hopefully all sense of fear will be lost completely as you journey on. However, if it shows up again having found a shortcut and met you later down the path just to test your patience, then it can influence you to stop in your tracks or turn back.

Now you could lead yourself to believe that Fear is a little bully and its only intention is to frighten you into submission. I am not quite sure this is the entire story. Fear is not dissimilar to many of your emotions that have a naughty side; it tends to have a history and there could be a reason that it keeps showing up. It mingles with Darkness and you could approach it in much the same way when you come into contact. Fear can also protect you, playing devil's advocate, as it thinks it is helping you before you take action so you can weigh up the pros and cons.

Unfortunately, Fear can go too far and you end up thinking that Fear is stopping you intentionally from doing something. Fear is reactive and doesn't stop you without your help – you allow Fear to stop you. You may not believe this when you are in the throes of having an anxiety attack because a black hairy spider has crossed your path. If you did 'stop' to ask yourself why you allow Fear to interfere, just when you thought the way ahead was clear of emotional attachment, you may find that there are plenty of reasons competing for your attention.

The eight-legged creature which stopped you from walking down the stairs, because it perched halfway along the ceiling minding its own business, is usually blamed for arousing a wave of fear throughout your body. I am not an expert on understanding the cause and effect of phobias but I know that I can be affected by this sort of scenario. How do I manage my reactions? I don't look; I scurry past and try not to make eye contact and then grab the nearest nebuliser to bring myself back to a sense of reality! Maybe I should look Fear directly in the eyes but at the time it isn't easy to be rational as Fear gives rise to emotions.

I personally don't recall if a childhood experience influenced me at some stage to feel as though someone had flicked my kneecaps to one side leaving my jelly legs to wobble in fear of a spider attack. I just believe that even if we don't know how a fear came to surface we have a duty of care to ourselves to work out how we overcome it, if it is causing us emotional pain. I remember when I was on a campsite in America, there were so many spiders that I got used to having them around so Fear toddled off and left my kneecaps alone. Equally, the idea of putting ourselves in a perceived form of danger – just to overcome a fear – isn't logical to me either. I would have to find a compelling reason to conquer a fear. If I didn't, then I am not going to get on a rollercoaster that will end up inviting half a dozen other emotions to climb aboard at my expense. I have always wanted to visit the Amazon and I admit that this idea has been squashed because plate-sized arachnids exist in its forests and apparently jump around. If I decide that my desire to visit the Amazon turns into a necessity and becomes one of my top ten things to do before I die, then I will seek to overturn my fear and post the experience on whatever the latest social network site happens to be at the time. I am sure it takes practice to conquer a fear but then it could be like hiccups – all of a sudden they are gone!

Imagine you are struggling to jump out of the aeroplane for the first time. Practice isn't going to be an option. You are planning to raise money because you haven't done it before – and not because you were ever part of the Parachute Regiment! Maybe your jump will be more lucrative in the long run with Fear strapped to your back as you descend, all because the charity working to save lives will appreciate your vulnerability and courage! So Fear is not all bad and can in fact get us to do the things we may never have dreamt of doing – but the part you play in this instance will be to remind yourself of the invaluable end goal. This is what will help you overcome your fear on the way down (you won't have much time to analyse the landing – until later). Look at it another way: your fear has been bought off you for a worthwhile cause. Donations are literally falling out of the sky!

Let's recapitulate (I've been dying to use that word!). Fear tends to stop us from doing something. Alternatively it can hold us back until we can find a way to challenge it and kick it aside, and even then it can show up again just when we thought it had disappeared. Fear can appear from nowhere, taking us by surprise, or dominate our emotional space when we are phobic. Fear can cause confusion as it prompts us to sense danger and protects us from harm; we may choose not to proceed if the alarm bells ring.

Imagine, again, you are in a fishing boat and the weather is turning. Fear starts to well up inside as you feel the waves getting bigger and the skies darken. This isn't about conquering your fear so as to keep you in the waters to fish! This is now about your gut instinct telling you that danger is looming so it's time to pack up and get back to shore before the boat capsizes.

Fear would like to be respected, but it is only once you have been out for that drink after the next match that you can ask which rules apply and then decide if it deserves your respect. You have to be in charge of your own rules but if you can recognise what mood Fear is in, when it arises, then you can decide if you want to play. You can't keep running scared – Fear is always going to participate in your life – so become acquainted.

I have a few ideas to explore. When we are worried that something untoward is going to happen (or could go wrong), even when we have no supporting evidence that it will, we are encouraging Fear to show up before it is due to make an appearance. This level of fear could be enough to stop us doing something that we would like to do and we may go on to manufacture a whole list of reasons why we shouldn't do something. Fear may not have kicked off but if you send out mixed signals it will enthusiastically clock into work and show up early; it will only say, "I thought you told me to!"

Why do we stop ourselves doing something we either want to do or would serve us well to try? You confess boldly to other people, "I want to go on holiday on my own but I am too scared". You haven't actually gone on holiday yet! You are imagining all the things that could make you fearful in relation to going on holiday alone and in doing so you are experiencing a form of fear. You have given it an assignment when it could do with a couple of days off, so what on earth are you thinking?

Fear begins to grow stronger as you think about all the things that could go wrong. Assuming you haven't got that far we could cut Fear a little slack if it is only a lack of confidence that is holding you back and what you may be feeling is 'apprehension'. You want to go ahead and book a holiday, so you haven't lost all sense of adventure, but in order to get there you will have to deal with the negative feelings that are bouncing around. If you continue to feed apprehension with negativity then it could start to exaggerate and turn into full-blown Fear that behaves like a ringleader controlling your other emotions.

Confidence may not get a look-in and as we learned a while ago, negativity can fuel negativity. Positivity hasn't managed to put its trainers on either, tripping up on your own shoe laces, which you haven't tied, so you are not setting a great example! Where is Trust when you need it? If you could trust yourself and believe that your holiday will turn out just fine, then you could avoid bumping into Fear. Change your thought process, do up your shoe laces, take positivity by its hand and don't let go until you have surpassed Fear. Do this in time before Fear stops you booking that flight to sunnier climes and you end up booking a week off in Surrey or Southend – pretty as both places may be.

Oh no, Fear kicked off, didn't it?! OK. Now you may benefit from taking time to reflect on why and what it is that keeps you in a place of fear rather than on the warm white beaches on the other side of the planet. Fear may only surrender if you can find a way to help it let its guard down. It may also depend on whether you are bothered about missing out on a foreign holiday or if you feel upset that you have let yourself down because you couldn't get past that first hurdle. Once again you renew your annual National Trust permit in readiness for the next Britain in Bloom contest down South. Yippee – another excursion to Kent to explore the UK's largest English Garden and that's before you explore the sexes (Essex, Sussex and Middlesex – why, what did you think I meant?).

It is more about being honest with yourself and only you can keep Fear and your limitations in such close proximity. The golden rule is: if you firmly believe that a fear needs to be conquered because it is holding you back, then change your thought patterns and even seek support. It is like we said at the very beginning of the book, don't give Fear (in this case) a trellis and it will not climb; find another garden to walk in, find the strength and you will find your own way. By the way there are some beautiful gardens abroad too!

Congratulations: you booked a flight and so it would seem you ventured out of the front door and this first hurdle posed no problem. Why is Fear kicking off now…? What… you are on the aeroplane and forgot you had a fear of flying? Oops! And you need to do what? (I know… I'm aware that this dialogue has suddenly adopted a momentum that Sooty and Sweep could relate to, and you may be pausing to do the same or google what on earth I am talking about!)

As our thoughts return to the aeroplane, you still haven't quite learnt what to do about Fear's rude interruptions, so you take a couple of miniatures from the bar and manage your reactions the best way you know how: through avoidance! This is a prime example of knowing your limitations and choosing to accept them; just don't become an alcoholic in the process!

When Fear kicked off this time you weren't in the most ideal of positions to simply walk away. Remember, you are now on the aeroplane; you cannot 'just get off' (unless your fear of jumping out with a parachute has been resolved and is less scary than gliding on the outer edge of space in an airbus you can't control). You have to land first, so you invite Trust and Hope along, even if Fear decides to remain with you until the wheels touch ground. Fear is just sitting beside you, kitted out in its shorts and shades with its seat belt on, diving into an in-flight meal as you remain pensive and white-knuckled (as if two miniatures were really going to pacify Fear for long!). You really are in a tight spot, aren't you? Fear is likely to win you over for a while and all you can do is look at it with contempt as it flirts with the other passengers during turbulence.

Unfortunately we don't have time to explore the various techniques that do exist to help you get out of a tight spot. We recognise that Fear exists on different levels. We know it can be influenced to behave but we need to learn how to do this. We have also learnt that Honest can be directive and that Fear responds well to communication. If you are the type of person who approaches your fear with logic then maybe Fear will back down. If your instincts have become silent, only speaking to you with a muted voice that can no longer be heard, then Fear is probably playing havoc with your personal compass and no doubt instincts will kick in again once you have calmed down.

When there is less cause to feel fearful then I think you have more opportunity to remove the fear before it becomes exacerbated. You had never been on holiday on your own, yet sadly you felt fearful about something you hadn't actually done, but you could counter argue that's a good enough reason to feel fear. You were turning the idea of going on holiday into a nightmare, writing the script before you got there and casting Fear without giving it an audition. It's more like watching a horror movie and getting drawn in, being scared to go to the bathroom in the interval in the event you get ripped to shreds by zombies – it isn't real (yet), and you can turn the film off.

Your imagination is powerful and if it can create Fear (like a character in a movie) then shouldn't it be able to eradicate it in much the same way? I don't like watching horror films because even when I turn one off, I am stricken with fear for some time after… Even when you stop mentally torturing yourself about the holiday that hasn't happened, it may take a while to clear your mind as it prepares for a new script. Change a couple of words in the next script and send out a positive message.

Fear isn't something to be taken lightly and it may seem that it has been trivialised. On the contrary, if Fear could be compared to sugar then it would be described in terms of its molecular structure that is commonly described as simple or complex. "Sugar…?", I hear you say in unison. Fear isn't sweet *per se* but you should have seen its little Hawaiian shirt that it wore on the aeroplane that shouted, 'Complex!' The only thing light about Fear is the artificial sweeteners it takes in its coffee; other than that, there isn't anything simple about Fear. Sugar is an anti-nutrient and so is Fear – there lies a commonality of interest. Actually we sugar-coated Failure last time and we often feel guilty when we consume too much so we could perceive that sugar hangs around to take the bitterness out of these emotions, throughout the section.

It can be very difficult to understand Fear and it may take a while to get it out of your system but this sandwich is simply about awareness. Next time you have an opportunity to jump safely out of an aeroplane I am sure this activity will release more from your system than you bargained for and you will feel lighter on the way down as a result of conquering your fears!

G*U*I*L*T

It's About the Response-ability

As the bus departed from the station, the travellers on board were unsure of where the excursion would take them and what tour they had actually signed up for that day. They soon learned they were being sent on a guilt trip. The tour guide announced that everyone had to participate in the activities along the way or be responsible for ruining everyone else's adventure, berating them for opting out before any had got underway. A tad controlling, they thought!

Wow. I think Manipulation snuck on board, having been kicked out of 'Charm School' for its lack of social skills and hooked up with Guilt at the bus stop! Maybe the driver should enforce a few more security checks before allowing trouble aboard. A new double act had formed and was going on tour. It could be possible that Guilt isn't always recognisable at first glance and it can manage to sneak on the bus anyway – somehow. It slips on discreetly clinging to buckles and belts, working its way down the aisle until it is finally caught out sitting in the back row, conducting the passengers – having orchestrated the entire event.

Guilt wears a few disguises and doesn't always present itself immediately. When you look Guilt in the eyes you will see that it has more than one side either born out of fact or feeling. You could be looking at someone with guilt in their eyes or you could be looking in the mirror and see Guilt staring straight back at you, reflected in your own. The difficulty with understanding Guilt is that it doesn't always tell you the truth and will give you mixed messages which have to be deciphered.

Guilt isn't always around as a result of misconduct. Sometimes when you think it is guilty, you later find out that it isn't and it was just putting on a show to entertain. As it turns out, Guilt was attention seeking, and led you and everyone else up the garden path and, as you later discovered, there was nothing to feel guilty about in the first place! It can show up in our lives for all sorts of reasons and we usually churn them over in our heads until they are exhausted. Until we are exhausted.

By now, most of the passengers on the bus were looking out of the windows wondering when they'd get to indulge the tour guide in one of their 'activities'. A forewarning, half an hour ago, had left them shaken up and flabbergasted at the prospect of being pulled into a set of mind games. Now, it felt a less daunting proposition. They had learned, since, that they could play on their own because going on a guilt trip wasn't reliant upon others to have a good time, after all. Guilt loved a good game of Solitaire too.

It was the quiz which got them thinking about the limiting thoughts they carried aboard. Guilt, the master of perpetuating the type of conversations that take up more time to hold than is warranted, was about to be questioned.

Answering the first question with a degree of certainty, Guilt confessed that if you are truly guilty of doing something wrong, you'll know about it. You will either 'have served your time or will be serving your time' – emotionally or otherwise. It is possible that you'll have an opportunity to make amends for whatever it is you are *certain* you have done 'wrong' so that Guilt moves on to becoming an experience that finds peace, rather than a shackle that forever holds you back in life.

Guilt was asked to consider its own association with the word *wrong*. It came up with the idea that when something is required from us and we let someone down, not only can we feel guilty, we *are* guilty of not fulfilling an obligation or a contract. The other person in the relationship can be affected. The emotional contract is broken! In this instance your own guilt will be clear on how it decides to reveal itself. Guilt – the one sitting on the bus being mischievous – went on to tell everyone (poised in their seats) that it becomes transparent. The other person can see right through it. Feeling guilty about not achieving what you set out to do, either for yourself or other people, is something we all deal with on one level or another. It is life – we all 'do things wrong' sometimes.

Society allows for a margin of error and various levels of tolerance exist. You are likely to find out post-deed, following an inquisition, if you were within or outside of the acceptable levels of tolerance. Most times we are expected to use our common sense and if we don't know what is acceptable, we should seek to find out. Otherwise, accept the penalty by way of atonement. On that note, the quiz finished. The passengers were left to play Solitaire.

The legal system must use some kind of 'tolerance chart' to determine the length of a sentence based on first, second or third offences... surely? We have probably overheard someone at some point remark about their luck in either getting off scot-free or being 'sent down' for half the time they expected. Would the penalty then influence how guilty someone goes on to feel?

I am just wondering if we feel guilt more or less, depending on either the severity of the action or how severe the result of the action is 'perceived' to be. For example, would a bank robber suffer less guilt from breaking into a bank without stealing anything because his action, whilst illegal (assuming it is a he), only caused an inconvenience? Or would the robber feel guiltier when he found out that the money he stole turned out to be the life savings put aside for a child's operation the very next week?

Does the level of guilt experienced fit the crime? Or, is guilt, guilt? Whichever way you approach it, it doesn't come in different shapes or sizes. It is clear that some people experience very little guilt for their crimes or certainly don't outwardly project the 'symptoms'! Attempting to rob a bank is in itself an act that should see Guilt sitting in the getaway car in full tuxedo because the intention was there all along – to steal the money – so what difference would it make how much and whose money it was? Guilt is a personal emotion and can be introvert or extrovert depending on its mood. Now let's consider another example that doesn't involve stealing!

If you dropped a clanger and someone said to you, "Don't worry about it, we all make mistakes", you may expend little or no time feeling guilty because another person has 'given you permission' to put guilt aside and move on. You may have to make amends but you don't need to carry guilt around with you on this occasion; it can sit on the emotional reserves bench until it is needed.

If the person said to you, when you dropped a clanger again for the second time, "What on earth are you doing? This is now costing me money", Guilt will return as quickly as you previously let it go. The result of your action is now perceived to be wrong and it would seem to have had a negative impact on the finances

It's About the Response-ability

of the person who trusted you at the beginning. In this case, the penalty may be simply an uncomfortable conversation that leaves you feeling mortified or as a worst case scenario leaving you never to be trusted again, by the same person who is out of pocket. Guilt will be looking at you now with its eyes speaking volumes, almost apologetically telling you that you are lumbered with it for a while until you ask it to leave, but it's your own fault!

We allow ourselves an element of leeway when we have knowingly crossed a line. If we erected the original goalposts, we will have set our own tolerances. Maybe we miscalculate on occasions and maybe society simply doesn't accept the formula we use in order to calculate how far we think we can go at any given time. We tend to know what our own experience of Guilt is going to feel like when it surfaces, because we learn 'what makes us tick'! (Remember?)

The levels of guilt we feel can be fuelled by external responses and we allow them to influence us – to 'feel guilty' (and on occasions that's not a bad thing!). The person who told you that they have lost money because you did something to support this accusation has, intentionally or unintentionally, 'made you feel guilty'.

Does someone make you feel guilty? We are responsible for our feelings; once felt, we react to the response and choose to feel guilty. They will only be responsible for 'delivering a response'. You will be responsible for accepting the response, like the handover of a baton in a relay race. If someone runs up to you with every intention of handing you the baton and you take it, you have taken responsibility to accept it. If you decided not to put your hand out to take it, then you cannot hold the baton and it will fall to the ground.

Guilt cannot be handed to you directly, because it doesn't

exist as something to give away. The person who lost the money couldn't give you a measure of Guilt to take as any form of punishment; he/she could only provide a response. Nonetheless, something amazing happens in that moment when the response is delivered and received. Guilt has transported itself from the bench on the sideline through a vortex, like a virus that is downloaded via the internet without any protection. Guilt starts chipping away and you now own this emotion so you need to start cleansing. Atone away!

As a general rule, we accept that mistakes will be made. It is how we manage the situation that follows a temporary lapse in good judgement and it is how we pick ourselves back up after dropping a clanger that is important. Feeling guilty is an emotion that we know will accompany us on our journey in life but it is how long we are prepared to let it hang around, once we have looked it in the eye and accepted it had a point. Once the point has been made and you are not in denial of any wrongdoing, you can look to move on and learn your lessons. Well, this all sounds jolly simple!

If the rules are that simple why does Guilt bother us so much? Maybe we are talking about another kind of guilt that is backed up by very little evidence and has absolutely nothing to do with committing a crime; the only crime it is guilty of is incessant attention seeking and should just give it a rest from time to time.

Even talking about 'feeling guilty' becomes a habit and the learnt phrase is commonly used in our everyday language. If we stop to think about what it is we really mean, when we say, "I feel guilty...", we could end up giving ourselves a life sentence for all the imaginary crimes we hold against ourselves! If we continue to be the judge, jury and executioner then we have no hope in

It's About the Response-ability

breaking any negative forms of behaviour and Guilt will keep reoffending. Let me clarify those last few words: Guilt is simply role-playing over and over. It is overreacting because it doesn't have a cause, most of the time, for getting so wound up and it pops up all over the place collaborating with other emotions, causing confusion. We have already acknowledged that it may not be supported by any facts whatsoever. And, do you know what the most frustrating thing is about the word? Guilt shows up in our vocabulary like a conjunctive that is over used; Guilt shouldn't be there half the time and we are completely responsible for allowing it the space!

We even provide Guilt with its own dressing room as it behaves like a right little diva – it is dramatic when it has the chance and it doesn't stop talking. It is aware that without an audience it has no reason to perform and so if you are willing to play host to it, then it will thrive and put on a display for other people. The issue with putting on the same show for the same people every day is it will become boring and they will lose interest – you may lose friends! New people will engage with your insecurities for a while until they witness a pattern forming. Some will join in so you can saturate your conversations with two helpings of negativity and put the world to rights.

Remember that Guilt is just one of your emotions that can become an obsession to have around and as with many obsessions you begin to think you need it in your life. As we begin to look at the things that we can allow ourselves to feel guilty over, Guilt will start to behave irresponsibly and we can explore a few examples together shortly.

How are you doing so far? Still with me?

Guilt will always have a place in our lives, *not* because it is *needed* but because it tends to occur naturally as a result of poor judgement (I am sure we could live without it). Actually, I would go further and say it can exist when we make a good judgement. We can feel guilty about doing the 'right thing' because we may be aware it will upset someone else and this is a prime example of when Guilt is surplus to requirements. We simply don't *need* it to weigh us down.

Any thoughts about the latter? Do you find it hard to do the right thing sometimes, knowing it could upset someone else? It would be interesting to find out how Guilt associates itself with the word *right*… Another time, maybe.

When we lack Time, Patience and Trust there are no end of situations that can unfold which provide Guilt with an automatic invitation to get involved and do a sales pitch. Fear and Failure are just as bad – both guilty of allowing Guilt to exploit their vulnerability.

As we explore this character I notice it is quite a good little networker! It rubs shoulders with everything it meets on its travels. No wonder it got on the bus at the beginning, with a box of tricks up its sleeve. It really can be a bad influence and impact on so many aspects of your life. We allow Guilt to lead us unnecessarily at times and whilst we can accept it is going to exist (or wants to exist) we need to set a few limitations and give it a cut-off point should it get out of control.

Can we look to abolish Guilt altogether or is it an emotion that allows us to learn and it is appropriate to experience it when there is evidence to support its existence? To what extent should Guilt linger around in your life in order to meet those learning objectives? I am sure it has to be proportionate. Even the word *should* is not a word I like to use too often; in this instance, it sounds as though something 'must' be present and it is possible that you can still evaluate a mistake without having to assign Guilt.

It's About the Response-ability

We cannot assign a value of time to a sentence of 'guilt' as it can be assigned to a length of community service, awarded by a court of law. Guilt is either experienced or it isn't. In keeping with the theme which has naturally evolved around crime in this sandwich, let us consider a criminal who displays no remorse for their criminal act – they may not feel guilty. A judge cannot order a sentence of guilt because this would be letting them off lightly. If on the other hand, a criminal suffered remorse and felt guilty for the consequences of their crime, whilst this may not be a sufficient level of punishment for the victim, friends or families, it will be an emotional punishment that will imprison the accused, possibly for a lifetime.

The type of guilt I would like to focus on now is the guilt that we all know too well exists in our lives. We touched on it earlier when we found it in places it had no business to be. Guilt takes you up your own garden path and, if you remain strong, you can force it into making a declaration that it misled you all along; you have better ways to spend your time than frolic with Guilt on a sunny day!

We mentioned that Guilt can be manipulative but it is people who manipulate, using Guilt as their weapon of mass destruction. For some reason, humans have a crafty ability to send people on a guilt trip so they can focus on their own agenda or achieve something that would not be achievable if they didn't take advantage of other people's good nature. I think this is also called taking advantage of other people's weaknesses. We are not all cut out to be this sly and, no sooner do you send someone on a guilt trip, you may well feel guilty for buying them the ticket on the bus in the first place.

Guilt loves a bit of sympathy but it doesn't always get it. Let us take a really simple example that anyone working in a group environment will either have been involved in, or overheard, at one point in their working lives. It is 9am and they have already started: the conversations about food!

"I felt really guilty last night because I ate chips," she said.

"Why did you feel guilty about that?" he said.

She goes on to reveal all her dietary habits from the day before and how the dress won't fit for her best friend's wedding, which is in two weeks' time (although it didn't fit for her sister's wedding six months ago either). She feels guilty because she lacks discipline and she hates going to the gym. When it gets to 11am and the day has already taken its toll, the whole team begins to debate what they are going to eat for lunch. Of course, they have already discussed the snacks they have eaten up to then, between 9am and 10.59am, polluting the atmosphere with guilt that even has the oxygen in the air reaching out for a mask to avoid suffocation. The discussions held on calories and nutritional labels, not to mention the portion sizes, have all undergone a journey through a quagmire of contradiction and hypocrisy in less than two hours. Gosh! We know that Guilt travels around in disguise, but in this example it has surely kicked the tour guide off the bus and is narrating the entire guilt trip single-handedly.

If Guilt could write a travel guide on your journey to losing weight at work and call it, *How to Lose Weight on a Guilt Trip Before You Reach Retirement*, it could be a millionaire. The fact is: Guilt won't make a penny! The 'guilty person' will start off believing that guilt is going to be the answer to shifting the next pound of weight, because obsession must in part be responsible for setting yourself limitations. What Guilt hasn't taken into account is the fact that free will encourages the weaker side of discipline to compete and intervene, if only to

It's About the Response-ability

justify that it really is OK to eat what you want and burn off the calories during an attempt to think yourself thin! After all, a little bit of what you fancy won't hurt from time to time… in this case, it would seem to equate to all day long when you should be working!

Don't worry; if I have encouraged you to feel sorry for Guilt and belittled its hard work thus far, you can be reassured that it will pipe up again after the next act of indulgence has concluded. It will catch you up and get you back to feeling guilty by 3pm when you end the day with a discussion on what you can't eat for dinner, assuming that you joined in with their discussions about food. Guilt wins you over for a while; it hovers around because you are feeding it throughout the day. It will never be rich but it doesn't need a penny because you are supporting it and it is living off the state… of your mind.

The travel guide that Guilt wrote will be an interesting read and, in order to learn something too, we need to move on from simply reading to taking the words off the pages and arrange them in a way that we can suitably reapply them within our own lives. This is the part we tend to overlook.

If we want to make a constructive difference to the way we live our lives and form a healthy relationship with Guilt, then we need to consider forming a healthier relationship with all of our limitations and accept that sometimes Guilt isn't the answer to all of our misgivings. Feeling guilty every time we don't reach the end goal that we set out to accomplish will only serve to hold us back the next time we try again.

What is it that we actually *need* to prove or find ourselves *needing* so much of throughout life? We would be wiser to question if the *need* is based on a desire or a necessity. Maybe if we recognise what influences us to feel guilty about the things we don't need to feel guilty about then we could find more of the happiness that Darkness can sometimes overshadow.

So, diners, have a think about this emotion and how it relates to your own lives. I don't want you to make a meal out of it, as self-reflective interventions can be heavy going. I would like you to put Guilt into perspective and become more aware of how often you use the word and why during everyday conversations. These may be held with other people or in your head!

Oh, and by the way... please stay away from any public transport that has guilt written into its journey destination; it will take you all around the houses and probably back to where you started! You will simply go around in circles and no doubt feel guilty for wasting an hour of your life in the process.

N*E*E*D

Desires and Delusions

Don't you just love an adventure? We all need a little adventure in our lives – don't we? Packing the suitcase is one of the hardest jobs because you never know what you'll need until you get there. Maybe you have been on a similar adventure but invariably your needs change, as what was once needed in your life is no longer required.

Naturally you can plan ahead and do plenty of research, while reading up on someone else's experience to help you to prepare. But even this is only helpful if you actually know they've been to the same place that you are intending to visit or find yourself unintentionally drifting toward. This is also assuming that you do know where you are heading because if you don't, then all the preparation in the world may not prepare you for a subtle diversion appearing midway. There may be little point in packing the things that someone else required if the path they took to get 'there' differed to the one you will end up taking, as a result of a detour.

Need is a character that changes its mind as fashion changes its shape from season to season. As the original design comes back into fashion, you find yourself wondering why you never liked it before. This is a common reaction because you may have suffered a memory lapse in between and undergone a stage of emotional development. This may have caused you to grow up and notice that shades exist in between black and white. You may have forgotten the reason you rejected your previous thought patterns. Now, several years on, you could be correct in thinking that had you been more adventurous, instead of judging how something looked on the hanger without even trying it on, you may well have needed it in your life more than you realised. This is, of course, hypothetical and without a crystal ball you may never know!

An adventure is really just one stage that you embark on and move through… until it comes to an end; you will find yourself going on a series of explorations throughout your life. An adventure will begin as soon as you set off, taking you on a journey to wherever 'there' happens to be. So, you will look to cram all the things you think you will need into the luggage space available and have a fair idea of what will be a necessity and what will be useful to have along the way – just in case.

Even if you are simply packing for a holiday, through previous experience you are certain that what you needed during the last trip will be needed again this time. I frequently leave behind what I need and pack what I don't, wondering what was I thinking of at the time! As a reasonably experienced traveller, I should know better but I blame the airlines for putting pressure on me to pack light or else pay a premium that at the time seems extreme; this is until I land and spend more than double on buying the things that I didn't bring. Although, I am sure if I took more than one suitcase I would only fill each corner with the things I didn't need as I frantically tried to rearrange my packing last minute, emptying the entire wardrobe in the process. Anything I did end up buying on arrival, to support my wardrobe malfunction, would either be left for the next tourist or replace the clothes I didn't need in the first place. Decisions, decisions!

I think there is something about going on holiday that has us hooking up with an alien-possessed mannequin! We seem to lose all sense of perspective and I have even heard an airline attendant say something to this effect: "Tourists: they leave their common sense at home!"

I have only just begun to explore 'Need' and I am already feeling like I am using it disrespectfully. I feel like I am making a fool out of it because Need doesn't know what it wants half the time. I don't think we always know what we want as we set out to explore new territory, never mind knowing what we really need along the way. It is often through trial and error that we become familiar with what it takes to have our own needs met and how best we can help other people meet theirs.

Incidentally, Need is following me around the page with a coyness that is so endearing I have to assume it is female. It is literally walking in the footprints I am mentally leaving behind as I work out the direction I would like to take this sandwich. It is doing that 'butter won't melt in its mouth' performance; hands are softly clasped together behind its back, rotating its torso from side to side with its head slightly tipped to one side to follow suit. If ever you've seen that look, which has been designed to make you feel guilty, then Need has just delivered it between a set of fluttering eyelashes that are saying, "Don't you want me…?" Talk about feeling guilty!

Need doesn't miss a trick. Throughout your life it will have been brainwashing you into thinking you *needed* to do a multitude of things that were probably not a necessity at the time. Need is a fantastic word to use when you want to convince yourself that an end goal is heavily reliant on the fact that you *need* to do something – or it simply won't work out. It is also great at stepping in to stop you doing something, as you tell yourself that you need to do something else first.

It is a versatile word that often goes hand in hand with your excuses and we can twist it to suit the context, blaming it quite easily for influencing the way we make a decision. As we have just seen, if we base a decision on the idea that we need to pursue something else first, whilst it could be a legitimate reason, it may only be a desirable course of action to take.

The word *need* is used in our everyday language to emphasise the fact that something may be missing in our lives. If this is so, then the lack of it may have an impact on something else that will end up being missed out on if the first need is not met. When little 'Missy' comes along and starts getting emotional it doesn't take much to confuse Need who has a soft spot at the best of times. It can mislead our friend Need and have it thinking it is a necessity rather than just desirable.

Need has a strong relationship with 'expectations' and it is prone to exaggeration which can get you into trouble. Need has a bad habit of believing that if an expectation isn't met, then this particular disappointment will be responsible for a wealth of other things not happening; you have created an excuse – how convenient. Need works so hard in order to help you fulfil your expectations that it convinces itself that it is going to be responsible for letting you down if it doesn't keep coming up with ideas and roping you in to all sorts of thoughts and actions; it is a workaholic. Goodness me; now 'Need' is feeling guilty too! You don't need to take Need literally all the time.

Take your time to understand this perspective; it doesn't matter if you have to read this section twice. If everything we learned came to us that easily we could miss out on the reflective aspect that accompanies learning. This allows us to stop for a moment and see whether we do in fact agree or if we could improve upon an idea because it makes more sense to us. When you break down any form of reasoning into smaller bites it can seem quite long-winded but that is often because we don't scrutinise our every thought, as it would be emotionally hard work to do and takes up our time. However, if we did look a little deeper into our motives that drive us to think a certain way, we could trace those small bites of reasoning back to the root of a problem and protect ourselves from further disappointment. We could learn to accept our own limitations if we understood why we set them in the first place and become more accountable rather than making Need our excuse. Need is enthusiastic and leads us into temptation, offering us options which don't always require pursuing!

When you miss something, does it imply that you had it previously but now you don't? When you miss something that doesn't appear in your life anymore it can be emotive, and whilst you may not be clear on your feelings, you are aware that it is missing. So this is one form of 'missing' that is real and is based on fact more than theory. We are not questioning whether missing something is either right or wrong or if any feelings that arise are relative as there is no context to discuss. It is purely to illustrate that it is plausible to miss something when it is gone.

Alternatively you may have thought about something so much that you are simply aware that by not having it in your life, you could be missing out. I would suggest you may have gone one step further and reflected all of the signs of a person who is missing something. Maybe you have looked into its known benefits and thought, *Yes, I would like a bit of that...*, or you have dreamt about how it will change your life if you have it and so you now need to pursue it until it materialises. This isn't a negative thought pattern, by the way. This is a good practice if you want to make headway in turning those dreams into a reality and it underpins the Law of Attraction theory.

I believe it's important to differentiate between what you really miss and what it is you think you miss. When you can do this and separate the two you will be more able to interpret your needs. You are likely to recognise if a need is a necessity or just a desire – a nice-to-have! What you think you miss only becomes a negative if you begin to yearn for it at the expense of making an unnecessary sacrifice and turn every need into a necessity to the detriment to your health, finances or relationships. If you have not had something before, you have no way of knowing if you really want it when you get it!

I have listed a few examples below, in no particular order, which could be considered a necessity or a nice-to-have in life and you will have plenty more of your own to add:

> I need a holiday
> I need a heart transplant… now…
> I need my kids to…
> I need to finish this first before I…
> I need to get married
> I need to eat healthier
> I need to stop smoking
> I need a new car
> I need to start yoga
> I need to learn a language
> I need to leave work on time or…
> I need you to tell me the truth because…

> I need to work in a team
> I need to get up early as…
> I need some decent clothes
> I need to save for a rainy day
> I need to get a divorce
> I need to start doing…

As basic as these examples can seem on the surface I bet some of these will be a necessity to someone because of the positive impact they could have on other areas of their life. Your necessities could be superficial to someone else because you both know so little about each other that you are making judgements based on a limited set of facts. We don't always know why one person will place more importance on needing something in their lives unless we learn more about that person.

When does a need become your priority? When does something you want become your need to have? How do you interpret your needs as a necessity or a desire? Does needing something, without knowing why you need it, taint your ability to recognise when a need really is a necessity but you have cried wolf so many times you even question your own motives and wonder if you are calling your own bluff?! Do you begin to lose sight of what is important to have or to do in your life to such an extent that you try to meet every need and feel exhausted in the process? How often do we create a need and hold it responsible for the events that follow when it isn't fulfilled? It's when that initial need gives rise to a fruitful knock-on effect and life just gets better – then you will be happy to brag about how you made the right decision. Whether it was based on logic or a gut instinct, it has paid off!

"I need to buy a sports car otherwise I won't attract the

'one and only' into my life. If I don't find true love then I won't have anyone to share my life; I may not get married; I won't have children and no one will look after me when I get old. If I don't buy that sports car then my life may as well be over!" Oh dear; I think he/she needs the sports car because they have led themselves to believe that they will appear more attractive, and just look at all the things that this person will not be able to achieve if they don't find a way to buy one!

"It is important to me to buy the sports car, so I am going to have to find a way to meet this need. I will take a second job and work all the hours I can. I will stop going out at the weekends so I can save the deposit and hold back on spending my money on things I don't need". OK, so the car is important and I like the idea he/she is prepared to make a few sacrifices to reach a goal – commendable.

"It has been six months and I am exhausted. I haven't had a day off for weeks, I feel ill, I haven't seen my friends for ages and I have forgotten what it is like to have a good night out." It appears that the desire to have a sports car is now hindering his/her health, relationships and social life. Is this car really a necessity? If someone wants it enough and they are willing to make sacrifices it has probably become a necessity to them. Whether it is a wise decision to someone else will be irrelevant.

"Hey, how do you like my new sports car? I've painted the town red since and fallen in love. I feel great about myself and I am the proud owner of the dream I made come true." And so the plan worked. I love a happy ending. It could have gone the other way but who wants to hear that side of the story.

The message is clear: we do what we feel is important at the time and hope that we make the right decision. If you believe you have a need and you have convinced yourself it has to be met, then you are likely to focus and do your utmost to reach the end goal. Unfortunately we tend to need too many things and expect them to all serve us well but they don't. Need gets greedy and we can lose perspective on what is important. Everything becomes important and if everything becomes important then we are going to be on a treadmill for a very long time!!

There will be hundreds of examples that will demonstrate how often we rely upon doing one thing in order to achieve a number of others. On occasions this will be the right mindset. If you were building a house, then there will be plenty of things that need to be done first before you can complete the other tasks; these are called dependencies. You will be dependent on one thing happening before you can move on to do something else. Sometimes you have to do them the right way around. If you want to put the roof on a house first, then go ahead and give it a go. Prop it up with a few poles and build around it – but I can't quite see how that will work. If you want to become a doctor or teacher then you will need to train first. If you want to set up a business then it is likely you will need a product or service to sell and have to think of an original idea. If you want to have a baby you will need to… and you get the gist! Certain things can only work out if you do something else first to make it happen. Necessity comes to mind. It is quite possible you didn't need to build a house, become a doctor, start a business or a family, and these were just desirable initially but once the desire became more than an idea, necessary steps needed to be taken thereafter.

Why are some of us so needy?! We all know someone who needs someone in their life – all of the time. Do they need someone or have they simply got used to having someone around so that when they are not there, they will look to find someone else because they need a companion or someone to validate their actions or even their feelings? We may convince ourselves we need a particular person in our life – but maybe we lack the confidence to live a life without them. Personally, I always feel lonelier being around people who don't make me happy (although I still wonder if anyone *makes* us feel anything, emotionally). If I am unhappy on my own, at least I only have myself to blame! However, being around the right people, at the right time and for the right period of time has to be fulfilling. We all need to feel loved… some of us just don't know it!

We may be thoroughly happy with being conjoined, and needing our own space isn't a concept that we would need to entertain. Space, for some of us, is a necessity if it means we are more able to cope with having a relationship or keeping one alive! What we need from other people in our life will vary; we need different things from different people at different times. We don't all have the same requirements and this is why people tend to make judgements because they may not have the same need. I think we are all guilty, at one time or another, of saying something like, "What does she need that for?" or "Why does he need to do that?"

Sometimes we 'feel a need'; it heads our way and we just have to do something about it! "I need chocolate" – but you probably don't. "I need a holiday" – and you probably do! We all need to eat, love, work, cry, laugh or scream. Sometimes a need passes; it heads towards us and just as we are about to embrace it, the feeling that has been driving it in our direction disappears. We either forget we ever had a need to do something or we are left wondering how we can need something one minute and not the next.

Need – I told you it is prone to exaggerating and you can't always take it literally when you hear it muttering in the background. This is why giving in to temptation is as a result of thinking you need something: the chocolate because you have just fallen out with your best friend! Maybe you need to resolve the friendship and just share the bar of chocolate! You see, we do need each other really.

We know we need other people to do things for us and we talked about that when we explored Trust. We trust people to do a job for us and we may need other people to do those jobs for us; we have become accustomed to having our expectations met. We can't do everything on our own so as a society we have collectively created a whole bunch of 'needs' (that may not be truly needed), all of which have evolved into norms. Needs in one section of society are considered a luxury in another and what is a necessity for the people in one country or on one continent is simply a desire for the other or doesn't even appear on their 'need' radar.

Interaction with other people throughout our lives is needed to help us to learn, develop and grow into the people we would like to be. We make comparisons and we form opinions; these help us to recognise our own personal needs and we decide if they are desires or necessities. We make our own choices and we are presented with opportunities to learn lessons.

Life is one big adventure and if we set ourselves unnecessary limitations then our suitcase will not contain everything we need for our journey. I know it's a good idea to travel light sometimes but, let's be honest, blaming the airlines for setting a weight limitation is not the answer. It is all about accountability: the sooner you accept that you are responsible for your actions and your own feelings, you free yourself from limitations that are weighing you down.

That is why they always say to you at the airport check-in desk, "Have you packed this yourself…?" They aren't silly!

Course 5

Fillings to Educate the
Taste Buds

Learning and Development

'A humbling experience empowers you to connect with your feelings.'

Before boarding the last ride in this playground of perspectives, it is worth noting that life asks rather a lot of us, don't you think? Equally we ask a lot of it too and so it is no surprise that we seek to blame something or someone when it all goes pear-shaped.

So far, you've had plenty of opportunity to discover and explore. You may have wandered into new territory and with little warning found yourself being interrupted by a past experience. Without wishing to seem rude you invited the old perspective to join you, making it clear that it was only welcome to tag along while you were comparing notes. There are bound to be times when you do look back and see all your old learning curves bobbing around in an ocean of memories, having served their purpose and made an impression.

After rounding up all the lessons that invariably get left behind, we can then choose how to put them to good use. Learning involves reflection. How, where and when we reflect is not prescriptive. Stumbling onto a spiritual path, believing that the sheer act of baring your soul will somehow make you feel so much lighter, may later leave you exposed wishing you could quickly cover it up again. Maybe you simply overlooked what it means to connect with your true self and thought it was about giving up something rather than enjoying the emotional freedom you have to gain.

It is time to educate the taste buds and confront the fillings that are held together with an arrangement of ifs and buts that dent our pride, make it hard to swallow and play havoc with digestion. They are not, however, about being subservient or overtly apologetic.

H*O*N*E*S*T

Choosing the Right Policy

Accustomed to taking responsibility, Honest sat quietly on its throne preparing to self-reflect. It came face to face with people every day and it wasn't unusual for this reputable character to suffer from self-doubt like everyone else, but not everyone appreciated that its intentions were always sincere. Honest tried to use its better judgement and regularly made sacrifices, but it couldn't seem to please all the people. However, it vowed to tell the truth and took pride in having a trustworthy reputation.

Honest was often challenged by Dishonest and having grown up together they were both able to differentiate between a truth and a lie; they just didn't agree with each other's motives. Even when Dishonest knew that it was lying, because at other times it really believed it was telling the truth, it usually had a hidden agenda and set about confusing its audience. The two rivals came to the conclusion that if an audience couldn't differentiate between a truth and a lie, the people would have to default into making up their own minds like a jury that had been asked to deliver a verdict. There will always be court jesters running around at the same time with the sole aim of causing distraction!

Trust would be asked to work overtime so that Honest could contest its innocence and the next round in the game would take place between Logic and Instincts. Unfortunately when the latter two characters get together, the final result may be based on interpretation of the facts presented at the time – if indeed facts are what they are! Sometimes we believe what we want to believe and sometimes we believe what we are told.

Challenged by Dishonest, who behaved like a competitive sibling that had to challenge for challenge's sake, Honest took comfort in the fact that it had led people on countless occasions to live a life based on honesty. It wasn't going to stop now! In its own kingdom that was founded on respect, it understood that dishonesty was never going to be ruled out. Honest was always living under the threat of being overthrown and as a natural born leader it would focus on leading by example.

Honest would endeavour to remain unbiased and work with the facts it had to hand at any one time. It would strive to resist temptation to blame; it would encourage people to learn and develop using empathy instead of sympathy as a tool for compassion. It also discouraged people from 'acting a part' in their lives that would compromise their own truth and mislead other people into thinking that they had it all figured out – when they hadn't. We can all be forgiven for wanting to make a good impression but not at the expense of forgetting to walk our true path and being dishonest with ourselves along the way.

Even though it wasn't going to be easy, Honest wanted to practise humility. When Honest was given an opportunity to speak the truth, because someone asked it for advice, Honest felt humble and this validated its entire reason to exist. It made every effort not to brag when it knew it was right, even though at times it was hard to hold back from saying, "I told you so…"

Holding its tongue, when the last word has already left the brain and is about to roll off the tip like a diver about to dive off a springboard, is illustrative of a good leader. As Honest diverts the incoming traffic to the back of the queue, the silence thereafter speaks volumes.

When we are given a chance to be honest, there is a fine line between answering the question you have been asked and taking advantage of saying more than needs to be said without permission.

In a courtroom, the judge intervenes and says, "Please just answer the question you have been asked", which you will have previously sworn to answer, telling the whole truth and nothing but the truth. The barristers will want you be honest but they don't need you to elaborate on the truth because they are not seeking surplus information that will only confuse the jury. Instead, they want an honest answer that will either confirm what everyone already knows, or can be used to persuade an audience during a closing argument. Ironically the whole truth may not have a chance to surface because the barristers in control will be directive and limit the 'volume' of spoken words, giving them a cut-off point. A fine line exists and you need permission to cross.

A scenario below presents opportunities to cross a fine line on more than one occasion and points out a few reasons as to why you could be held back from crossing. Your honesty is requested through invitation and you have been given a licence to use free speech within your reply. But does that mean you can 'speak your mind' freely? Freedom of speech falls into a grey area for discussion that requires a certain amount of grey matter to both get started and conclude respectfully.

Let's choose a simple example because the theory is the

same if you want to consider it within a more complex situation for yourself. Your friend (who we will refer to as a 'she') has asked you for your advice about what to wear at the Christmas party. She asks you quite openly to be honest but how honest does she want you to be when allowing you to rattle off your reply?

Do you simply recommend an outfit based on your opinion (because that is what she asked) or do you elaborate and tell her all the reasons to wear one and not the other? Did the invitation to be honest come with an opportunity to explain how you came to a conclusion or did you just deliver it along with your opinion anyway? What is it that stops you saying more than you need to say because it is superfluous?

Instincts may warn you to stop talking if there is a chance that your reasons could open up a can of emotional worms for your friend! Equally, wasn't it up to her to set the boundaries so you would know if you could cross that fine line in the first place? I am not sure that such a rigid approach can be taken in this particular instance. You could be the type of person who says it 'how it is' or you could be tactful in your delivery, in keeping with being honest – and know when to stop talking.

However, Honest may be unduly influenced by several factors. If Dishonest poked its nose in, you could have told her what she wanted to hear (which may not be your truthful reply) – which arguably isn't giving her the honest answer she asked you for originally. If you provide your friend with more information than she needs it could lead to confusion and mixed messages; she will be none the wiser after asking.

Why not tell her which outfit to wear and only give her the positive reason for wearing it? A winning reply; not only did you state which one to wear you provided a clear reason as to why.

Does she need to know why the other options aren't suitable? Probably not, unless she asked!

It is unlikely you are a mind reader and as this is an out-of-court settlement… crossing the line will be usual practice. The only bar you will be allowed back into, should you have overstepped the mark, is a public bar to buy her a drink to apologise if you have been too honest!

When we ask people for their advice or opinion we tend to expect it to come from a source of honesty, even if it isn't what we wanted or expected to hear at the time. We ask teachers, doctors and lawyers to give us their honest opinions and they will follow a professional code of conduct. We ask our friends and our family for their honesty and may give them a little more leeway to insult us with the truth or trust that they will be diplomatic! We hope that people will think about how they communicate their honesty and whether they need to dress it up to suit the occasion or simply deliver it with no frills attached.

*

One day, Honest was pondering over a situation it had been asked to resolve. It looked into the mirror and said, "I am not sure if I can be honest enough with everyone today so maybe I have to be more economical with the truth". It felt emotional and torn because Honest didn't lie. Honest could shape the truth to fit but this was only a temporary method to avoid confirming the truth that still needed finalising. It wasn't prepared to lie and lose the trust of the people, and it certainly was not going to move over to the dark side. If Honest was ever misguided and found itself on the wrong side of right, it would like to think it was down to an innocent mistake that it could afford to explain and not because it was overthrown by Dishonest. It would rather choose to die with honour and be remembered for its good values than be accused of foul play at the last minute.

Honest has to do the dirty jobs sometimes and unfortunately someone can get hurt. In an attempt to be economical with the truth, Honest will upset someone. It can be misconstrued as a lack of honesty, which isn't the same as being dishonest. Dishonest usually equates to telling lies whereas a lack of honesty implies that it was simply missing in the first place. No one was necessarily being lied to, but Honest didn't show its true colours. It hid back from the front line to observe. Some may consider this cowardly but what was Honest supposed to do? If it led everyone into battle it could have been accused of sabotage without any supportive evidence that going into battle would have been the answer. If it remains in its ivory tower watching everyone below run around confused, negatively discussing Honest behind its back, then by the time it does come down to meet its people, it is feeling guilty of malpractice! As it bumped into Guilt on the winding staircase, on its descent, it took the baton and is now under its spell (until it drops over the railings). Not everyone appreciates the dilemmas Honest can face in its day-to-day work and sometimes it has to make difficult decisions.

Company mergers and acquisitions are not decisions that can be taken lightly by the board of directors that are buying or selling a market share. Honest will be invited along as part of the package, playing an integral role throughout, and it will be relied upon heavily to influence both parties involved to make the right decision.

Honest may decide to be economical with the truth when it comes to working with Human Resources – HR as it is commonly known. It is used to working with royalty day in and day out, and whilst HR is not royalty *per se*, anyone who has worked in an HR environment may say there is little difference between the two hierarchies! Honest will have to be evasive and remain calm and respectful when challenged by the workforce without actually caving in and telling the truth or a lie! HR will need to inform everyone that business change is imminent and these changes will impact on the organisational objectives. Of course, what they are trying to do (which is understandable) is avoid misleading the employees and creating anarchy. HR hasn't got all the answers yet and could end up swimming for dear life in murky waters, becoming entangled in the reeds, if it makes a poor judgement.

The company cannot afford to make announcements that are not yet formalised. Therefore being economical with the truth will ensure that Good Judgement has a chance to develop. HR must ensure that PJ doesn't run around like a free radical leaving a mark on each employee with whom it comes into contact – maybe we should have put PJ in with the other anti-nutrients; it can cause damage when it doesn't have controlled access! Just in case you have dipped into this sandwich without trying the others, PJ stands for Poor Judgement. It sat alongside Good Judgement in the foods enriched with good nutrition section; it just needs a little education. I don't know about you but every time I talk about PJ I get this sense that it is a serious attention seeker. I can't help but picture it walking around with shoulders hunched and hands in its pockets, its cartoon face having eyes far too big for it, verging on a caricature depicted in a children's cartoon. It has an angular face with a jutty-out jaw and a baseball cap back to front that makes you want to reach out and give it a big hug – but PJ would be too embarrassed. After all, it is trying to befriend Dishonest, so it won't appreciate any sentimental interventions!

So Honest is taking instructions from HR who, in turn, is taking its instructions from the board of directors. Honest has to make sure it keeps up with all the ifs, buts and maybes that will be batted around, so it will be important that it thinks before it speaks and remains impartial just until HR has been given a free rein to speak to its people with confidence.

The last thing we would want to see happen is for Honest to be denounced before it has had a chance to acquire all the facts and deliver these with the support of its emotional fellowship that has been forming in the background. If it didn't let Dishonest dethrone it at the start, it is not going to be dethroned by a bunch of employees who aren't yet acquainted with the truth. If it pushes Honest too far it may end up colluding with PJ who is now bored of being good like a child who has been sitting in the back seat on a car journey for far too long. Honest could end up being influenced to tell a little white lie or bend the truth to get them off its back!

People don't always appreciate honesty but they don't always want to be insulted by having the 'economical with the truth' side of things bestowed upon them, as if softening the blow now will somehow change the shape of the truth when it finally arrives! Although this is an assumption that may never be proven, the bendy truth is like a credit card which can be helpful in the moment but has to be paid for later. The moral to this story is be careful how far you bend the truth before the card snaps rendering it useless – even though it's credible, if it's broken you can't bend it back again and no one will ever know the truth!

People don't like dishonesty even if they practise dishonesty; it is a one-way street. I am sure you've all seen the films based on a New York drama that underpins the darker side of Italian life on the streets that usually has me smiling because they are often up to no good and mischievous. The dialogue is accentuated and I end up trying to impersonate one character or another because they sound so 'cool', even if they are running around with sawn-off shotguns and beheading their rivals because they said the wrong thing at the wrong time. You don't want to be dishonest to these guys!

So what is it exactly that people want you to be? What if it's not about you?! What if they are asking something from you that you cannot give and it is clear that it probably wouldn't matter what you said – you won't please them. It's often about the other person and their expectations. Maybe they don't like to hear the truth and therefore you have to allow them to go and work out what they do want – for themselves. You may want to be helpful and justify your train of thought but *help* doesn't work if it isn't recognised as a form of help to the other person, and who says that what you are offering is helpful?

Can we say that honesty is the best policy? Some would argue not… Some would probably say that Honest is behaving economically most of the time in each corner of the world and occupies space for a very good reason. Honest and Dishonest are on opposite sides attracting and opposing each other, keeping the planet spinning on its axis so that an element of the truth, which sits somewhere in between on a budget, can be appreciated. These two extremes may meet halfway and blend together to compromise the truth which can work sometimes, depending upon each other's agenda and any settlement involved. Other times emulsions, formed in the heat of the moment, begin to separate like oil and water, as both sides choose to resist one another's charms, realising that they aren't compatible. They simply cannot work together!

Everyone will have a different relationship with the word

honest and, depending on their own experiences, they may decide when honesty is the best policy or if circumstances can keep it under wraps until the time is right for it to reveal itself – if at all.

We have learned that Honest isn't a ruthless character and seems to understand the complexities that exist while delivering its honesty. Sometimes, it could do with a little direction when its blunt delivery of 'a matter of fact' rattles the cage of its recipient, saying, "I am just being honest with you!" There may still be a fine line to keep in mind but maybe you don't feel the need to wait for permission on every occasion. In fact, in some instances – if you waited for permission to be honest with someone – you may wait a very long time. Honesty may still be based on perspective – so tread carefully!

One of the other points the alien made in its report on Failure, which wasn't elaborated on at the time, was that human beings were either prone to misinterpreting supportive information and feedback, or they were justified in being confused or upset because it wasn't well communicated. There is nothing wrong with making judgements or being honest but there is a way of doing this and sometimes humans need to learn to do this better.

*

Yep, it's all well and good being honest with other people but how honest are we with ourselves?! Some of us are much better at handing out free advice and then sidestepping any opportunity to share some of the same magical stuff with ourselves. This may have something to do with the idea that if you are honest with yourself – about 'whatever it is' that isn't going that spectacularly – you will *actually* have to do something about it! Well, you don't have to… but, having brought any of your own areas for improvement into your awareness, it would be a betrayal of yourself not to give them some attention.

When you gave out your free advice your part was done. You got to walk away with your halo alight, having done the job that Honest was enthroned to do. It was then up to the other person to take action (if they chose to do so). But if your honesty was reflective of passing judgement that needed to look in the mirror, then be prepared, in case honesty decides to do a U-turn as guided by your opponent and come back to find you!

Challenging and managing conflict, though, is a huge area to explore. If you have been silently tolerating someone else's poor behaviour or listened to comments that have become tiresome and always seem to be directed towards you, then it may be time to challenge. Once you have found the courage to be honest with yourself, then being honest with someone else, as a result, can set you emotionally (or physically) free. This is especially true when one person is having a profound impact on another person's wellbeing. The reason you challenge may have something to do with recognising that it may be time to be honest with yourself and take positive steps to change a relationship with someone or something that isn't working for you in your life.

Being honest with yourself in how you choose to live your life – how you decide to walk your path – can be challenging. The thinking part and the doing part that accompany being honest have to meet at some point otherwise honesty may not fulfil its purpose. If it happens to be misdirected or misinterpreted, then, yes, there may be consequences – that's when the learning takes place for everyone involved. I suggest it is more about understanding that through being honest with yourself you may be able to make more informed decisions about what you want out of life. This could be a useful practice which encourages healthy, open and honest relationships to develop in all areas of your life so you have more emotional freedom.

Honest was coming to the end of its reflective practice for the day and had welcomed the peace and quiet. It came to the conclusion that self-doubt or the lack of confidence to speak its mind was holding it back from being able to speak the truth to other people. Nonetheless, what it discovered to be just as important, or perhaps even more important, was the truth it spoke to itself.

Leading by example wasn't just about gaining other people's trust in order to sleep well at night! Honest had to promise itself that it would apply the same level of integrity when it came to being honest with itself so it didn't have to share a bed with Dishonest and be led into temptation when they were alone together!

B*L*A*M*E

Lying Down On the Job

Frequently, you will find Blame sitting on a chair in detention at school because the headmistress has asked it to take time out to reflect on where its responsibilities lie. Blame is allowed to exist. No one doubts that assigning blame is a natural reaction when things go wrong, but it has to learn to be honest and prepare to challenge and be challenged.

On one occasion when Blame found itself in detention, leaning against the back wall in the science lab, it wondered why it was easily influenced and if there was indeed any scientific explanation for its actions. It noticed that in one situation it would be accountable whilst in another it couldn't seem to accept full responsibility and got into the habit of finding someone or something else to take ownership. In the midst of deep contemplation, it started to think about the different positions in which it could lie. It only had an hour, so it chose to generalise knowing full well it would have an opportunity to put another spin on it – at a later date.

Generally speaking, Blame was aware it was a bit of a lazy character and took the easy option, when it could. It is usually guided in one direction or another, so it can justify anything when it is being asked to assign the blame and has been given instructions to get away with it on your behalf. It tends to stick close by to excuses and they are often found together, working out their next plan of action.

The main reason Blame gets confused, when it is connected to a perceived failure, is because it is shuffled around so many times and undergoes so many reassignments that it can forget whose truth it is defending. Blame is just the messenger – you can't shoot the messenger! Do you shoot the postman when he delivers you your credit card bill? No, you don't! Blame lies down at your front door as you collect your unwanted post because it has nowhere else to lie on this occasion.

Blame knows when you are using it as a scapegoat, passing the buck and attaching itself to an excuse that simply doesn't add up! We are aware that Blame takes its instructions and executes them like orders that have been passed down from a senior officer to his/her troop – the soldiers have to carry out the orders but this doesn't mean they are always understood. When Blame is under assignment, it may feel uncomfortable and have an ill feeling about its mission. This is more noticeable when it senses that the blame has been misplaced.

When it is asked to explain itself it hesitates, spouting nonsense, and it is at this stage that it realises that it hasn't fooled anyone! The line of questioning it undergoes proves hard work and it is only pride that stops it apologetically retracting its finger and asking for forgiveness. When Blame gets it wrong, and it does, then it has to learn to be humble and swallow its pride so it doesn't look foolish for hanging onto a thin thread that could barely hold its accusation together in the first place. Whilst it is only the messenger, it can still be shot down in flames if it doesn't surrender when it faces resistance. Camouflage may fool the enemy for a while but Blame only has to look in the mirror and it will be hard pushed to fool itself. Its reflection will be saying, "Come on, you know it's your own fault".

Sometimes people don't like to take the blame or they decide to bear the blame as if it were harbouring a fugitive that was on the run from facing justice elsewhere.

Consider those times when something goes well for you in life; usually, you take the credit or assign it to someone or something else involved. So, when something goes wrong you either take responsibility or look to assign it elsewhere. These two approaches seem reasonable on the surface, don't they! If honesty has anything to do with it then it shouldn't be too difficult to make the right connections to ensure responsibility is correctly assigned. This may not be as straightforward as it sounds.

Firstly, take Honest and imagine it has to be compliant with a code of conduct in order to sanction blame. If Honest is open to interpretation and has no set of procedures to follow then it cannot be accused of non-compliance when blame is misplaced. Versions of honesty conceal the ultimate truth, appearing as lame excuses, and the quest to appoint blame correctly leads to a motion to dismiss.

So in the belief that the truth will surface, the next question to consider is whose truth will be right? All the evidence points to the accused but what Blame didn't take into account was that the accused had its own piece of evidence up its sleeve and another heap of blame was being catapulted back. Blame gets swung back and forth and, as a result, the dizziness begins to cloud its judgement and, depending on what or who is on trial, the motion to dismiss probably couldn't come quickly enough.

Blame is constantly being held to account and gets involved in a range of conscious or unconscious cover-ups. These can take place in a courtroom, in a relationship, at work, in business and, low and behold, everyone has the capacity to look in the mirror and blame the reflection for being a victim of mistaken identity!

Blame has raised a few valid points so far and it would seem it is a rather pragmatic character. Although it is led by you, and has to do as it's told, I also get the sense that it is a clever accomplice and knows whether it is acting inappropriately. Maybe Blame has an ability to transmit its concerns back to you, in the hope that you will reassess your original line of thinking, when blame is misdirected.

Sometimes Blame is made redundant. It is asked to sit on the outer edge of the circle that is formed by a group of people who have been given permission to lay Blame to rest. Organisations that have the resources to invest in employee development and improve morale in the workplace will be doing so in order to prevent a blame culture from developing. Blame is a negative practice when it is allowed to run riot, and has to be explored in order to be understood and managed.

However, putting Blame back in the jar and screwing the lid on tight doesn't resolve underlying conflict that may find another way to surface. It is much better to have Blame sitting (restrained if necessary) in the circle where it can join in conversations and air its opinion, as good communication is half the battle. If Blame can learn to be diplomatic and exchange feedback using self-control, then barriers can come down as two sides to a story are explored. Blame is open to changing its mind when it has a good reason to back track and is more than happy to share responsibility if the other side to a story can restore harmony with no hard feelings.

In a team environment, I think the idea is to move the team

members on from a place of appointing individual blame that is associated with an unsuccessful activity and, instead, become collectively accountable. Even if there is room for Blame to be assigned, the preferred option above encourages people to look at what lessons can be learned in order to make the activity successful in the future. In this instance, 'deferred success' will escort Failure and Blame off the premises.

Blame observes and gets restless in these situations. It doesn't mean to be defensive but it doesn't always understand why it has to share the blame when it isn't at fault. Blame has to learn that sharing responsibility in an overall objective, especially at work, may be part and parcel of keeping the peace and keeping your friends (even if this concept sounds like blackmail!). Blame came to the conclusion that it wasn't suited to the corporate world which wasn't too impressed with Blame either.

It is understandable why Blame gets upset because it is taught to be true to itself and challenge but it feels it has to change its behaviour when it goes to work and then again, when it returns home or sits among friends. Regardless of whether it is actually right or wrong, or finds itself in places it shouldn't be, this doesn't change the fact it feels it has to constantly adapt. Maybe Blame could take a few lessons from Judgement and Honest which both agree that it isn't always 'what is said' but 'how it is said'. If Blame gets confused at times it could be down to a lack of direction.

Sometimes Blame is known for saying what it has on its mind. So when it presents the facts as supporting evidence, it doesn't understand why it's cautioned. A good example of this can be illustrated between two siblings who are having a quarrel. The parent pipes up and tells them both to stop arguing. One sibling defends its honour and states, "But it's not my fault, he pushed me first". The parent turns around and says, "It doesn't matter whose fault it is, just stop arguing". Well... does it really matter whose fault it is and would the argument have drawn to an amicable conclusion had it been mediated in a constructive manner? It didn't matter whose fault it was to the parent but the sibling under attack reckoned it was important!

Blame started pacing the perimeter edge of the science lab trying not to sulk, wondering what was the point of being honest if that didn't lead to justice! Honest, who was an expert in experiencing rejection, just added to Blame's confusion by advising it to be humble and accept that the truth isn't always outwardly revealed, but sometimes knowing and living by your own truth, which exists inside of you, will be enough. Blame wasn't entirely convinced. It felt that fluffy responses are usually a sign of not knowing the answer, but coming from Honest you'd think they'd be well founded.

It thought long and hard about the message recently delivered by Honest, which was also insinuating that instances existed where it was desirable to accept a share of the blame – even if it wasn't your fault. It had learnt that there were usually two sides to a story and a 'two-sides-to-the-story' argument unfortunately allows both sides to be right, until one of them is found guilty. Blame is often open to interpretation. If humbleness is too hard to swallow then Blame is asked to lie low and behave unless a twist in the storyline surfaces and pulls Blame in one direction or the other!

As Blame parked itself on the workbench, thinking retrospectively about life, it started playing around with the Bunsen burner that clearly displayed a warning sign: 'Not to be used unattended'. *Fair comment*, it thought. Blame could accept that if it blatantly did something silly then there would be no denying it was to blame, especially if it got burnt. Edging away carefully, concerned that pointing its finger in the wrong direction was enough to set the burner alight, Blame often compared itself to a misunderstood character out of a comic book. Sometimes it found its fingers smouldering even when there was no sign of fire, and skipping science class to avoid bumping into PJ still landed it in trouble. And landed it in detention.

Once, it took a course, studied hard and failed the exam and had no idea who to blame so it decided that the teacher hadn't done their job properly! The teacher challenged and Blame reciprocated their kind gesture by challenging them back in return. Despite all the studying, something else outside of Blame's awareness had to have been involved. That's it – it's a no-brainer – the test was too hard, the marking guidelines far too ambiguous, so who can take responsibility on this occasion? Where is Blame going to sit now and can it be assigned to the exam writers? After all, they wrote it and evidently didn't write it very well! Blame recalls pacing the corridors up and down, in limbo at the time, pleading for an alternative assignment because it couldn't work out where to lie.

Who or what is actually at fault when these sorts of situations arise? In many instances, there seems little evidence that an offence has been committed. During that period of time, Blame studied hard, the teacher taught well and the examiners marked in accordance with a set of guidelines. Everyone was compliant. A 'failure to comply notice' could only be served if Honest was under scrutiny but there was no indication that it was at fault. Sometimes things just happen. Sometimes one of the mixed seeds in the pack doesn't develop particularly well and something obscure, that we don't understand, grows out of shape. We don't know that for certain and so we learn to accept that Blame is homeless once in a while.

I am writing this section giggling through a grimace of pity for this character. Blame is endearing yet vulnerable. If it can't be assigned, then it has to bite its tongue and consider looking on the bright side… Maybe it was time to walk a different path if this one was clearly going to be too disheartening. Why make its life more difficult and go through the humiliation of resitting an exam that could equally turn out to be a waste of time? No, it was certain that it wasn't cut out for academia. There was an upside to this experience. If it could blame itself for this glitch in its education, sometime in the future, and reserve it for a period of reflection in a time of self-doubt, it would be able to secure a couple of months in sheltered housing! Blame just needs to lie somewhere in order to secure accommodation. In fact, practising self-pity (when it didn't have anything else to blame) meant it could go and play with Guilt, in its free time, to see if it had anything else to explore while it was in a self-deprecating frame of mind.

Guilt can encourage us to keep on blaming ourselves, in the present, for creating a situation in the past that appears to still be having an impact on our lives. Carrying the blame (founded or otherwise) through into another point of your life at a later date is neither right nor wrong and it would be flippant of me to say differently.

Past experiences which involve 'mistakes' can have their place in the here and now. When we learn to keep the emotions previously associated with them detached in the present moment, we can use the learnings as a result of those experiences to our advantage. This does not trivialise their importance, after all they were a part of our lives. However, in order for them to serve any purpose now, as you recall the experience, they must remain less emotive. No doubt you will have enough emotions to deal with, surrounding your new experience, never mind expending energy on pacifying the past – again.

When we recall a time, either recently or in the distant past, whereby we made a poor judgement, it is likely to surface when something in our current world isn't going too well and we haven't quite worked out how to deal with it. While we take the time to get our 'sensible' head on – the one that will help us to find a solution – we can regress. Whatever it is that isn't going to plan now may or may not be connected with an incident from the past, but our mind wanders and frantically tries to find a connection and something to blame. A couple of things can happen if it does do this.

When we track a connection down we can press the replay button and remain in a negative state that relives the past. The past is unable to make any positive contribution to your present circumstances, because it is quite literally behind the times and you haven't brought it up to date. If you don't offer those past experiences, which manage to push their way to the forefront of your mind, any form of rehabilitation, then why bring them back up again? If you are looking to find excuses for a present malfunction in your life – underneath the floorboards – then it sounds like you have reunited with the Chinese whispers from your last voyage as you worked alongside Darkness. They will tell you stories.

Alternatively, we can trace our steps and look for a link to our past that will be unsentimental and use it to help us find a solution. In doing so, we can recognise the errors we made back then, avoid making them again and learn to do things a different way. If we are going to blame ourselves then we may as well get something positive back as we put ourselves through the mill, one more time.

The past could be very recent! Something may have happened last week and you think, had you done it differently, you wouldn't have ended up in this mess this week. Even if you did what you thought was right at the time we have a habit of overturning it when something else comes along to undermine the original decision. This is a clear situation in which Blame is misbehaving!

When the past has nothing new to say, that hasn't been said already, and can't help you anymore, shut it out or tell it to be quiet until you have dealt with any consequences requiring your attention as a result of the decisions made. Besides, how much time can you afford to waste now colluding with Blame? You have more important and current things on your mind.

It is OK to accept responsibility and admit to making mistakes, or shall we call them 'your less than finer moments'. Process them – work through them – then do something positive to keep moving forward. Blame may be linked to your history but once it has made any overdue contribution just ask it to camp elsewhere. Find the arrow sign on your map that states: *You are here.* Knowing where you are is a good place to be and offers you a recognisable place to move on from. In time, you will only sense how far you've come without the need to look over your shoulder.

It was nearing the end of detention and Blame was feeling in a good place too! Despite being in an ideal environment to explore the cause and effect of the big bang theory, it knew that it couldn't explore all perceptions of Blame in one detention. It had always wondered if the Big Bang Theory was to blame for lifeforms appearing on earth or if something else was responsible.

Blame is usually associated with something that is perceived to have gone wrong. In this case it would depend upon whether someone thought that the formation of the world, as we know it, was indeed a good thing or something that went terribly wrong! Blame would have to look at its own family tree, to see if it was involved, and that would definitely entail looking back through history and making some links. Blame could go on to become a historian if science didn't work out… so far it wasn't faring well!

Blame had really enjoyed its hour in detention after all, and thought for a moment about how Guilt had been previously associated with a fact or a feeling. Blame could identify with being torn between the two, agreeing it functioned in much the same way. Sometimes a person was to blame for a jolly good reason and other times only felt they were to blame until they realised they weren't! If Guilt sticks around long enough too, it will embellish the truth (the perceived truth) and Blame will be remanded in custody until the person's imagination has created a new version of the truth and set Blame free.

The million dollar question is: How long do you carry the blame around once you have accepted that something is your fault? You are not asking to be exonerated but the healing process has to begin. Usually we look in a mirror at some point during the day. This may be intentional or unintentional, providing an opportunity to make eye contact with the only person in the whole wide world that will be around for as long as you are alive and knows your truth: yourself. Blame will come face to face with its opponent as it stands in front of the mirror which will help transcend any limitations imposed by the self. Sometimes things are not your fault and threadbare accusations can simply fall and rest in another place.

In life, sometimes we have an idea that we could fall without being pushed but hope we stay upright, with or without crutches. Sometimes we trip over something that got in the way and caught us unawares. It is hard to come to terms with the fact that we often set ourselves up to fall. We go about our daily affairs and we brace ourselves for the journey across the undulating landscape, along our path. No one likes to fall but words get said and things get done that create an imbalance which, at the time, cannot be immediately restored. The restoration part has to be worked on as you attempt to get back up, and it can take minutes through to years depending on how far you fell and how strong you are physically and emotionally.

Blame knew there would be repercussions from playing truant and probably set itself up for a fall. It accepted the blame after it had spent a little time trying to avoid it! Once it was caught by the headmistress, it had to take responsibility and deal with the consequences. It was healthier to move on and swallow its pride; otherwise it would only become a victim, enslaved by its own inefficiencies and feel sorry for itself, forever more!

As you have probably discovered by now, having witnessed Blame engaging in an hour-long session of profound reflective practice, it is a reasonably level-headed character and didn't fall too far on this occasion. It found that experimenting with its feelings was productive and this particular experience was great for self-development.

If something we are feeling is disturbing us then we need to change the feeling so we are no longer disturbed. Blame is a natural reaction but if all of our natural reactions run around freely then they will find someone or something else to disturb. Not all of our natural reactions will be negative and they may well influence in a positive way. Remember 'natural' doesn't mean it is always OK – it just means it occurs.

F*O*R*G*I*V*E

The Multi-Step Equation

Forgive didn't profess to be 'up there' sitting alongside Pythagoras and Archimedes but it did see itself as a philosophical mathematician. Philosophy didn't seem to do either of those famous chaps any harm as they hopscotched numerically through life, shining light on each new discovery.

Forgive is an immortal character and has witnessed a multitude of sins unfold throughout the ages. It has been privy to secrets and sadness, which at times forced it to question if the forgiveness it was dishing out was unconditional or if that could be challenged. Surely it is down to personal choice? It may take someone a long time to arrive at a decision to forgive. However, sometimes little thought may go into making this decision and no sooner one is made, forgiveness is later retracted. This is when something just doesn't add up!

Returning to the blackboard, Forgive makes further attempts to understand why the maths logic it applied earlier didn't produce the intended results. Maybe it got the methodology wrong or it simply put an integer in the wrong place. In maths an integer is a whole number but it is also something that is complete in itself. Forgive wondered if a part of the decision-making process, that led to forgiveness, was incomplete. If the decision was made simply because it seemed the right thing to do, then the person may not have been thinking holistically. They didn't take all their feelings into consideration and this oversight had left a hole in the formula. They imagined that forgiving would help them have closure and feel complete. Sometimes it just takes longer to figure out how to forgive and mean it.

Getting caught up in drama and feuds, Forgive often represents a bright light at the end of a tunnel, which steps in to restore harmony and peace. It is called upon to reconcile differences, having an innate ability to blow arguments out of the water when trivial disputes get out of hand. Every so often, Forgive holds it breath and then exhales once it goes off duty wondering if it acted inappropriately just to calm the waters. It didn't consider itself to be dishonest, although it was aware that, in a teeny-weeny way, it may speak to appease a situation. It simply had a secret love affair with Peace and being calculating had its advantages. Keeping the peace can be a commendable thing to do and Forgive usually went about its business quietly!

A simple phrase of kindness can often neutralise the irritation brought about by either human error or a minor act of mischievousness that went slightly pear-shaped. Forgiving can be an honourable thing to do and a humbling experience for both parties involved. Sometimes we just forgive naturally and then no more gets said on the subject; soon after, the dispute is forgotten. This is of course until a similar situation arises and the previous business that had been dealt with so eloquently suddenly grapples with an ego that had stayed remarkably quiet but decides to re-engage in churlish behaviour. This isn't the case for everyone. This behaviour may just reflect a lack of sincerity that was lurking behind your initial deliverance to set someone emotionally free. The fact that a similar situation has arisen is an indication that an earlier dispute is unresolved. Either that or someone is taking someone for a ride – they keep making the same mistake and you keep on forgiving. A temporary stopgap in a relationship is entertained by forgiveness.

Unhealthy relationships can thrive on Failure, Fear, Guilt and Need. Forgive works alongside these characters, appealing to their better nature to work through their insecurities. They have each been through battles in an attempt to understand their own limitations and strive for acceptance. Forgive is always learning and developing, as it too has to come to terms with its own feelings and the impact of its actions. Forgive couldn't be malicious if it tried. It has a sense of duty to work with all the emotions along your path. This is because underneath every emotional obstacle which houses conflict, Forgive asks you to take the opportunity to look at it from two angles. Firstly, is there anything about yourself that requires 'your own' forgiveness and secondly, does the area that feels most conflicted include someone else?

Forgive performs at its best when it collaborates with Honest and Humble. Do you need to forgive yourself for being... 'too hard on yourself'? This merely clouds your judgement and makes any chance of seeing the wood for the trees impossible. If, on any part of your journey so far, you sense that you have held yourself back, can you now allow yourself to be forgiven and move forward? How we communicate with ourselves is interesting. We are capable of working out many of our issues on our own. What are often in the way of making room for any sensible conversations with our higher self are those trees! We tend to focus on the limiting emotions that branch off in all directions and we miss the beauty that lies within the flora and fauna below our feet, which help to keep us grounded.

If you feel conflicted and recognise that the challenge to forgive someone else is going to be the hard part, then you can start by forming a self-help group! Gather up all the emotions you reckon are involved in this burden and get them talking to each other. Find some common ground and look at any dependencies between them that need to be broken. Respect your emotions and listen to their stories before you drown them with any self-importance. Then you are ready to make a more informed decision.

Now and then, Forgive is asked to conjure up sizeable amounts of forgiveness when it simply isn't ready to do so, although forgiveness itself probably only comes in one size. Once it has decided to present forgiveness as a gift, then the amount provided is irrelevant. The focus is more likely to be on the chain of events that will lead up to that decision being made and take the most effort. It is the amount of time taken up, included in the internal and external dialogue, which goes into the pursuit of finding inner peace.

A person can either forgive or they can't. Forgiveness is either at the end of a short or lengthy process – or it isn't. If, after an emotional rollercoaster of deliberations, forgiveness is not the answer or a person is not ready to forgive, then it isn't something that can be quantified. It works like Trust and cannot be partly awarded. Forgiveness is not something you must do but, rather, something you can choose to do because you want to or need to; the reason for either decision is up to you. Is the need to forgive a desire or a necessity? Sometimes forgiving is hard to do and it doesn't always come naturally. In the case it feels unnatural, then plenty more can be said and things are less likely to be forgotten in a hurry.

Up until now we have seen that Forgive, like all of us, has

good days and bad days. Some days it toddles off to work and irons out a few hiccups and no one gets hurt. It swoops in like a superhero and saves the day leaving little collateral damage to tidy up. On other days, it gets involved in a difficult project only to discover that it ends up questioning itself and the integrity of the task in hand. It debates whether to forgive or not and when it concludes that forgiveness is the best course of action, it can find another reason to retract its proposal to forgive and has a dilemma on its hands.

This dilemma persuades Forgive to remain indecisive until it is finally assaulted by an influx of emotions whose sole purpose is to put its intentions to the test. Once it overcomes that barrier with flying colours and has convinced its heart, first and foremost, that it is going to execute its plan to forgive, then another challenge arrives.

What is the methodology required to go from A: choosing to forgive through to Z: delivering the package? What does it need to consider by way of coping strategies as it comes out of its comfort zone (a place in which it understood its own emotional boundaries) and puts itself amidst a head-on collision with vulnerability, as Forgive hurtles towards goal Z?! Who would do such a thing?! I use the word *hurtles* because in this context when you move out of your comfort zone, everything around you can appear to move so fast. It is a new experience and requires a little kindness on your part to guide you through the maze, until your balance is restored.

So now you are back on your feet, having lingered long enough in Tree Pose, you can fully embrace the journey ahead along a new stretch of path. Everything you experience hereafter will collectively add up and help you reach your end goal. You may feel like you will lose a small part of yourself along the way, yet gain something else in return for your efforts. You will multiply all the times you said, "I can't do this", by one hundred and then divide that answer by one common denominator: Resilience. Resilience says, "Yes you can..." and it gets personal!

It takes personal resilience to come out the other side of any painful experience. If survival alone is your end goal then finding the courage to journey on, when there is no room to accommodate the word *forgiveness*, will remain your first priority. However, if you feel burdened by your own misery which seems to be in the process of multiplying tenfold and weighing you down, then you may need to clear some head space and make more room for negotiations between Misery and Forgive. Even if this initially applies to forgiving ourselves for umpteen things for which we probably didn't need to chastise ourselves in the first place.

Forgive is turning out to be quite the 'applied mathematician' after all. Applying maths to other disciplines in life is right up its street. For example, it suggests that if you can forgive, then you may feel better about whatever it is that made you unhappy. What if the magic formula looks something like this: To forgive = feeling better in some way! It doesn't identify who for and it doesn't provide any granularity in this equation to how forgiving does bring about that particular result. It is a sweeping statement that happens to have the equality sign sitting in the middle as if each side of the equation is dependent on the other being in existence.

What part of yourself do you 'tap into and work alongside' when you contemplate forgiveness? You lug around your emotional toolkit on your entire journey, mainly because you don't know how much of yourself to give in order to forgive. It can be difficult to travel light, although the idea is to feel lighter once you have processed your thoughts and offloaded a few emotions that were weighing you down.

It doesn't matter if you are striving to forgive someone else or yourself. An act of forgiveness has to start from a place of sincerity and what better place to start from than within you! Honest will aim to keep you on track as you attempt to understand why you are considering forgiveness in the first place and it will keep Blame at a healthy distance. Patience is heavily involved and will be supportive when the climb seems too daunting; it will sit with you as you contemplate and reflect.

Forgive thrived on self-expression. It sat on a logarithm, on the forest floor, and wondered how much effort it would take in order to get to the stage of feeling comfortable with serving up a portion of forgiveness. In other words, how many sensible conversations does it need to multiply in order to answer this question? It always had its maths head on and even if numbers didn't provide all the answers they usually crept into a methodology somewhere.

A numerical expression is a mathematical sentence that contains numbers. It is not, as I first thought, anything to do with a number pouring out its feelings or voicing its excitement as it proclaims that "one add one equals two". A number doesn't get caught up in semantics, unlike words which have a habit of being put together only to be torn apart again by people who just want them to say something else – other than what they are saying at the time. And, we know by now that it is often the meaning of a sentence that sits under the microscope as the poor little words get manipulated.

Arithmetic deals with the manipulation of numbers and when this happens, an arithmetic operation will have been involved (addition, subtraction, multiplication and division).

There will always be a 'given', which is the result. But is a number just a number, no matter which way you look at it? How you reached that number is probably what counts; did you add 'five to five' to reach 'ten' or did you tot up 'six and four'? Did you add 'three to eight' rubbing the last digit off in frustration, because you got your sums wrong, adding a zero instead?! Double figures can prove quite complicated. Using too many words can be equally exhausting. We have all come across people who have swallowed a dictionary. They are able to poetically populate a sentence with really long words. You can be left wondering what they all meant once the full stop silently props them up for evaluation.

Can we create a numerical expression for a set of feelings? I suppose if we could offer up a number to reflect an emotion then we could go around speaking and expressing ourselves in code, but would we really be understood? Maybe some of us are not particularly understood now using linguistics, never mind numbers – although numerology gets a little credit and is explained linguistically. Playing with numbers can be as much fun as playing with words. When it is simply the case of moving a few around, in order to come up with a successful formula or methodology that works for you, a Eureka moment can be quite exhilarating.

If forgiveness is the given (the result), then what is actually involved in the process leading up to forgiveness or in the act of forgiving? If feeling better is the given, once forgiveness has marched forth and multiplied, what has to actually take place in order for you to feel better?

Maths abides by rules which can be followed in order to bring about a specific result. Life itself doesn't always appear to work in this way. Events unravel in no particular order – or do they? Life unfolds and sometimes the order of things, in which we would like them to happen, turns out to be somewhat different from what we had planned or originally intended. We grumble and wish that something else had happened first – but it didn't! We want something to magically appear so we can do what we thought we wanted to do – but it doesn't. Sometimes we are pleased about that, later on in life.

Sometimes dependencies have to exist. A+B needs to happen before C+D can take place. Maybe you want to reach F quickly but you have to let E run its course. If you add A+D then E can't happen and if you let B+C get together you could have an explosion on your hands. What if you never reach F? What if F stood for forgiveness and when you do manage to hold it in your hands, it doesn't end up making you feel better when you finally give it away?!

Is it about the order of operations? Is it about processing your thoughts in any particular order or following a sequence which underpins your methodology? Think 'maths', for a moment, and consider the two numerical expressions below:

Figure 1:
$1 + 2 \times 3 = 9$

Figure 2:
$1 + 2 \times 3 = 7$

What did you see at first glance? If you calculated them both in sequence then you will be accusing me, within seconds, of making an error in Figure 2. But the latter is correct. A keen mathematician would know that you work it all out in order of operations and multiplication comes first. Of course, adding a couple of brackets into the equation, around the '1 and 2', may have been useful, in Figure 1, if we wanted 9 to be the answer.

Maths lesson over!

My point is: we don't always see things correctly. Later, we may come to realise that some of the answers we saw, at first glance, simply don't add up. Sometimes in life, something may catch our eye (or we hear a word) and we can jump to conclusions and get in a muddle. If someone is colour blind, depending on which colour cone cells are defective, this may determine which colours they see. When someone looks at a sentence, depending on where the commas are situated, the meaning may be open to interpretation. Also, just because a word is used in a sentence the full meaning may still not be understood (as the writer intended) because it lacks context and can be taken to mean something different to different people.

When you lay all your facts and feelings on the table in readiness to forgive, what you do in order to bring about that result may not stare you in the face and sit in any logical order. What if you don't know what to add or subtract? What if you don't know how much white to add to red to make it a rosier picture? What if the words you wrote down, as you emptied your mind, suddenly sound different once they are airlifted off the paper and vocalised? You spell the letters out, counting them all in case you left one behind, and realise that joined-up writing never did make anything easy to read – or understand. A squiggle here and a loop over there – a seven begins to look like a one. You need to attend a TEFL (Teaching English as a Foreign Language) course before you can even coach others on personal resilience overseas… and teach maths!

We interpret things differently and deal with conflict in a variety of ways as we pack our emotions into our toolkits in unequal measures. Another perspective may help or, at the very least, give you time to decide if your first thoughts were, in fact, correct. Later, you may choose to ignore any feedback, yet feel appreciative that the advice offered served as a positive interruption, allowing your own thoughts the space to reflect.

Incidentally, if you do wish to improve your maths, because you want to become an architect or an accountant, please find a professional teacher as Forgive hasn't qualified yet and I'm a bit rusty in that department.

*

Operation Forgiveness

It is understandable that there will be glitches in the process. We are human. What sounded like a good idea last night as you soaked up a glass of Chablis or bathed in a bath of bubbly seems quite unreasonable the next day. Doing things in the heat of the moment to keep the peace, as you chant "I forgive you" three times, isn't always good practice but you decide to start somewhere anyway.

Events in order of operation could look something like this:
(A + Exfoliate − Toxins + Patience) / Reflection x Honesty = Z

Exfoliate

People romanticise and like to encourage forgiveness without knowing the full story and it is often conjecture. You know if something is forgivable and the lengths you are prepared to go or the feelings you are prepared to let go of in order to forgive. You are the one who has to work through the layers of oppression before you feel comfortable in your own skin. Having removed a few dead cells which were blocking your pores, you can let your skin breathe and begin to glow; this will help the toxins rise to the surface and say farewell.

Remove toxins

The notion that forgiving can cleanse implies that impurities exist and have to be removed. If forgiving can help purge the soul then maybe that would allow you to walk a more peaceful journey. For some people, forgiving can be cathartic. Forgiveness doesn't mean you forget but maybe you feel compelled to draw a line under a situation. This can prevent any further emotional contamination as a result of misguided emotions crossing over into another relationship and becoming toxic.

Be patient

It usually takes patience to work through feelings. If you are not a feely type of person, you can still allow Patience to guide you through the process that will lead you to a sustainable end goal. The one that says, "Yes I forgive and I promise I won't retract that or bring it back up when we fall out again!" Patience just asks you to try… that's all. Patience says, "Give it a go and see how you feel".

Reflection

No one is duty bound to forgive. If you are religious and believe this is the right thing to do, it doesn't mean you will find it more or less easy to do than someone who is spiritual, agnostic or an atheist. Practising a faith doesn't imply that the journey you take from A to Z can be trodden without a full emotional toolkit intact. Emotions may appear in different intensities and some may be diffused or disregarded more quickly than others. Some emotions remain suppressed in order to cope with the bugbears that are associated with forgiving and probably accompany you in the forest too! This may question if you truly forgive. Maybe you need to feel 'whole' first so that the formula doesn't fall apart.

Honesty

At all times, be honest with yourself. Are you forgiving another person in order to bring about closure for you? Do you need to forgive yourself for feeling unable to forgive?! Telling someone you forgive them is likely to make them feel better; this is great. Telling someone you forgive them may not make you feel better. So why would you take the time to do this? Ask yourself if you are ready to forgive and listen to the answer that speaks the truth.

If someone asks for your forgiveness, it sounds likely that they have accepted the blame and Blame needs to be released from duty now. Where does that leave you? It may depend upon what the consequences were to their actions and not everything can be forgiven easily. We approach such matters very differently. There are different acts of injustice to take into account and what one person is able to forgive will be unforgivable to someone else.

Testing your methodology

Playing the martyr isn't an attractive quality; yet, I can understand that giving 'forgiving' a go may seem a first step –

if only for experimental reasons or to gauge if you are actually ready to forgive. You may have already experimented a little with this idea and been in what you thought was a healthy place emotionally to forgive, only to find out later on that you weren't really ready or you just didn't want to forgive… yet.

If you get to the end of a journey and decide that forgiveness is an unrealistic proposition, for now, then it is not unreasonable to ask yourself to accept that some things just aren't forgivable – choosing simply to forget instead. And, even if you don't entirely forget, then peace may have already collected you from those dark corridors, drawn back the curtains and shown you that life still has more to offer from a room with a better view.

Forgive is a natural source of light and we all have the power to tap into its infinite wisdom and look for answers. Physicists will tell you what light is, and how it behaves, and the dictionaries will, in turn, provide you with clarity – in their usual succinct fashion – about what light itself can mean. Forgive also stimulates sight within each of you, allowing things previously unseen to be seen.

All journeys allow you an opportunity to consider different perspectives. Maybe yours will allow you a chance to look at things from a different angle whilst taking the time to have those 'internal conversations'. Perhaps you see something about yourself now that you didn't see before. It is quite possible not to like the things you see but shedding light on them allows for healing to take place.

All this time, the alien visitor had been shadowing Forgive on its journey through the forest. It wasn't stalking and had only returned to see how emotional conflict can be approached using inner strength. It was also interested to see how our emotions can keep us in the dark when they are not given an opportunity to be released safely.

It observed and decided that **F-O-R-G-I-V-E** stood for: **F**inding **O**ur **R**esilience **G**ives **I**nner **V**ision **E**mancipation. It wanted to use the 'E' for 'Elbow Room' until it realised it was made up of two words – though that could be workable if you happened to be a 'forgiver'. There you 'R'! In other words: it suggests that if you can find your own ability to recover quickly from difficult situations this will allow you to look deeper within and give your inner vision the freedom to see more than it could see before.

As an aspiring mathematician, Forgive knew that it has to be about living your truth. Sometimes it is simply about forgiving yourself for putting the decimal point in the wrong place...

H*U*M*B*L*E

Making a Connection

As the egos walked through the door, Humble greeted them all in turn and kindly asked them to take off their hats and leave them outside. It spoke with a softness that was kind and respectful, using a tone of voice that could only be described as one which belonged to an old soul who had been sent back to the here and now, to enrich those of us who are still finding our feet.

The egos turned to one another and looked inquiringly. Whilst they didn't question the instruction given to them in that moment, they all huddled together later to discuss how vulnerable they felt; it was as if they had removed a layer of protection.

All egos behave differently. Whilst some of them can be grouped together because they display similar signs of behaviour, behind the scenes their stories tend to be quite different. They each have their own history which influences their shape and size. Humble couldn't take a 'one-size-fits-all' approach in the workshop it was about to deliver. It would most likely look at a few different scenarios which could resonate, in one way or another, with the delegates and then they could share their own experiences.

The workshop was set up in an outdoor marquee that felt

warm and smelt of damp grass which complemented the earthy vapours that snuck out of any space where they could find a hole and be released. It happened to be a sunny day so the egos couldn't complain of being cold. They seemed a little cold towards one another at first. This is likely to be a side effect of walking into an unnatural environment which could stir up emotions. However, the space soon became their new comfort zone as the icebreaker melted the barriers which, for some of them, had been up since they arrived.

They attended voluntarily. It wasn't mandatory to sign up for an outing in the countryside and undergo a bout of self-development that could cause them to feel vulnerable. Putting yourself in a vulnerable situation within a learning environment is a rather brave thing to do. Who knows what to expect at first. Assumptions and nerves can get the better of you, and the key is to overturn any negative feelings that surface and approach the experience with an open mind sprinkled with humility.

Everyone was intrigued to find out what Humble was going to teach. A couple of scenarios to help the egos explore their own potential and evaluate past behaviours through open discussion was on the agenda. As they looked for nuggets of fresh ideas, during their conversations with new people, they could look forward to making self-improvement as knowledge became accessible. They may not have been directly involved in the types of examples Humble planned to use but knew someone else who had been affected.

Humble was most certainly deserving of a place among the 'Fillings that educated the taste buds'. Attending its workshop with a view to trying out a new flavour, even if you didn't like it, was all part of the fun. Just being open to new ideas can give Humble the impression that your learning shutters are up. What you choose to do with those learnings is really up to you and will depend upon whether you perceive them to be useful in your own reality of the world or not. The first scenario focused very much on how, as individuals, we approach a learning opportunity.

Learning can be fun if you can find the courage to laugh at yourself a little while you learn – especially when your brain hasn't yet managed to understand a thing! You look at the subject matter through glazed eyes and with the word *confusion* imprinted across the forehead. This is usually supported by a frown which only disappears once the penny drops.

It is easy to focus too much on how your ego is feeling during the process and you convincingly tell yourself why you can't learn rather than how you can! Drumming up excuses to hide a number of these reasons is understandable. Although, unfortunately, a delay in facing them now, head on, only magnifies their discomfort for you when they do eventually surface having lost their disguise and run out of excuses of their own.

Facing up to your barriers to learning isn't something to be ashamed about. It can be a humbling experience which will often be interrupted by your own defensive messages trying to get through and throwing your emotions into turmoil! That's the ego taking you on a rollercoaster. Your darker emotions tend to appear as silhouettes on a bright background. Having the humility to work your way through your emotions, to overcome a barrier, allows humbleness to shine in the background to support them. Simply cut out a softer-shaped silhouette, enjoy the process and turn the learning outcome into a work of art. You have artistic licence. Didn't you learn to do that in your art exam, earlier on, as you engaged with Patience? Go on, tell me you took the maths exam instead to catch me out!

When you find yourself in any new situation, be that in a classroom or out and about on your travels in life, the experience can take you by surprise. It is possible that you feel unprepared and didn't expect to react the way that you did or anticipate the reactions you received from other people. We can only mind read for so long, before our predictions may lead us into trouble or we wade further into the unknown and out of our depth. Return to base, clear your mind and take a different perspective.

If you haven't studied for a long time or you are a mature student who has found yourself amidst a youthful bunch of technological whiz kids (or those that sit somewhere in between) then it isn't surprising that you may feel open to the elements. You walk into the class with an open mind and then find that the very same mind closes straight back down, all too quickly; just like a blind that rolls back down as the result of a broken cord. You find yourself in unfamiliar territory that can make you feel intimidated.

Does a situation make you feel that way? The situation just exists. You walked into the situation and felt a certain way. Something about the situation will resonate with something inside of you and act as the trigger. A situation is made up of hundreds of tangible and non-tangible components. What are you going to do: blame every one of them for the way you feel? Suppose you do go ahead and sign up for a new course; if you took away a couple of the components would you feel less intimidated? If you could activate your smartphone, in advance, in order to change the colour of the walls, delete a few delegates, swap the smartboard for a flipchart and reprogram the teacher… would this be helpful? It is highly unlikely that if you changed any of these things you would feel any less intimidated and only appear less teachable.

The truth may be that you haven't studied since you had the children; or your IT skills are below average; or everyone seems to know more than you, when in reality they may be feeling much the same as you. They may simply be hiding their pre-course nerves extremely well or have learned to laugh at their insecurities without taking them personally.

All the egos in the marquee had put themselves in the same situation for the day. They all had the same teacher (Humble); they all had something to bring to the workshop (life experience); they all enjoyed the outdoors. Good! The environment was conducive to learning, supported by pockets of freedom to explore their ideas in exchange for Humble's gifts of wisdom.

It would be interesting to see which egos denied any involvement in the scenarios altogether, categorically stating they couldn't relate to any of them. It wasn't unknown for some of the egos to forget to take off their hat as they got caught up in the excitement of meeting new egos at the entrance, earlier that morning, and chose to practise selective hearing. Other times they simply snuck a spare hat in their backpack, squashed up against their emotions, so they could put a hat back on as a defensive measure during activities. These usually appeared crumpled, so Humble had a good idea which ego was feeling vulnerable. If the ego chose to keep its hat on, the hat would probably serve as a useful resource during some of the exercises and even then, when that did happen, Humble wouldn't need to do anything. It wasn't necessary to cause any further embarrassment. Passing on its experience and suggesting better ways of behaving or approaching a situation that required an element of humbleness was sufficient. The egos had to learn in their own way, through experience. Learnings would unravel as they were meant to, and end up forming part of the overall lesson.

Learning just goes on and on; it doesn't stop. You stop learning if you think you are always right. You stop developing if you feel you have developed enough. If you stop learning and developing then you are no more humble than you are wise. Wisdom appears as tiny droplets of instinct, surfacing once they have had the luxury of rolling around in knowledge first. Wisdom doesn't have to exist in any particular quantity to be considered useful; it expands its own horizons because it is willing to learn.

Humble is slightly transparent, wearing just enough to cover up its modesty. It isn't dressed in attire you'd imagine for something considered to be quite healing and is found clothed in nothing which resembles a white coat or flowing robe. It doesn't swan around as royalty or appear as a godly being that has any desire (or ego) to emulate any other powerful being. It doesn't expect to lead or be followed intentionally and has simply learnt to be the leader in its own life, choosing to pass on its knowledge, when it can. This may be why during everyday life, when you look closely at what is going on around you, you can see Humble gently moving around, attaching itself to situations and supporting the people in them to cope better. It radiates and you get the feeling that it knows something about life that you don't and it would be foolish not to consider its advice, when offered. That is being humble, isn't it?

Humble started that day with an introductory presentation. It was made up of imagery and text which required further explanation in order to be understood in context, rather than a list of dos and don'ts. It was there to guide rather than prescribe. The day ahead was heavily reliant on exchanging points of view and it wasn't all about Humble standing on stage and doing a monologue which focused on its own self-importance. What kind of example would that set for the other egos listening?

Emotional Sandwiches

When Humble attended a recent conference on control issues, the James Bond lookalike, who held the presentation, had everyone filling up on a portion of humbleness for breakfast. His icebreakers were thought to have the potential to melt the North Pole! The ploy worked; everyone appeared to behave less egocentrically and looked thoughtful and engaged as they listened intently. The North Pole, however, remained frozen. Well, it certainly hadn't melted any further because of his presentation. Humble wanted to have a similar effect, while working with its own audience, but without feeling as though it had inadvertently hypnotised everyone in the process. It was setting out to teach and not preach; and anyway, it wasn't a conference – it was an interactive self-development session.

The challenge Humble was now facing with 'the audience of today's world' was that it struggled to keep up with technology and discovered that the way the world absorbs information was beginning to change. So, it thought that by displaying 3D images, instead, which rotated and flashed prematurely during its profound introduction, would help to convey its messages more effectively. But it didn't. This advancement in information technology didn't help Humble tune into its higher self or enable it to linger longer on the poignant moments. It preferred the good old-fashioned methods of teaching using chalk and a board without choking the delegates and bringing on a series of asthma attacks. There were always one or two waiting for an excuse to surface, and Humble trusted that those who did suffer were clued up on what to do, should one happen. Such an excuse could exist to mask an ego's sudden urge to evacuate the marquee when the lessons became too intense as a result of having an aversion to learning after all.

Who knows? Maybe by the end of the workshop Humble

Making a Connection

could demonstrate a little humility itself by agreeing to be mentored by one of the egos. There was bound to be one that was heavily into IT, who could offer to teach Humble how to use an interactive smartboard in its future sessions without exposing the egos to dust particles in the process and without compromising the all-important tuning-in process.

Humble is always an undergraduate; it continually studies humility and has seen humbleness practised both naturally and also with great effort! On both counts, humbleness will be considered for the value that it adds in any given situation, no matter how much effort was involved. A person may learn something from being humble as will the person who is on the receiving end of an act of humbleness, if they choose to notice.

The egos had been listening for the best part of the morning, while watching Humble collect its thoughts and skilfully present them back to the group in a highly intuitive and surreal manner. They eventually demonstrated signs of becoming receptive. Humble knew, by their faces during break, that they were ready to start engaging with each other and strike up a healthy debate. This led Humble rather nicely into its next session and went about splitting the egos into groups. Time for them to do some work now.

One group decided that an act of humbleness can take place right under their noses and none of them would be aware! Maybe you can be so natural at being humble that it can pass unnoticed. Sadly, on other occasions it is quite possible that the other person has seen Humble perform, lapping it up and mistaking its appearance as a sign of subservience that can be exploited.

The second group came up with the idea that when you seek to learn from someone else and ask for their support and point of view, then this can be a humbling experience and Humble is working to its strengths. It focuses less on itself and more on the person who is giving you that support. Sometimes people find it difficult to ask for help and see that as their weakness.

It would be unwise to mistake Humble for Innocence or even Naivety. It is a free spirit and can be practised by anyone and everyone. It isn't something in your emotional toolkit that you only search for when you have to apologise or happen to be feeling less important than someone else. If you feel less worthy or suffer from low esteem, then this would be a good time to look at what it is that is making you feel this way. You may feel humble while discovering what that's about, as you explore your feelings, and find that it has more to do with a lack of confidence. It is a good first step to remove the ego long enough to be open to exploring any underlying reasons.

Owning the decision to make a positive change about you and seeing that through can take courage. When you feel silly for doing this, then you've probably still got your ego attached, no doubt worrying what other people may think or feeling too embarrassed to own up to the fact that you are more human than you originally thought!

Humble rounded everyone up and explained to both groups that people can get the wrong impression of what it means to be humble, perceiving it to be a vulnerable character, and they couldn't be more mistaken!

When you are feeling in an uncomfortable position, one which you have either put yourself into or found yourself in – as the result of being in the wrong place at the wrong time – Humble can come to the rescue. Humility is one of the qualities to have which will carry you through the difficult times; it won't necessarily solve your difficulties. Guilt and Blame tend

Making a Connection

to miraculously enter the stage, each playing a martyr for their sins. So they need to be explored as well in the event they are having an impact on a situation. If they arrived unnecessarily, by default, competing for attention while starring in the play *Martyrdom – Death by Exaggeration*, just kick them off stage! Graciously of course.

Feeling humble when you have upset someone is understandable. Although, playing a martyr to Subservience that has eaten too much Pie just weighs Humble down. Needless to say it can be quite exhausting emotionally.

"What can I expect to feel when I am being humble?" Interestingly, this had been asked by Benjy, one of the egos that hadn't spoken a word all morning.

Happy to hear a question that demonstrated the workshop had moved on to the next level, Humble summed up its initial answer in one word: 'Empowering'.

Little did the egos know that the walk in the countryside, after lunch, was going to expose each of them to all kinds of emotions and if they wore their hats, any sudden gust of wind could blow them sideways. Intent on venturing off the beaten track, Humble wanted the group to feel slightly vulnerable, while keeping them safe on the chosen path. The idea behind this cunning plan (if you can equate Humble to any form of deceit) was to guide them to a place where they could be in awe of something, for a moment, and allow their own importance to step aside at the realisation that they were part of something big and connected to more than the eye could see. Humble would also make it clear that this wasn't the same as being dismissive of your own importance altogether! Feeling self-empowered is probably about having the confidence to know the difference.

Admittedly, they weren't following an Inca trail or climbing

Kilimanjaro but they were surrounded by landscape, all the same. One which owned its story that dated back thousands of years. Indigenous populations may have died out, leaving an unmarked territory on the surface to a distant eye. Yet, what lies beneath the land that simply hides and protects those stories may only be unearthed by archaeologists, with permission. Even then, the tangible items cannot bring along with them the feelings that had once been felt by those who previously held them. Polished up, they get to sit alongside other artefacts in a museum that promises to preserve their stories; or certainly offer an alternative resting place that will remind those inclined to visit, that an alternative reality once existed. It is at this point that you can become sentient and feelings can stir. Who knows, you may be picking them up from the past!

I don't know about you, but on the occasions that I have wandered through a replica of a historical village, designed to take you 'emotionally' back in time, I have truly felt humbled. The past happened. It just reminds me that while the present is a great place to live my life from, the lives once lived, across the planet, make up a past that I will never fully understand; yet, I often sense a connection.

Without a doubt, all this sightseeing left the group feeling humble. Considering the combined wealth of experiences that were lived before and the experiences that were yet to unfold – to be lived by someone else, somewhere – it seemed clear that the egos still had time to leave their own mark, too! That thought alone was empowering as well as somewhat overwhelming. So, that's what Humble meant when it spoke about feeling empowered. The realisation that we are all here to live a life and not simply to watch others live theirs (unless you are watching a reality TV show for research and it forms part of a comparative study) is self-empowering. Seeing the beauty when we stop to see it, or choosing to smell the residual fumes left by Time, as it travels alongside us at speed, burning up its fuel reserves so that stopping on the way doesn't become an option, is up to us to decide.

During the walk, Humble reckoned this activity had more of a ramblers' club-like feel to it as everyone walked at different paces. Some egos moved in front and others fell behind. Some took a break to have a chat with their feelings and emotions until they realised they were lagging behind. It was at this point that they took to running, in order to catch up with the striders ahead and as for the asthmatics… their inhalers could be heard sounding off in unison!

Sometimes the egos shared interests and other times it was obvious their personalities clashed. It is not uncommon to fall out occasionally when spending time in each other's space; you don't always want to walk or talk with everyone. It often takes strength to manage your emotions in a less than comfortable situation and, in turn, control your reactions. As Humble witnesses your distress, it prompts you to look inwards and decide if it is something about yourself that is coming to the surface as you spend time with others. Egos may act as human shields but they also act as mirrors. This was one of Humble's ideas, anyway!

Curiosity can work to your advantage when you find yourself in a situation that causes internal conflict. On the walk you can choose to ask the right questions, only to find out that you discover something interesting about another person. Invariably, you can let your ego quieten down, as you take turns to listen to each other's stories. It is not unusual to find out that you actually have more in common than you first thought, after assuming the worst initially. A small disagreement may have happened when you met, triggering off a chain reaction of unease which simply had to be broken. What better way to do this than on a walk – on a sunny day!

As the egos arrived back at the marquee, a few of them exchanged contact details and acknowledged they had been too hasty in forming opinions about one another; others simply remained amicable, still finding it difficult to leave their competitive side out of the workshop. Bringing the session to a close, Humble reinforced to the group that it can take time to develop a mindset that finally allows you to take comfort in the idea that being humble can bring a sense of peace to many other aspects of your life, where it has been absent.

Leaving the marquee, the egos went to pick up their own hat. Some of them picked up two! They appeared to look at them slightly differently and with less desperation than earlier that morning, parting with a sense of achievement. It wasn't difficult for Humble to notice that the hats that had been left behind were nothing more than a veil that, when worn, hid the insecurities which lay beneath. It was lovely to see that some of them didn't feel the need to take them back or, perhaps, had simply forgotten to pick them up as they left, still caught up in the events of the day. Humble wouldn't turn off its phone just yet, in case it had some distressed callers on the other end requiring immediate protection, once the novelty from the day had worn away! Aware that egos are part and parcel of who we are, it didn't really expect any of the delegates, from that day or any other, to discard their hats forever but simply to be mindful how best to wear them.

Learning how to cope with true disappointments in life when they lay beside you, asking to be understood, is not dissimilar to when Darkness just wanted your attention, whilst

Making a Connection

fidgeting endlessly! The ego rattles on and on leaving your mind, quite literally, full of ifs and buts… and maybes. Certain that the egos didn't attend the workshop because they wanted a sermon, Humble sensed that they did want reassurance that there was something else, outside of themselves that could teach them more than they already knew. Some of them arrived inflated and needed to be compressed whilst others were able to sit comfortably without falling over. It would like to say that there is no room for egocentricity in its workshops but alas, that is exactly what shapes them and makes them more interesting.

As it packed up for the day and opened the door to leave, it hoped that it had entertained the group and also charmed its readers just as much as all of the other characters had entertained – if not more!

Nearly jumping out of its skin, it heard in its head the words, "Hey, Humble… take off your hat… you can't say that…"

Benjy had been sitting quietly by the door waiting for a lift home and must have become telepathic as a result of opening up his senses to the elements during the day, speaking to Humble without appearing to move his lips! Benjy had only spoken out twice during the workshop. If he had communicated to Humble through non-verbal channels then he was about to witness the humility expressed through the voice of a master.

Humble blushed as it saw Benjy, and replied, "Oops… Sorry…!"

Benjy smiled and speaking softly, replied, "Don't worry, no one's perfect. And by the way, I teach IT!"

The Last Word

"Cut…!" shouted the director.

Congratulations were in order as all the characters breathed a sigh of relief, in chorus, greeting Humble outside of the studio on what had been the final day of filming. *Emotional Sandwiches*, which was sometimes shortened and referred to by the cast as ES, had indeed been an interesting documentary to make.

Most of the characters were pleased that they didn't get involved in the original plot with the French detective. Coincidentally, he had been filming in the studios around the corner along with his cast, and was now shooting his third series! It seemed a long time ago that the Emotional Sandwiches went for their very first interview. It wasn't something that could be easily forgotten! None of them realised, then, that the book would blossom into a 3D adventure and spark further interest requiring them to take a crash course in method acting skills. They had learned over time to become more emotionally involved and hone in on their character's strengths and weaknesses. During this escapade, bringing the first book alive had been truly an adventure.

The book could only provide a flavour, designed to leave a tingle on your tongue and a mark on your mind that persuades your own questions to cross boundaries, and search for more answers in your own time. The documentary could only capture so much detail. And as with many programmes, which explored the meaning of life in one sense or another, there was often more footage made which would never get shown, yet still takes its toll on the actors. A sequel would have to be made if there was any chance of exploring a character in depth. Patience had already auditioned and she was lined up, by the same director, to work in a new series alongside Time. That title was still under wraps.

It wasn't quite over yet! The director wanted to film some of the events that followed Humble's final scene to give the audience greater insight into the characters' own experiences. It would most likely present the ideal opportunity for them to share their frustrations; although, what would give them cause, in the first place, to become frustrated?

Well, in order for the producers to take a look at a handful of perspectives, in the allotted time, they risked skimming over a few others which seemed equally valid. As a result, emotions among the cast rose to the surface as disagreements took place. It was difficult for the crew to prepare for their entrances and they had to deal with the emotions as they appeared. When they stir they begin to stimulate reactions. These may be internalised before they graduate to the next level and either display signs and symptoms first, or rush in with no warning, leaving the owner of that emotion bereft or amused. These emotional states, felt or witnessed, are known as feelings. A word about these, before we get back to the 'end of show party' and hear some more home-grown truths!

Feelings

Feelings can tie you up in knots or go around in circles until someone or something encourages them to break the cycle and behave in a less self-centred way. A feeling is naturally self-centred and oozes signs of promise or despair. In between both suggestions appears an abundance of emotional markers which prove useful on our path in life, helping us to make comparisons and fine tune our thoughts.

The impact of a feeling is often explored when it is adversely affecting a person's behaviour. They may negatively hold that person back from reaching a goal (a goal, for now, could be absolutely anything of your choosing). You could be striving to overcome agoraphobia and experience a feeling of fear in open spaces and this holds you back from leaving the house. Alternatively you may have lost your confidence and feel nervous about filling in the next job application, which holds you back from getting a foot in the door, on a new career path. Gosh, you could even be climbing Mount Everest and the feelings of fear have you turning around and running back down the mountain, emptying your entire emotional toolkit along the way! Feelings can be held accountable for many trials and tribulations and we are responsible, in the end, for how we feel.

Is there a beginning or an end to a feeling or is it constantly revolving around something or someone and can we enter a cycle at any point to engage and have an experience? Feelings are like London double-decker buses: you can hop on and off a bus pretty much 24/7. They go round and round the city centre, inhabited by different people, at different times, and no two experiences are identical, even when the journey feels the same. There is usually something on board which colours in each experience differently and the length of time you are on the bus may vary. If you get stuck in traffic, the ride can feel intense. Sometimes you can find yourself changing buses, more than once, to make the overall journey smoother, moving from one to another to suit your mood.

Eventually, through experience, you begin to work out that your own feelings can arrive at specific times during the day, the month or year – just like buses. You may not be sure at what time they are due to depart! Feelings may coincide with the moon's cycle, an anniversary or even a point in the day that has reserved its spot, making a regular appearance. And, there may be nothing you can do about that! When you are hungry for food or anything else that makes your tummy rumble with butterflies, you can have feelings that transpire from nowhere. Well… certainly kept hidden from us at the time and possibly understood in more detail at a later date.

Some feelings, though, crop up out of the blue, randomly throwing us off guard while others have a habit of returning frequently, yet still can't be pinned down to a particular time. Very few feelings can be captured in a timetable, informing us of an arrival or departure time. Just like buses, sometimes our feelings don't show up when we expect them to. Then, guess what, a few of them come waltzing by, all in a row as if they have been asked to attend an identity parade. You look at them thinking, *Yep that's the one… or is it the other one I prefer… or shall I let them both pass by and jump on the next one coming around the corner?!* Feelings – who needs them?

Of course some feelings are so great that you spend little time wondering how they came about! It is only when you sway from a high to a low emotionally with no reasonable explanation that these may need to be investigated. Assuming that all your happy and contented feelings can be traced back to the source, I suggest you keep doing what you are doing and stockpile them in the event of an emergency. They can't be bought but they can be shared. Actually, can they be bought or do we buy a commodity that will influence our feelings to behave in one way or another? Why don't you have a think about that one the next time you eat a bar of chocolate or drink a pint of beer?!

*

All the characters from the set of *Emotional Sandwiches* met in the lobby area of the adjacent hotel. This is the one which had stood witness to the rollercoaster of feelings over the last few months and were exhibited most evenings by one or more members of the emotional fellowship – if not the entire crew. The cast was ushered through to the lounge to pick up a glass of champers and seduce their appetite with a few hors d'oeuvres.

The cast had also popped in from the show next door. They seemed happy to tuck into the bite-sized delicacies (no… the canapés, not the sandwiches!). While the French actor recalled their first encounter, making up a few of his own stories along the way, the interviewer was prepping in the background for an informal event, which would take place after everyone had eaten. Overhearing some of the loose-lipped fabrications coming from that side of the room, he now had a better understanding about the leading actor and why he was known for his extra-curricular skillset among the ES cast. *Gossip is often hearsay*, he thought, *and shouldn't be read into*. Once the guests shot off, no one left behind felt any the wiser, only mildly disappointed, for not knowing if the rumours floating around were actually true. After all, the Frenchman was a tad dishy!

The ES cast were asked to remain in the same room. Yep, in the same room all together at the same time… on this occasion! Up until now, they had all been used to working either alone or with a few sidekicks. All of them seemed jolly pleased not to have been thrown together to fight it out amongst themselves, from the start – which, incidentally, is exactly what appeared to happen at the auditions led by Monsieur what's-his-name.

The interviewer was about to give everyone an opportunity

to say something regarding their feelings that surfaced during their recent journey into self-awareness. It allowed everyone to describe their feelings in their own words. Feelings had been present in every scene and will have been wafting throughout the book too, finding emotional cycles to dip in and out.

There are so many feelings associated with all the words that colour our language. No doubt you could look through the dictionary and link a feeling to some of the more common words that exist in your everyday vocabulary, and these will be personal to you. Other words may need to be translated first, before you get any inkling that they could provoke a sense of desire or misfortune. As it stands, for now, we only have time to listen to a few, summarised by some of the hardest-working personalities in the business during their final interview.

So turn the page and take the time to pay them a little attention, giving each character a voice that allows them to make a stand and tell you, in their own words, that they have feelings too!

The Final Interview

"One-two-one-two; can you all hear me?" said the director, using a surround system to show off her authority.

"All good over here," shouted Trust, raising a hand, who you knew could be relied upon to give an opinion that counted, while sitting beside Honest as a show of solidarity.

The interviewer took the microphone and introduced himself as Pete. His real name was Pierre but after overhearing the recent rumours about the actor he didn't want any glib jokes being made while he was aiming to be professional (not wishing to let the director down!). He had been dying to ask his first question and decided to just throw it out to his audience, knowing full well that this would shake things up a bit from the outset.

"So, what did it feel like – to play a sandwich?" said Pete, smiling cheekily throughout the time it took to ask the question. "Yes, Normal… what are your thoughts?" noticing the puppeteer absent this time!

"I think I can speak on everyone's behalf when I say that we didn't waddle around in costumes smothered in sauce!" Normal rolled her eyes to ensure her point was being taken seriously. "I liked the fact that, between us, we were able to push boundaries. The 'in the moment' experiences which exposed our feelings, at the time, pushed our buttons too!"

"And we weren't all running around in Hawaiian shirts, either," Hope added, laughing as he pointed across to Fear whom he'd had to sit beside throughout the plane journey, during one episode, witnessing it at work in full disguise. Hope felt like he had played a silent part, as the good guy, next to his troubled partner, Fear, who, as an aside, didn't take off his shades the entire flight!

Fear quickly retaliated: "Behave! One night, you had Wardrobe literally throw together a Hawaiian costume for Need; she ended up flirting outrageously with the crew dancing the Hula well into the early hours of the morning." Defending his corner, Fear knew that he wasn't the only one who had a soft spot for Hawaii. Or for Need, come to think of it. He couldn't resist watching her blush with embarrassment as they all went on to recall the moment it fell apart, cracking at the seams as she lost her footing, landing conveniently in the arms of her admirer.

Pete listened as they all took turns to say what had obviously been on their minds as they decided to go public with their jokes. "So, if you weren't really 'sandwiches', why do you think the writer wanted to represent you as such? You don't look edible to me."

Humble stood up and spoke a few poignant words and the laughter rapidly died a death. "When we use our senses to explore further, we can often discover more than what appears to be present on the surface of any situation in any given moment. Food is able to illustrate this rather well. In just one bite you can open up your senses. These include your sense of smell, taste, what you see, what you feel and what – believe it or not – can be heard. You become mindful, in that moment, and realise that the art to trying something new isn't to 'force' yourself to like it, afterwards, but to know that you had the courage to try something new in the first place. The outcome is another story."

Everyone looked astonished; yet that in itself was surprising. After all, Humble was a profound teacher and featured in 'Fillings that educate the taste buds', so what did they expect to hear?

Humble carried on with its performance, despite being averse to doing a monologue, earlier, and began to pick up momentum in what was fast becoming a speech: "Sandwiches are usually food products that can also be multi-layered, appear multi-faceted and contain plenty of potholes that get you wondering what it is that you have actually bitten into at the time. The flavours rise out of the crevices and catch you off guard, the ingredients make you sneeze and suddenly a whole new perspective is born – just because you took one bite!"

Only stopping for a second, to draw breath, Humble edged closer to his captive audience, animating while talking them through the process of engagement. "Imagine it's your first attempt: you only have to lift up one layer of spongy carbs to take a sneak preview, and any number of things can happen. Whichever way you hold it, eyeing it up from a distance because it looks too big to handle, then approaching it from the bottom (instead of the top) to make an indent, simply adds to the overall experience. However, planning to hold it with both hands and heading straight towards it, only to find that you bounce back off again, is not dissimilar to a stunt performer who crashes into a skyscraper in an action film. They misjudge the point of entry, thinking it is an open window. You can feel overwhelmed or…" Humble paused and, suddenly, seemed lost for words.

No one was quite sure what to say next! The room had gone exceptionally quiet until Darkness piped up and attempted to complete the analogy to avoid a cliffhanger ending. The sandwich had been described so vividly and sounded rather enticing; it would seem a shame if it became out of reach.

Sounding more like Churchill addressing the nation, Darkness stood up to address the room and declared, "And remember! Our path in life is full of delights and obstacles. There is often another way to get around an obstacle. You will not feel dismayed for long..." Breaking character, Darkness chuckled as he was clearly lacking the profundity that Sir Winston had managed to find, suggesting that opening the window first before making an attempt to dive through it could be helpful. And making a sandwich smaller without the scaffolding to hold it up could mitigate the risk of a collision at its borders. Joking aside, this is one character which encourages obstacles on our path in life to become better understood by getting to know their darker elements, in order to be overcome. Oh, and the stunt performer was fine.

"I had the impression you wanted to keep us all in the dark," jested Control. Pete cringed as he covered his eyes, choosing to listen instead to Darkness about to return fire. This was while the rest of the cast watched in anticipation, their eyes darting back and forth to see at what point that was going to happen.

"I DON'T keep you in the dark. Haven't you understood a word that I've been saying?" Sighing heavily, Darkness went on to admit, in less frantic tones, that he knew he could be annoying and his sensitivity to light didn't help matters. Of course, he didn't mean to scare anyone or make them feel sad. They usually did that to themselves. Sitting down again, he said (with more profoundness than when he started off), "An emotional state is something you get yourself into. I know. I watch people do it!"

By now, Pete had a fair idea how the characters felt during

the filming of ES and that it was becoming clear that they each had their place on our paths.

"I felt challenged," confessed Control.

"That's often how I felt too!" declared Blame, standing up to shake its legs. It was still seeing the chiropractor for a bad back after reshooting scenes which demonstrated the numerous ways in which to lie; it would defy anyone to curl up in a jam jar – gasping for air – until the lid was unscrewed. It took hours to unfold.

The director agreed that it had been emotional to film. She sighed and looked at Confidence asking, "Come on then, what are your thoughts? You've been quiet tonight or are you merrily enjoying the bubbly with Patience, which incidentally I can see needs topping up!"

"Well," said Confidence, "I wanted to take part in the storyline to demonstrate how easily I can be influenced – probably more than people realise. I felt dragged into endless double-act scenarios and now I know how Control must have felt," looking over to him with compassion. "I felt lost at times and have Patience to thank for helping me to cope with those periods of waiting. Granted, a person waits for Confidence to find them; but I wait too and hope to be found."

Those last words, spoken by Confidence made the director smile and Pete nodded in agreement as he took back the microphone to see if anyone else in the room had anything to say, aware that time was getting on. Actually, Time was sitting asleep on the sofa and had suddenly aged. He must have been sapped of his strength while putting in the hours.

Patience looked up and in slightly slurred speech told everyone that she felt undeserving of being put on a pedestal. But she thanked Confidence, anyway, for her kind words. She did agree, though, that her role involved waiting, reminding those in the room still listening, that this was usually while others took their time to buy into (or give into) her school of thought. Once they'd made a commitment to join her, she would wait alongside her new recruits and explain that 'doing nothing' is often the right thing to do. The latter had to be handled with care to avoid Doubt from creeping into their relationship.

Rounding off a confident performance with an unexpected afterthought, Patience spat out her final words: "And Time will tell you that too!" Sounding desperate for his approval, in case no one would believe her, Time was, without doubt, her soulmate. Sometimes, between them, they only had a few seconds to make an impact and waiting longer for something to happen was not always an option.

Pete had planned on getting them to open up on their feelings a little more, but they had seemingly been washed away by barrels of beer and magnums of champagne that had forgiveness written all over them from the start. That reminded him of something: "Hey, Forgive," said Pete, looking around the room, "is there anything you want to say?"

Forgive had resorted to Chair Pose now, in the corner of the lounge, and could quite safely say that it had left tree hugging well behind, in the forest. He showed signs of being ready to perform *a cappella* with his roommates who, unfortunately, looked as though they had just undergone a session of hypnotherapy. Forgive's plan, to have them all sing along to a version of 'Feelings', was short lived. On reflection, it wasn't the most uplifting of songs for 'an end of show' party! A renowned empath, Forgive had more than enough experience in engaging with feelings on a day-to-day basis and was probably due to have a rest from them.

Guilt had irritated Need far too much during filming and couldn't resist teasing her now, asking her to challenge herself more about her reasons for existence. Interrupting Guilt's flow of hypocrisy, Need spoke up in agreement. "Actually, I was asking Fear, only the other day, that exact same question. We agreed that we both face this dilemma and have choices to make. Sometimes we simply make the wrong ones."

"And what feelings come up for either of you, when you are faced with this decision-making process?" asked Pete, looking smug because he'd read about Choice. Noticing that neither the documentary nor the book had turned Choice into a cheeky chappy, giving him a voice *per se*, he still managed to keep the army of opportunities active on the path throughout the entire script! Choice had left the party early with Sometimes. Despite being picked to launch the show, she had felt more like a side garnish in each episode as opposed to the temptress she'd envisioned playing. But appearing in the same section as Choice was a good career move and they worked well together – so far.

Fear had been hesitating to speak, unsure if Need wanted to say something else first, then filled the silence. "I feel a degree of empathy for the person I tag along with and would like to think that everyone can choose to work through fear or walk away from fearful situations. I know this isn't always the case and so I am not going to insult anyone, who has come this far on their journey, to think that my last words are meant to be derogatory. A big word admittedly for this time of night as I have since had a few extra miniatures from the bar! But I can be useful to have around…" Fear definitely had a sentimental side to him.

Judgement woke up as Fear was in mid-flow and interjected, reminding everyone how we are all more than capable of judging ourselves a bit harshly at times.

"Yeah, yeah, point taken," said Fear, wishing that Judgement had remained asleep. Now was not the time for another speech. Any games of Pass the Parcel would have to wait for another time so wrapping up any advice now (kind or otherwise) wasn't going to protect Fear from experiencing a hangover the next morning; early signs had already threatened to run wild. Fortunately, Judgement didn't go on to discuss any more points of view, settling on one generalisation as his only contribution for the night.

Failure couldn't argue with the fact that this had been a great evening and there wasn't much that it wanted to add – only telling Pete that it had been upstaged by the extra-terrestrial. It felt that the alien visitor had said plenty on the subject and Failure wasn't sure if that was only a ploy to become more widely recognised, on Earth, through appearing on our TV network. Pete thought Failure was sounding a little envious but saw from watching and listening to how this character spoke, that Failure wore some interesting shoes which were probably ill-fitting at times. It was often called names. The alien kept spelling his name out, as if Failure couldn't hear, making it mean something different each time. It seemed to like the 'F' word!

Clearly, this bunch of characters could contribute to global warming all on their own, just by talking! Pete nicknamed the documentary 'Green House Emotions', hoping that his own imagination would win him the opportunity to return during the next series. Maybe they could call him Pierre, after all.

Well, it was getting on for midnight and even though this was early for the emotional fellowship, it was clearly a Cinderella moment being felt by all and time for everyone to retire. There was one final observation, to consider…

Path had been lying around all evening propping up most of

the cast as they became mildly intoxicated which it had chosen to do since day one. It hadn't really got much of a mention in this interview and it didn't volunteer either when Pete, soon to be Pierre, willed them all to be honest and open about their feelings. Talking about Honest, where had it been all evening?

Honest was keeping a low profile and just as Pete was about to ask it a question, Honest put its finger up to its mouth and whispered, "Shhhhh… not now, sometimes the truth hurts", and Pete got the message.

The director, who also played the master of ceremonies for the evening's activities, was about to leave. After saying goodnight to the cast first, she went on to wish Pete a safe onward journey. Knowing that the book had given Path more acknowledgment in its closing chapter, she said no more and preferred to share a final moment with Path, alone, as it led her to the exit and on to her next journey.

Then the doors shut.

The Folders of Your Mind

Looking up at the sky there seemed to be plenty of activity going on. A flock of birds appeared to be heading off in a direction that made me wonder if they actually knew where they were going! One or two were gliding in the opposite direction an inch below the other formation; well, that's what it looked like from a distance, and neither one looked like they were on a mission to get anywhere fast. An aircraft intercepted their paths with no repercussions and the clouds passed between them as though the gaps had been made just the right size to prevent a catastrophe.

I soon came to the conclusion that I had safely returned through the small arched doors. I wasn't cut out to be a director anyway – but what a ride! I could only assume I had made it back to reality; the one where you had just polished off your fifth course and I had rudely interrupted your imagination, taking us both on a detour. Sorry about that!

An interesting challenge that I face, sometimes, is deciding whether something is realistic or not. I'm a born optimist. I wake up in the morning and have a new idea that alters the perspective on an idea that I had the day before. It wears me out! But isn't that what learning and developing is all about? We can change our minds – because, as humans, we are gifted with this wonderful ability to learn. We are capable of challenging our own points of view and, in turn, we might change our perspectives. How many times have you done this with these Emotional Sandwiches?

Also, I'd love to see past the first layer of action in my field of vision and learn more. If I could look up and explore the solar system without using a telescope, whilst continuing to lie flat on my back to avoid falling over (only cricking my neck to view another planet), I'm certain I would see pathways lit up by the stars. These would beckon me and I would follow, and I'd probably remain their travelling companion until I had no more reason to follow. Alas, my sight is limited. I can only see what I can see and the rest that is hidden may be left to my imagination or witnessed through my third eye. Perhaps we aren't meant to see everything and maybe that is a good thing.

Path, on the other hand, has been witness to plenty of shenanigans without the need for magnification. It usually wanted to chuck the Emotional Sandwiches off for misbehaving but, given time, some of them went on to find their own way. In contrast, Path has seen Beauty and Darkness meet somewhere in the middle and become friends, suggesting that people can turn a corner in their lives and find peace. They can find a star to guide them on. I was going to say home but I believe it is more important to know there is somewhere else we can be if home isn't all that appealing either. We don't all have a home. But maybe home, in this sense, is where the ego hangs up its hat to retire for the night or it may be a place we aspire to go when all has been said and done on Earth. You choose.

Path has recently had the time to listen to incredible stories of love, triumph and hardship. Each story packaged up in different ways, depending on the circumstances, as their followers all walked the distance which was never predicted nor measured. Path saw the waterfalls and couldn't do anything about them because it wasn't its place to predict those either, leaving it up to us to do that and avoid them when we can. Maybe our own path can, but doesn't feed back that information in the way that we understand while we are busy planning our lives but not necessarily living out those plans. We become less aware of any connection that we once had as we choose to ignore our instincts and allow logic to undermine what may have been the truth, all along. It is possible to become less self-aware as we immerse ourselves in the battle to find more of what is absent in our lives before getting to know if what already exists is sufficient.

Do we walk a destined path? Hence why it doesn't have the ability, all on its own, to change the landscape without permission? If destiny is involved, then this may explain why Path indulges our tantrums and supports our dreams – because it has nothing to lose! Path tends to narrate rather than voice its opinion in case its direct approach stops you from taking an adventure. It will always be facing in one direction or another, turning around only to see if you are still strolling behind or if you have taken a detour. Then it would be down to fate, to read the signposts accurately and lure you back onto the right track, in the event that you went off at a tangent.

The path that looks after your emotions is ageing all the time. It keeps on going (until it has to stop) and as such, tends to get tired the most, finding humour to be something that can take the edge off the bitterness that lingers once it has been bitten.

*

So, how can we wrap up the fillings together and, in summary, portray them in a helpful way with a respect they deserve that still awards them with a little latitude? After all, they all play a role in our lives. They just happened to have been characterised and unusually depicted in this arrangement to entertain but remain a bunch of words – thrown on the pages – all open to interpretation.

As we have ventured from one filling to the next, you may have seen that some of the characters had the potential to move around and no doubt you will rearrange the sandwiches into different groups to suit your own relationship with each word. You will know who gets on better with whom in your own world and where those encounters lie. On reflection, I could have put the sandwiches on a buffet table from the start and you could have picked out your favourite ones. My only concern, if I had done that, is that some of them may have been left out, on purpose, all because you weren't too happy with a previous encounter. But if you don't happen to have any particular issue, *with any of them,* then you can look upon this entire journey as a milestone that tells me you are doing something right!

Indulge my imagination one last time and picture a large and empty tortilla… Create your own wrap, layer up the fillings in desirable quantities and let the flavours speak for themselves. Then you can go about adjusting those amounts in order to get the balance right for you! They will wriggle around and look for an escape route when they know they're going to be challenged, hiding behind each other or camouflaging themselves against the greenery to avoid being seen. Relish the thought that you may even want to heat things up and throw in a jalapeno to get them all engaged – this would be one heck of an icebreaker! Whichever way you choose to roll yours up, aim to keep the fillings under wrap long enough to create a sense of self-awareness and a connection to your thoughts and feelings about what these words mean – to you. Then you can explore them in whatever order you decide using logic and instinct.

I've a couple of ideas which you may be interested in developing further, on your own, and I'll share these with you in a moment. By now, I hope I will be known for using simple and subtle analogies which allow messages to filter through and gently wake you up. I didn't see any point, in this book, concocting worst-case scenarios that may serve as a distraction instead of functioning as a platform from which to explore a word. You will have your own stories, some of which will be new while others may revisit you from the past and surface in order for you to learn from them, rather than be relived.

So for better or for worse you could, pretty much, take any scenario in your own life and apply all twenty words, either in sequence or shuffled around to help you review a past or current situation. There is no hard or fast rule and their relevance or importance may alter depending upon the situation. Once you are able to better understand the relationship that you have with these words, you may be able to put a situation (or your entire life) into perspective and realise that in any given moment you may feel more drawn to one word than another. You begin to understand any importance behind this discovery and this may be a revelation for you or a simple reminder that your levels of self-awareness are on the up!

I have looked at situations in my own life and (while it can take time) I have been able to talk myself through a situation using each word effectively, calling upon the Emotional Brigade to come to the rescue. It was interesting to see that one word would often appear more obvious, maybe because of the scenario I was exploring. It wasn't unusual for another one to come forward and ask to be explored too because there was an association or a link being made that needed addressing. Sometimes there was a mutual dependency and sometimes one word would attract the other, just because it could; I'd notice double acts unfold in front of my eyes!

I found myself giving them all a voice, using both logic and instinct to decide if any of them could be moderated to improve a situation or did I need to reduce or increase their presence to bring balance back into my life? We all have an opportunity to choose to improve the way we think, express ourselves or reflect.

So, if I left you with another idea that we all have an Emotional Sandwich within our own vocabulary yearning to be explored and better understood, what would yours be? It wouldn't surprise me at all to learn that you even have your own selection of words to explore. These will most likely be communicating with you on an entirely different wavelength, sending you messages that may well go unnoticed. Still, not every word in your selection is suffering from confusion or on the verge of having a breakdown. They may only be fighting to get your attention because of their capacity to understand and support those that need more attention in order to be understood!

Well, have you thought of one yet? If you haven't, then just choose an ES off the existing menu for the final illustration. It's not unusual for one of your favourite words to suddenly lose its enthusiasm and misbehave in the future, instead, choosing to orchestrate your emotions to play 'Chopsticks' – as opposed to Beethoven's calming 'Für Elise'. Sounds can vibrate at different frequencies and confuse you at the best of times. Words, too, vibrate at different frequencies as they try to tell us something now that they didn't say before and may never say again. The next time they speak to us, they may have forgotten what was said, even though they seemed so important at the time. Contexts change. Words don't want to be stereotyped; although, it is useful to get to know the words that discolour your language and then your feelings may stand a chance of being understood.

How can you get started?

After great deliberation, I've decided just to include a few initial pointers in this book. Why? Because, I feel that some of you will find them interesting to consider, taking inspired action to unravel your next steps, while others will not wish to have their entertainment ambushed with a lengthy, unsolicited coaching exercise, and choose to skip the ending altogether. No, no, we can't have that. So, let's keep it light hearted and I will reserve the detail for another time.

The folder

Create a folder in your mind and call it M-E-S-S-A-G-E: **My Emotional Sandwich Selection and Gorgeous Excuses**. Then put your Emotional Sandwich into the folder and call it '**MES-1**' or by name – make it personal.

How to approach your Emotional Sandwich

It's time to run off a little diagnostic assessment. The idea is to cross-check your **MES** alongside both words in the course titles and determine if it fits into any theme before deciding whether to explore it further, or delete it altogether from the folder. For example, using the ES, Confidence, you would link it up with each word separately: Confidence/Balance; Confidence/Management; Confidence/Understanding; and then do the same with the others (Respect; Limitations; Acceptance; Learning; Development).

Run it through an MOT (Message On Trial) test

Now you've linked up your MES with the eight words, as shown above, it is time to do the cross-check. The idea is to spend a few minutes on each set and ask yourself (without over thinking): "What are my thoughts and feelings telling me as I allow these two words to resonate together?"; "Are there any underlying messages that are asking to be understood?" Decide if the feedback warrants your energy. And if it does, then schedule in some time to focus on your relationship with the word that is frequenting your path. In this book, I put Confidence in with 'Balance and Management' – you may want to put it in with 'Respect', already understanding it perfectly well, once it's been on trial.

What if nothing comes to mind immediately?

No worries! Time and Patience will support you when you're ready to engage with your senses. Now may not be the time. Eventually, they will open up to you – like a good friend. We are often more than capable of finding our own answers within. Sometimes, we can sense them coming to the surface relatively quickly. Other times, the answers lie in wait, beneath, taking forever to let us know that they're there. As we close our eyes, screw up our face, grit our teeth and slowly inhale – nodding our head back and forth, just a fraction, hoping to shake the answers loose (while playing 'air piano') – it all begins to feel like hard work. *Within* can't be that far away – can it? Go on, do that sequence and smile – because you know exactly what I mean!

Equally, you could learn something about an ES in every theme – in which case a full service comes to mind. In fact,

The Folders of Your Mind

if you're feeling brave and since discovered that you've more than one ES on your mind, then why not put your entire **MESS** (My Emotional Sandwich Selection) into the folder and brace yourself for an emotional cleanse! Scrub-a-dub-dub! And if ever there was a perfect time to add a caveat, which cannot be accused of drivel on this occasion, I ask you to cleanse safely. In other words: don't climb a mountain alone, if walking with a group feels safer.

Interestingly, our emotions can come to the surface along with the solutions out of the blue. But putting the situation on trial, instead, may be easier for you to do and is in keeping with my first analogy. Simply call in the Emotional Brigade; run the situation by each ES in this book to see if they have anything to do with how you could be feeling.

All good? Great!

Finally, consider something that may help you to take the seriousness out of the experience or put it back in when the experience replies unkindly. Here goes my conscious friend…

Self-awareness is going on all the time. Becoming more self-aware may or may not be an effort for you. It can come easily and be satisfying to some of us; yet prove to be something quite alien to the rest despite the fact we are all an embodiment of knowledge and practise self-awareness to lesser or greater degrees. It belongs to each of us and communicates on so many levels. It is worth taking the time to listen to what it has to say and notice how any messages (which it has been itching to deliver) can make us feel – without getting too hung up on incidentals. Otherwise, you could be contemplating all day long and who has the time to do that? Cryptology has its place – just ask Confidence! It's what we choose to do with the information we receive, using all of our senses, which may make all the difference to how we live our lives and interact with others that cross our path, regardless of who bumped into whom first.

By the way, I think the alien visitor would certainly approve of the mnemonic: *MESSAGE*. I know 'mnemonic' is one of the more unusual words I've introduced so far, having made a conscious decision, from the outset, to leave the less popular ones in my vocabulary out of this book. Fraternising with a dictionary, every step of the way, would only distract me from writing from my heart and I wanted to ensure my underlying messages were within reach (and not too alien for the human mind). Why complicate it, I say?! Incidentally, I don't even know if the alien visitor had a name; I could have nicknamed it AV – if only to reflect its audio and visual capabilities.

Self-awareness isn't something that can only be accessed by passing through a void that takes you somewhere that doesn't appear to be here. You remain conscious and you will know when you are being self-aware because you are either questioning yourself or agreeing, having got in touch with your feelings! If you want to tap into the subconscious mind or take a trip into another dimension, via a meditative activity, to bring about a greater self-awareness then by all means find out which one of those floats your boat and give it a go once you've learnt how.

Before I forget, did you read about Fate in the last section of 'Article 22'? This is after airlifting the magazine off the table, which was actually marked up: 'Please take a free copy'. Oops, I think I forgot to tell you to imagine that bit. Sorry! Look on the bright side. You've had a chance to put together your own two and two and draw your own conclusions, something you may not have thought about doing had you felt well that day. You've now had an opportunity to explore the impact that the 'Power of *your* mind' can have on the 'Folders of *your* mind'.

Guilt may subtly choose to remind you about this awkward experience the next time you visit the surgery, when the CCTV camera turns towards you and the receptionist greets you with the same watchful eye (as if they are both plugged into the same system). But you've since learned that you had nothing to feel guilty about. Right?!

Maybe Fate does play a hand and destiny puts just the right amount of mixed seeds in Fate's palm so that when they develop, there is just enough space either side for learning to take place allowing room for improvement. The only thing catastrophic that may occur, in the process, is that you forget to dream. Alternatively, the space you currently occupy on this planet may be all you need, in this lifetime, without going off into the galaxy looking for trouble. Daydreaming and searching for something else, outside of your current vision, may only lead to unrequited love between you and the Universe, which is a catastrophe you would rather avoid. And I get that too; it's OK. We don't all enjoy puzzles.

Nonetheless, whatever you choose to do with your space, whether you are in it alone or sharing it with others, be sure to walk a path that feels good for your soul and remember to 'Coach the artist within you to create…' [and you can fill in the blank].

NOTES